Intrepid's Footsteps
Sustaining US-UK
Intelligence in an Era
of Global Challenges

INTREPID'S FOOTSTEPS SUSTAINING US-UK INTELLIGENCE IN AN ERA OF GLOBAL CHALLENGES

Anthony R. Wells

Print information available on the last page.

Rev. date: 08/01/2023

To order additional copies of this book, contact:
Xlibris
844-714-8691
www.Xlibris.com
Orders@Xlibris.com
852674

CONTENTS

DEDICATION

Dedicated to my four children, John, James, Lucy, and Fiona; and my eight grandchildren, Jayden, Anthony James, Korban, Virginia, Mason David, Lydia, Elizabeth, and Annalise.

Also in memory of "Intrepid" himself, Sir William Stephenson, CC, MC, DFC (January 23, 1897, to January 31, 1989), a Canadian soldier, fighter pilot, businessman, and Sir Winston Churchill's personally appointed spymaster based in New York City during World War II. Sir William worked personally with Pres. Franklin Roosevelt and his key staff at the most sensitive intelligence levels. As the senior representative of the British Security Coordination based in a highly secretive location in New York "Intrepid," Stephenson's codename, he did extraordinary and invaluable work between the United Kingdom and the United States, helping to ensure that the western allies defeated Nazi Germany and Japan. Intrepid was awarded the Presidential Medal of Freedom and was knighted by King George VI as a Knight Bachelor on the nomination of Sir Winston Churchill. He was also made a Companion of the Order of Canada (CC), and as a young man, he was awarded the Military Cross (MC) and the Distinguished Flying Cross (DFC) for bravery in action.

Sir William Samuel Stephenson, Knight Bachelor, CC, MC, DFC

PREFACE

This book links the critical World War II roles and missions of Sir William Stephenson, "Intrepid," with the decades since, until the present, showing the extraordinary continuity of cooperation of US and British Intelligence. Intrepid set in action from his secret location in New York City a pattern of working together that is unprecedented in the annals of intelligence. His work was unique in every way and laid the foundations and set a huge example and standards for his successors over the following decades.

The author followed directly in "Intrepid's Footsteps," the only living person today who has worked for British Intelligence as a British citizen and US Intelligence as an American citizen, spanning the period from 1969 to 2023, fifty four years dedicated to the values, traditions, loyalty, and special relationship between the United States and the United Kingdom.

William Stephenson (January 23, 1897–January 31, 1989), whose World War II codename was "Intrepid," was a Canadian soldier, airman, businessman, inventor, and spymaster. He was Prime Minister Winston Churchill's handpicked security coordinator for the entire western hemisphere during World War II. He was born in Winnipeg, Manitoba, and died aged ninety-two on the Goldeneye Estate in Tucker's Town, Bermuda. He was Churchill's key person for delivering scientific and intelligence secrets directly from the prime minister to Pres. Franklin Roosevelt. He helped Roosevelt and his closest advisors in changing American public opinion from an isolationist position to a more aggressive stance regarding the Nazi threat.

Stephenson was adopted, and his name was changed from Stanger (his original parents were a mother from Iceland and a father from the Orkney Islands who could not care for him) to his foster parents' name, Stephenson.

He had a most distinguished World War I military career, winning the Military Cross and the Distinguished Flying Cross. After World War II, Stephenson had an outstanding business career and married in 1924 the American tobacco heiress Mary French Simmons. He built a large array of international contacts such that by as early as April 1936, he was voluntarily providing Winston Churchill with confidential information on Hitler and the Third Reich and the latter's military buildup.

Churchill used Stephenson's information to warn the British people of the dangers of appeasement. Against the objections of SIS (MI6) head Stewart Menzies, Churchill sent Stephenson to the United States on June 21, 1940, to secretly and covertly run British Security Coordination (BSC) based in New York City, over a year before the United States' entry into the war after the attack on Pearl Harbor, December 7, 1941. Stephenson and BSC operated from Room 3603, Rockefeller Center, officially known as the "British Passport Control Office," and was registered with the US Department of State.

Stephenson's operation handled highly sensitive information between British Naval Intelligence (Room 39), SOE (Special Operations Executive), and SIS (Secret Intelligence Service, commonly known as MI6), and the Americans.

He was also cleared by Churchill to pass selective Bletchley Park

"Ultra" data to President Roosevelt. It was Stephenson who advised Roosevelt to appoint William Donovan as head of the US Office of Strategic Services (OSS). Stephenson worked without salary and paid from his own resources much of the large administrative and personnel costs of BSC. When he was made a Knight Bachelor in 1945, Winston Churchill wrote, "This one is dear to my heart." In November 1946, he was awarded the Medal of Merit by Pres. Harry S. Truman, at that time the highest civilian award in the United States. Gen. "Wild Bill" Donovan most appropriately presented the medal to Stephenson. The "Quiet Canadian" was made a Companion of the Order of Canada on December 17, 1979, and invested on February 5, 1980. His book *A Man Called Intrepid* was first published in 1976.

Intrepid was close to Room 39 in the Admiralty in London, the headquarters of the director of British naval intelligence. The first World War II director of British naval intelligence, the DNI, was Vice Admiral John Henry Godfrey (1888–1971), promoted in 1939 to rear admiral and DNI until 1942, three critical years. In May 1939, Rear Admiral Godfrey appointed Ian Fleming to be his personal assistant. Godfrey and Fleming had very close working relations with Stephenson and as a group with President Roosevelt's fine choice for the head of the United States' Office of Strategic Services (OSS), William J. "Wild Bill" Donovan. On June 13, 1942, President Roosevelt issued an executive order creating the Office of Strategic Services. Donovan received a commission in the US Army as a general and became head of the new agency. OSS is regarded as the first centralized US intelligence agency, though the US Navy's Office of Naval Intelligence (ONI) is by far the oldest of all US-UK Intelligence organizations, founded in 1882 (150 years old in 2032). The roles of the British DNI, the director of ONI, and the future character and operations of OSS were greatly influenced by combined US and British naval intelligence. Admiral Godfry and Ian Fleming, with Stephenson, played critical roles in helping Donovan define OSS's missions and detailed operations in Europe.

What happened during World War II in US-British intelligence relations set in motion a continuity of relations that persist to this day. In 2023, the world faces extraordinary challenges. A war is raging in Ukraine. China is acting in aggressive and provocative ways that have destabilized not just East Asia but also the whole world. North Korea, Iran, Syria, the Middle East situation, and global terrorist and extremist groups are pervasive in multiple locations across the globe. It is essential that US-UK Intelligence holds fast in this new era of threats that will persist. There can be no weakening of links, no reduction in the trust and cooperation that has persisted since the halcyon years of Intrepid's time in New York City and all that the US Office of Naval Intelligence, and Magic cryptology, the British DNI, MI5, MI6, and Bletchley Park achieved in the years 1939–1945. The following chapters are dedicated to showing how and why these relations must be sustained for the preservation and protection of freedom and democracy.

"Intrepid's Footsteps" will indeed be followed, and readers are encouraged to participate in the dialogue and the didactic approach taken to create awareness and appreciation of the crucial roles and missions of US and British Intelligence in the modern era. "Intrepid" lives on in new and equally critical contemporary guises.

INTRODUCTION

The following chapters will not follow traditional approaches to analyzing and discussing what may be generically described as the history of US and British Intelligence from World War II until present. The objectives are different. We live in global challenging times, and every reader may participate in a serious dialogue about how two great countries ands allies, the United States of America and the United Kingdom, can continue to work together to preserve and protect our freedom and democracy.

Each chapter encourages participation in an age when the younger generation, highly educated and capable, not just living in the digital era but also making strides technologically every day, will inherent the responsibility of leadership. It is their future, their challenge, and their responsibility to preserve and protect freedom and democracy.

Each generation may participate, and the hope and objective at the conclusion of this book is for readers to appreciate not just the continuity of the past through to the present but also the "why, what, and how" US-UK Intelligence may work successfully in the future in the great traditions of the past and in the "Footsteps of Intrepid." Everyone can contribute through dialogue in an open society where security is still paramount and also where open dialogue is equally valuable and permissible, particularly in an era of "open sources." Media information is extensive, perhaps at times overwhelming, and technology permits commercial satellites and a whole variety of media outlets to inform and educate. Discretion, judgment, and evaluation are also needed in this technology-intensive environment. Information overload requires accurate knowledge and information. Disinformation is pervasive in an ever-growing digital world, and part of the emerging challenge is recognizing "truth from fiction," the latter in many guises often from discreet sources that wish to sow untruths and disinformation with buried objectives. Disuniting democracies via internet disinformation is a clear goal of several dictatorships that seek to destabilize democratic institutions, often by the classical technique of "divide and rule." Internal dissent can prevent unity in the face of external threats. US-UK Intelligence has to face a multiplicity of disinformation threats aimed at creating internal disagreements both within the US and the UK and between both countries, thereby potentially weakening potential opposition.

The chapters that follow seek to help readers not just appreciate the various aspects and traditions of US-UK Intelligence organizations and operations but also provoke and elicit insights into why and how we may progress in the future.

The general structure is as follows. Two aspects are joined in parallel.

There is a chronological aspect to each chapter, though this is not the dominating aspect. The latter is more thematic, making observations and drawing conclusions from events and intelligence policies, procedures, organizations, sources, methods, outcome, albeit over time. The aim is to provide the wider overview and perspective, with the passage of time, though time is not an overarching aspect. For example, intelligence successes, and failures, varied greatly over time. Sadly, some mistakes were repeated many years later. So a more generic view is sometimes necessary. Even today, some of the most successful intelligence operations of World War II may provide lessons and guidance for contemporary more advanced technologically oriented operations.

Chronology should not therefore inhibit a wider and much more valuable perspective on how we may progress in the future and how the next generation can examine and implement the future roles of US-UK Intelligence.

This subject is indeed of national importance. Much is self-evident. We all need to know the intentions, capabilities, and actions of those who are not well disposed to the US and the UK and their allies and our traditions of freedom and democracy. As Heraclitus wrote, "There is nothing permanent except change," so if changes are made in one key domain, US-UK Intelligence, that safeguards our freedom, then they should be made with as much knowledge and perspective as possible.

The key objective is for readers to participate, form their own views and opinions, and have a well-informed understanding of how the past and the present interface to help us all collectively decide the way ahead. The United States, the United Kingdom, and their allies and friends deserve no less.

CHAPTER 1

The Intelligence Requirement and Objectives

The functions and processes of intelligence have changed since Winston Churchill and Franklin Roosevelt met secretly in Placentia Bay off Newfoundland on August 14, 1941, just a few months before the Japanese attack at Pearl Harbor on December 7, 1941. They planned the strategy for ending Hitler's domination of Europe and later, after Pearl Harbor, with Winston Churchill's historic visit to Washington, DC, shortly after the attack, the response to Japan's preemptive attack. However, what has endured since that meeting is the abiding cooperation between US and British Intelligence. The British brought Canada, Australia, and New Zealand into what is now known as the "Five Eyes." In recent years, the Five Eyes share relevant intelligence with India and Japan, and the "Quad" of the US, Australia, Japan, and India is a growing cooperative body facing the challenges from China. The August 1941 meeting began the regular exchange of extensive intelligence beyond what already existed (the US and UK were exchanging intelligence before Pearl Harbor), particularly of the British "Ultra" data from Bletchley Park based on the critical "Enigma" intercepts of Nazi intentions and operations, and the US "Magic" data from Japanese intercepts managed by a legendary team based in Hawaii and in the Office of Naval Intelligence in Washington, DC.

The key objectives of US-British Intelligence have not changed over the decades. There have been modifications naturally over the past eighty-three years since the 1940 historic meeting on HMS *Prince of Wales*. The essence is to provide reliable, accurate, and timely intelligence to key policymakers and particularly those who managed defense and security programs, together with a wide range of multiple government departments and entities across the board, of which the US Department of Defense, the UK Ministry of Defence, the US State Department, and the UK Foreign Office are key. Technology, trade, critical minerals, water supplies, climate change, and the next generation of computer and communications systems and technologies are a few of the many domains that require up-to-date and timely intelligence of the highest quality. Globalization at one level has witnessed a significant shift, particularly because of the intensive controls and security systems imposed on international activities and cooperation at all levels by countries such as China and Russia. The peace dividends of the post Soviet Union and ending of the Cold War enjoyed in the 1990s seem to have evaporated in a new era, post-9/11, Iraq, and Afghanistan, into the challenges of the 2020s and beyond. The demands now posed on US-British Intelligence are challenging and nontrivial. New ways and means, sources and methods, together with sophisticated analysis tools, are the order of the day in this changed world. Dictatorships have emerged that threaten the western democratic order and value system. To stand still, to atrophy, will create a most undesirable situation. The great innovative strengths of Alan Turing and his colleagues at Bletchley Park and the brilliant team at Station Hypo in Hawaii in World War II will require reinvention and different innovations in the modern era. Times have changed, but the fundamentals of intelligence have not.

The physical world of international rivalry, conflict, and war has been changed forever by the digital revolution. The analog era is bygone. It is over. This has changed everything at all levels of international interactions. Technical superiority has characterized the outcome of national rivalries and, worst case, war itself. Scientific and technical intelligence has underpinned national superiority together with extremely adaptive sources and methods, together with expert analysis tools. All have been underscored by the fine minds and, simply put, brainpower of US and British Intelligence personnel and the industrial base that sustains all, including academe.

In an age when new innovative software, artificial intelligence, neural networks, and machine learning are becoming ever more powerful, there is an urgent need for policymakers in both the US and the UK to reassess not just intelligence functions and operations but also the timely uses to which intelligence products are put. The very best intelligence in the US and UK may possibly be either underused or not recognized by leadership unless the current and future leaderships of both intelligence communities have a continuing and regular interface with policymakers.

It is not the role of intelligence to make policy, rather to provide the accurate, unvarnished, timely, and unbiased intelligence to support policymaking and future critical investments. The role of precious metals in the key software industries is one example in the global supply chain that sustains the computer and communications industries, together with the global interfaces of voice, data, and imagery. In defense and security, the above have clear and ever-present relevance.

Response times have changed as a result of the digital revolution. By 2030, if not earlier, there will be a global competitive industry in artificial intelligence alone that will impact every aspect of trade and commerce, affecting the US-UK industrial base, its manufacturing, logistics, transportation, and the scientific and technical research that sustains these in a competitive world in which China seeks preeminence. Defense and security will be impacted dramatically.

From a purely military perspective, the basics are still present in terms of requirements, though the technology has changed dramatically. Intentions have always underpinned everything. What are China's intentions? In parallel, the need-to-know capabilities in fine detail has not changed since World War II, together with movement and locations and, of course, in conflict itself the real- or near-real-time location of enemy forces. The world of conventional warfare has changed because of the new demands placed on both systems and operations of counterterrorism and counterinsurgency. In all these very different conflict situations, there is an ever-changing need for innovation by US-UK Intelligence as the information revolution in private industry and private commercial enterprises advance at a faster pace than government can adapt, contract, and implement.

The future preparation of the battle space across all military operations will require US-UK Intelligence to adapt to a rapidly changing environment unprecedented in past conflicts. The ability for humans to interact and take action will be surpassed by digital machines operating at speeds beyond human ability. This will be akin to Turing's solution to dealing with the Nazi daily changing of the Enigma code. Another revolution is required. Workable intelligence at the machine speeds that will be available will have to meet the traditional requirements by the use of new and innovative data analytics.

Advanced software will be needed to analyze the vast trove of open-source intelligence as a result of the vast amount of data available. Unraveling data links across vast troves of data will require advanced AI tools because intelligence personnel will simply not be able to analyze in a timely manner. Human beings can quite easily make the wrong assessments because they cannot handle the amount of data plus the ever-present possibility of preconceived ideas and bias as to what may be occurring.

This does raise the issue of digital innovation and security in this new era. To improve the speed in the intelligence collection and analysis process, there is an urgent need for highly classified software tools, akin, for example, to Magic and Enigma/Ultra data in World War II. Even the existence of Bletchley Park did not become public knowledge until 1974. The new equivalent will require a similar level of security.

At the military level in real operations, what is called the Common Operational Picture will require total interchangeability between the US and the UK and their key allies within the Five Eyes and other nations such as Japan, South Korea, and India.

The above requires new and innovative forms of jointly integrated information systems across a multitude of sensors, with all the necessary intelligence analytical support.

One basic example in the maritime domain is the real-time collection, analysis, and dissemination of AIS data (Automatic Identification System) to all key operational entities. The information load is enormous, and this is symptomatic of multiple other sources. The commercial world has developed extremely clever and innovative tools for dealing with these types of huge and complex information sources. The war in Ukraine has, for example, shown how the command, control, and communications issues associated with the use of drones require new and innovative ways to both exploit their data sources in real time and to how intelligently use such systems in the most efficacious ways. US and UK companies will need to pool their brain power to produce the software tools that will provide cutting-edge capabilities to exploit these types of capabilities and others in the unmanned world. Unmanned underwater and surface vehicles are in this category.

Military commanders at every level will require the above types of innovative tools across the board. Intelligence personnel will need all the help they can get in this information-loaded environment.

In US-UK Intelligence, the past can be prologue in positive and creative ways. There are still lessons that may be learned from the past, and these may be overlain on the current situation described above. It is important to ensure that similar mistakes are not reproduced at every level, including the highest organizational levels, in spite of the digital revolution. Generic situations prevail today that did in the past, and there is significant value in reviewing and analyzing these. People remain the key element in the intelligence process. Let us look at several key past events, people, institutions, outcomes and try to infer important lessons that we can apply in the digital era.

CHAPTER 2

The Past Can be Prologue in Positive Ways

The year 2022 witnessed in Europe events reminiscent of the 1930s, with the invasion of Ukraine by Russia. At the time of writing, the war is still raging, and the Russian leader has been charged with war crimes by the International Criminal Court in The Hague. He is unlikely to be arrested and brought to trial given his location and security, unless he is removed from office and open to arrest and arraignment in The Hague. However, a much larger and internationally ominous event occurred in late March 2023.

The Russian president Vladimir Putin indicated to the world that he may deploy short-range tactical nuclear weapons to Belarus, a threat that he had consistently alluded to as the Russian military situation deteriorated after the initial February 2022 invasion. This raises questions about nuclear safeguards and the intelligence support that has gone hand in hand with US-UK nuclear weapons policies since the early postwar period when the UK joined the US as a nuclear power. Other than the Cuban Missile Crisis in 1962, the US, the UK, and the former Soviet Union managed a stable system of controls and communication. US and UK Intelligence was constantly vigilant in watching all aspects of Soviet nuclear weapons activities, including the protection of the US and UK's ballistic missile submarine force (SSBN) while performing round-the-clock surveillance of Soviet nuclear systems, including detecting and tracking their undersea fleet of SSBNs, some of which were regularly deployed under the Arctic ice cap to avoid detection and tracking by US and UK nuclear powered attack submarines (SSNs). American and British nuclear powered attack submarines were specially configured to operate under the Arctic ice cap and tracked the Soviet SSBNs. Nonetheless, the nuclear order was maintained. This has all changed with the Putin regime in Moscow. In addition, this situation has been exacerbated by other equally disturbing events elsewhere.

The North Korean leadership has consistently executed well-proclaimed and intensely monitored programs by the US and its allies of missile tests, including intercontinental ballistic missiles that can strike the United States and its allies. North Korea's neighbor has also developed an expanded nuclear weapons program in parallel to its expansionist military buildup, particularly of the Chinese navy. Traditional Cold War nuclear arms control agreements have gone out of the door with Putin's declared noncooperation stance. He announced in 2023 that he was suspending obligations under the New Strategic Arms Reduction Treaty (New START) with the United States. This is a serious setback and calls for the US-UK Intelligence community, together with the Five Eyes as a whole and other allied intelligence support, to reassess the traditional ways and means of performing nuclear monitoring and particularly the "Warnings and Indicators" aspects. The latter is particularly critical in a situation that by the spring of 2023 had led to a breakdown of US-Russian communications at the highest level. Your author remembers well discussing with the late dean Rusk, US Secretary of State during the Cuban Missile Crisis and the June War of 1967, the dialogues that occurred with the Soviet Union to avoid Armageddon. This situation no longer exits with a breakdown in traditional diplomacy between the US secretary of state and his opposite number in Moscow. The latter is worsened by similar nonexistent communications between the two countries' military leadership. This situation heightens concerns regarding miscalculation and misinterpretation of information regarding possible use of nuclear weapons.

Given the Ukrainian scenario, the lack of Washington-Moscow dialogue, and the absence of a new nuclear arms agreement between the United States and Russia, and one that would require the agreement and ratification by the US Senate, a situation prevails of uncontrolled nuclear competition between Washington and Moscow. US-UK Intelligence now has a heavy responsibility of collecting and analyzing critical intelligence of Soviet nuclear systems, command, control, and communications. This will have to run in parallel with collection against China's, North Korea's, and potentially Iran's nuclear capabilities. Add India and Pakistan to this already disturbing scenario and the joint US-UK Intelligence community has daunting tasks ahead. All this is achievable, and the past may provide insights even in the new technologically ever-changing environment and various ways and means to ensure that policymakers are provided critical timely and accurate intelligence. Avoiding false warnings of attack and other technical and communications failures and miscalculation, made worse by cyberattacks and non-state actors criminal acts, is paramount. The US-UK Intelligence community has to provide a new and innovative nuclear fail-safe system based on accurate and timely intelligence to avoid the very worst of all threats, an out-of-control nuclear catastrophe that escalates. Intelligence is vital in what will be required, a new and totally reliable fail-safe system that operates not just in real time but also with highly reliable communications to the US and UK national command authorities.

Without making a very bad pun, a "Start" has been made with the 2022 National Defense Authorization Act that provided for the conduct of an independent review of the safety, security, and reliability of nuclear systems. President Biden indicated that he sees nuclear security as paramount.

US and British Intelligence has to be at the leading edge of systems that will prevent accident, a miscalculation as a result of technical mistakes or failures in the warning systems, and the ever-present threat of terrorism, or, in the case of an unbalanced national leaders such as Putin or Kim Jong-un, a catastrophic decision that escalates to a nuclear exchange. The US and UK and the Five Eyes community as a whole is at the heart of new, innovative, and advanced technologies that can support national policies to both protect US and UK nuclear arsenals while guarding against the above potential catastrophic scenarios. Fail-safe measures in the cyber era are therefore heavily dependent on accurate and timely intelligence that will be quintessential in all regards. Fail-safe and intelligence go hand in hand in all regards. Such intelligencer will support the need for a more extensive and thorough revised Nuclear Nonproliferation Treaty, NP, that currently includes China, France, Russia, United Kingdom, and the United States, bringing in India and Pakistan as new members. All these nations have a vital national interest in preventing a nuclear mistake from turning into an international disaster that could threaten the world, with agreements particularly in the ever-present threats from the growing and powerful cyber domain. The current Ukraine-Russia situation highlights the urgent need for these changes and reordering US-UK Intelligence processes. The US-UK Intelligence community will need to monitor the activities and policies generated in Beijing and how intelligence data can be used by US and UK policymakers to influence the Chinese leadership together with other international organizations such as the G-7. Kyiv and Moscow will have to face the reality that it is in their best interests to avoid at all costs a nuclear exchange, and one that could currently emanate from Russia.

It is more likely than not that the world may see growth in global nuclear weapons inventories. The major policy document released by Moscow on March 31, 2023, approved by decree of the president of the Russian Federation, "The Concept of the Russian Policy of the Russian Federation," fails to address, not directly rather by implication, the two key facts that Russia has threatened the use of tactical nuclear weapons in the war in Ukraine, and at a time when the very president of the Russian Federation, Vladimir Putin, who approved by decree this document, has a warrant issued against him by the International Criminal Court for war crimes in Ukraine. In this challenging environment, the US-UK Intelligence community and their allies will need to provide the most accurate and timely intelligence to save the world from catastrophe.

Let us now examine how the past can, in "Intrepid's Footsteps," help in shaping the thinking that may form the basis for new and innovative intelligence practices and procedures that will help policymakers in their decision-making, not just over the nuclear weapons issues above, rather across the broad spectrum of policies and operations. Today, data analytics are vital when information complexity and machine speeds exceed the ability to analyze, decide, and act in timely and effective ways in potentially highly hostile environments. The Chinese threat to Taiwan is a clear and present danger and is very much in this category. The preparation of the battle space across multiple domains and with allies requires today systems that will prevent human error and misjudgment. This requires new and innovative software that can analyze data faster than operators in the intelligence community, however well-trained and experienced US and UK personnel may be. In the naval arena, the Common Operational Picture (COP) is the quintessential system for total maritime domain awareness and action. Allies within the INDOPAC command, control, and communications structure have to be on the same page and potentially in certain operational instances at lightning speed. Introduction in a timely manner of the latest software innovations is vital and particularly in machine learning tools driven in part by revolutionary artificial intelligence (AI) tools.

So, what does the past contribute in this complex data-driven new world? One critical aspect is ensuring that the right agreements are in place and that not just intelligence data sharing is continuous, rather the technological underpinnings are in place to facilitate rapid change based on industry innovation. The HMS *Prince of Wales* meeting in August 1941 off Newfoundland in Placentia Bay between Winston Churchill and Franklin Roosevelt showed the way for a new US-UK accord based on technological innovation and the application to grand strategy and operations. This is particularly so not just in regard to Russia, rather in the serious threats posed by China. The new twenty-first-century Enigma and Magic are the next-generation software and communications technologies.

People make things happen. Change is critical. It does not take an army, rather a few very capable men and women to lead. The careers and achievements of key people in World War II exemplify this point. Besides Alan Turing, there were many others such as R. V. Jones, Norman "Ned" Denning, Harry Hinsley, J. C., Masterman, and John Godfrey on the British side, and, of course, on the US side, the legendary Magic team in Station HYPO led by Capt. Joseph John Rochefort, a brilliant cryptanalyst. The US Navy's Office of Naval Intelligence, formed in 1882, predated British intelligence organizations. Today, a new generation similar to the above is required to innovate and lead. They are there, whether in Quantum Computing, advanced applications of Artificial Intelligence (AI), unmanned vehicles of every kind with advanced sensors and communications, the next generation of manned stealthy aircraft, and the nuclear-powered attack submarines (SSNs) that will be developed under the AUUKUS trilateral security agreement put into effect on March 14, 2023, by the leaders of the three countries to provide stability in the Pacific. In San Diego, California president Biden, with the prime ministers of the United Kingdom and Australia, provided details for a way ahead for building SSNs for the Royal Australian Navy based on demonstrating to China in particular that an alliance-based deterrence strategy was in being to prevent conflict.

Let us go back to Operation Biting in World War II, known as the Bruneval Raid, February 27–28, 1942, a British Combined

Operations raid on a German coastal radar installation at Bruneval in northern France. The objective was to seize and bring back to the UK a new German radar. Senior British officials such as the legendary scientist R. V. Jones determined that it was essential to examine the system to provide countermeasures. Although all those decades ago, Operation Biting still provides insights and critical lessons to be applied today.

What Biting still shows is that it is always important when looking at the investment nations make in their intelligence services to ask one simple question: What is the true added value, whether to national security, to national economic or political self-interests, or to the maintenance of the international order? In the long run, does intelligence make a difference? Biting shows how critical is the role of intelligence.

In 1978, I was privileged to provide a Royal Navy honor guard from the Royal Navy's Ordnance Engineering School for a special ceremony in Southampton to mark the anniversary of the commando/special forces raid of February 27–28, 1942, on the French coast at Bruneval to capture key components of the vital Nazi radar station. Operation Biting was stood up by the newly formed Directorate of Combined Operations, led by then rear admiral Louis Mountbatten. Knowledge of the Wurzburg radar's capabilities at Bruneval was regarded by the British technical intelligence community, led in this matter by the legendary R. V. Jones, Prime Minister Winston Churchill's special programs lead, as absolutely vital. This radar was thought to be used by the Nazis for detecting and tracking Royal Air Force Bomber Command's raids into Germany and also for assisting the Luftwaffe in its attacks on the UK. In 1942, the RAF was suffering heavy losses in its nighttime raids over Germany and before the US Eighth Air Force had arrived in numbers in the UK to begin daylight raids with B-17 aircraft. There was urgency in defeating German detection capabilities of RAF bombers ingressing Germany. Combined Operations determined that the optimal way to capture the key radar components and bring them to the UK was a nighttime parachute drop into the Bruneval area, followed by an attack on the radar site and then a naval evacuation from the beach. This was a daring raid and was 100 percent successful. In addition to bringing back the key radar components, the raiding forces also captured a key German radar technician.

British radar specialists were then able to design countermeasures against this and similar German radars.

The raiding force was led by Maj. John Frost's C Company of the Second Battalion, the Parachute Regiment, and a part of the British First Airborne Division.

Major Frost was to follow his exploits at Bruneval with yet more courageous acts.

In the fall of 1944, now lieutenant colonel Johnny Frost was in command of the Second Battalion, Parachute Regiment, and led his battalion after being dropped into the Low Countries to the famous Arnhem Bridge as a key part of the ill-fated Operation Market Garden. This was conceived as a daring thrust to capture the key Rhine bridges. This would be a precursor to invading Germany by a northerly route that would take General Sir Bernard Montgomery's army to Berlin by the fastest possible route before the Soviet Red Army could occupy key parts of East Germany and Berlin itself. The strategic concept was bold and imaginative but was fatally flawed. Frost's battalion held the Arnhem Bridge, waiting for the arrival of nine thousand men from the British XXX Corps that never arrived. On September 17, 1944, Frost's men, 745 in total, very lightly armed with no armored support whatsoever, faced the wrath of a full German SS Panzer Corps, a quite extraordinary feat of arms and heroism. Frost's men fought to the bitter end, a four-day battle that left only one hundred of his men facing a complete panzer corps. In 1978, the Arnhem Bridge was named the John Frost Bridge. In the movie *A Bridge Too Far*, the British actor Anthony Hopkins plays Lieutenant Colonel Frost.

In 1978, after Lord Mountbatten and Major General Frost had inspected the guard and warmly complimented the officer of the guard, Royal Navy Special Duties lieutenant Derek Rowland, on the fine turnout and performance of his men, I had the privilege of meeting the attending distinguished dignitaries at the reception following the parade. After pleasantries and a discussion on the modern Royal Navy, General Frost and I entered into a detailed discussion on the intelligence successes of Bruneval and the total failure of intelligence in support of Operation Market Garden. What did General Frost think?

General Frost expounded. All source intelligence went into the planning of the Bruneval Raid—from SIGINT collection, Enigma data, aerial photography and work by MI6 agents in France together with reports from the French Resistance.

Timing and the weather were everything, and the role of the meteorologist was paramount for the drop into the Bruneval area and for the Royal Navy's evacuation from the beach—wind, tide, wave height, moon status, and beach profile. The Royal Navy needed precise data on the whereabouts of opposing German naval forces, and Frost and his men needed not just estimates but also precise knowledge of the opposition that they would meet—force composition and locations down to the most detailed unit level—weapons, training status, combat experience, and likely state of readiness. Surprise and security were crucial. Intelligence never failed them, and the mission was a huge success and a great morale booster for the British public in the dark days of 1942. He stressed one critical, overwhelmingly important factor: the need for reliable, secure, and redundant communications that would hold up in any weather conditions and locations. Radio numbers counted.

It was no use having insufficient numbers when one radio failed or was damaged or the operator became a casualty or was captured. Multiple systems were required to ensure survivable communications. What General Frost described to me was what today we call situational awareness—the ability to know in or near real time the overall picture regarding the enemy. In 1942, British Intelligence gave Frost and his men the best situational awareness for the time and the best communications available. Simple techniques work well: just one code word can summarize a total situation; many code words can cover a whole range of contingencies and events so that reporting is kept to a minimum and limits interception and decryption. By contrast, Operation Market Garden was, to quote General Frost, an unmitigated disaster caused largely, but not wholly, by, extremely poor intelligence planning and execution, and the failure of the high command to accept the intelligence provided as ground truth. He said that underscoring this failure to appreciate the intelligence provided was a mindset that was so fixated on the strategic plan that the tactical level detail and execution were assumed to automatically follow as a matter of fact like day follows night. He was emphatic about the detail of failure. The key failure lay in the assessment of the location, movement, and strength of potentially opposing German units, and in particular German heavy armor tanks. These tanks proved to be the nemesis of the Second Battalion, the Parachute Regiment, at the Arnhem Bridge. Key telltale signs of the location, movements, and strengths of one key German panzer division were overlooked to the point of incompetence. Frost stated that insufficient thought and planning had gone into examining and creating a plan B should the original operational plan begin to fall apart. There was no backup and nowhere to go for Frost's brave men. There was no relief on the way because the British Corps that was supposed to drive hard and fast to the key bridges soon found itself faced with innumerable threats and sheer terrain problems that had not been properly thought through, and certainly not anticipated. Communications became nonexistent because of radio failures. What he stressed was that in the two-plus years since Bruneval, the knowledge and operational templates developed by Combined Operations had not become doctrine and had certainly not reached the mindset of Operation Market Garden planners. Most of all, vital intelligence was ignored.

One of the important lessons learned from this conversation was simple but vital.

As the years pass, technology tends to produce better solutions, and operational experience can be built into the doctrine, tactics, techniques, and procedures of fighting forces. However, if there is no organizational and cultural willingness to make changes and implement lessons learned, the same mistakes can be made time and time again in new and often different operational settings. Intelligence aims to mitigate failure by providing the very best total situational awareness with the best timely information flow that communications permit. The US and the UK and the Five Eyes have shared their collective experience, knowledge base, and technology via a wide range of formal exchange agreements and cooperation in field operations, whether military in nature or across the spectrum of intelligence collection operations. A powerful cultural element has been ingrained within the US-UK Intelligence community. The fundamental checklists that started in 1942 continue today, with the tragic lessons of Arnhem as examples of what goes wrong if the checklists are not meticulously followed. The US-UK checklists are all about why and what needs to be known for strategic and tactical intelligence planning and execution at all levels. US-UK Intelligence checks address likely threats, force levels and composition, deployments, basing and logistics, together with tactical development, research and development (R &D), acquisition, and, most of all, the intelligence that frames the choices, options, and decisions associated with the foregoing domains. The amalgam of the collective body of US-UK distilled and carefully analyzed intelligence is simply, in one word, prodigious.

Given the current situation in the INDPACIFIC theater regarding

China's military ascendancy and potential threat to a stable and peaceful East Asia and beyond, particularly the Taiwan scenario, it is critically important to learn from these past operations, their successes and their failures.

Today, the Market Garden and Arnhem Bridge disaster can be avoided in Asia by addressing the key domains of near or real-time intelligence sources and methods, coupled with secure command, control, and communications, uninhibited by cyberattack. Sustaining these elements are the underlying key needs for secure and reliable interoperability and interchangeability between the US and UK forces and their allies. Intelligence is the golden thread running through this whole picture of sustained intelligence support.

The strategic level vision of Market Garden had clear virtue, militarily and politically, yet the planning and execution failed because of the failure to observe all the critical inputs from intelligence, plus the lack of willingness to accept intelligence that did not paint the picture that the high command wished to hear. Biting, by contrast, was an outstanding success with minimal casualties because of the extraordinary quality and reliability of the intelligence inputs and the fact that it was indeed a "Combined Operation." The latter ensured that all key parties were joined in the planning and execution; they also shared intelligence without controls or any other reservations. These are very important factors to consider in the current East Asia scenario. Real-time shared US-UK Intelligence will be quintessential. Timelines will be very short. Decision-making and reaction times will have to be predicated on extraordinary reliable intelligence that flows uninhibited by communications disruption, whether cyber, electronic jamming, and deception. Likewise, the US and UK and their allies will have to be on the top of the intelligence process in terms of their ability to deceive and jam threat communications and electronic systems. The real-time flow of integrated multilevel all-source intelligence will be vital. All this needs to be structure, managed, and operated on a regular basis in exercises and in the detailed planning for every scenario likely to be faced in East Asia and the wider INDOPACIFIC theater. Sharing intelligence on a routine and regular basis with the US and UK allies will be absolutely essential.

Biting and Market Garden provide us with a good entry point into the strategic and tactical and operational issues now facing US and UK Intelligence in the context of the rising power and potential threat from China. Ensuring that both these levels are properly thought through and integrated in a coherent plan of action based on the very best US-UK and allied intelligence may make the difference between peace or war, and in the worst case of conflict, the difference between success and failure, winning or losing.

The John Frost Bridge at Arnhem, Holland (Wikimedia Commons).
A stark reminder for the new generation of US-UK and Five Eyes
Intelligence personnel of the critical importance of accurate and
timely intelligence in strategic planning and execution.

CHAPTER 3

The Strategic and Tactical Level Issues Today with East Asia as a Paradigm for the Way Ahead for Combined US and UK Intelligence

Current world events are so disturbing that a reevaluation of the United States' and the United Kingdom's strategic posture is necessary. The maritime dimension is crucial. In many places, there is not just discord and disharmony but also bloodshed on a large scale. The war in Ukraine focuses attention daily on a people suffering from the effects of Russian tyranny the likes of which we have not seen the evil days of the Third Reich. Putin is a despotic demagogue and a master of deception and lies to a people whose communications and freedom to think and express their opposition are totally controlled. Shades of "Mein Kampf." The Russian political ideology of Vladimir Putin is not far removed from the horrors of Nazi Germany. There are common bonds, values, and processes that unite the US and the UK and their allies as nations in facing the current threats to global peace and stability. The daily lives of Americans and British and our allies are directly affected by, for example, energy supplies at a time when a challenging winter has consequences in the northern hemisphere.

The United States' Middle East associations have recently been tested to the full. The OPEC decision and alignment of Saudi Arabia with those who challenge the world order is a lesson in itself. US and UK Intelligence have to advise who are truly friends, and whom can they trust? The United States' and the UK's most trusted allies remain solid.

The recommended answer at the highest strategic level for the current global situation and for the foreseeable future may be summarized in one key word, "deterrence." From the beginning of the Cold War and the formation of the NATO Alliance, the United States and the United Kingdom succeeded in keeping the world safe from Armageddon, including staving off, in the case of the United States, the Soviet Union's nuclear militarization of Cuba in October and November (October 16–November 20) 1962. President Kennedy and his highly capable body of advisors used naval deterrence to make it patently clear to Nikita Khrushchev's Soviet Union that deploying nuclear armed missiles in Cuba was a nonstarter. The disposition and power of the United States Navy came through. The president's team of Robert McNamara, Gen. Maxwell Taylor, Gen. Curtis Lemay, Admiral George W. Anderson, and the attorney general, Robert F. Kennedy stood firm and refused to be intimidated and bullied by their opposite numbers in Moscow, particularly Khrushchev's closest cohorts, Anastas Mikoyan, Rodion Malinovsky, and Matvei Zakharov. Admiral Anderson, the chief of naval operations, was in charge of the naval blockade of Cuba. Sadly, Anderson never became chairman of the Joint Chiefs of Staff, having differences with the difficult and controversial secretary of defense Robert McNamara. President Kennedy subsequently made Anderson ambassador to Portugal, and later he became president of the Foreign Intelligence Advisory Board. *Time* magazine featured Admiral Anderson on its front cover and described him as "an aggressive blue-water sailor of unfaltering competence and uncommon flare."

Sadly, this tradition and modus operandi has not always been continued in the modern era. Let us look at two critical events, one involving China and the other involving Russia. In the case of the former the United States, the United Kingdom, and their allies allowed the Chinese to unilaterally take over and seize key islands in the South China Sea in total contravention of international law and the rulings of the International Court of Arbitration. The rights of several nations were violated in the process, including the Philippines, Taiwan, Malaysia, Vietnam, and Brunei. The United Nations Convention on the Law of the Sea (UNCLOS) was swept aside by the Chinese in blatant naval actions against the interests of these nations and the overall security posture in East Asia. In addition to the militarization of these islands, the Chinese were clearly looking to secure access to the undersea oil and mineral deposits off these islands. UNCLOS provides a two-hundred-mile economic boundary around the coastline of signatory nations. This is a nontrivial area of ocean.

The United States, in particular, with strong allies in the region, particularly Australia, Japan, and South Korea, with a powerful and highly capable Seventh Fleet, within the US Pacific Fleet, stood by. The Chinese got away with all their seizures. If this had been the Cold War, it is unlikely that any American president and our allies would allow this kind of unilateral seizure of others' sovereign territory that had, in addition, serious strategic implications for the future of United States' and allied interests. Reliable intelligence was available from multiple sources and methods. The preparations that the Chinese made gave plenty of warning time. One issue that persists is why the United States with its key intelligence ally, the United Kingdom, did not produce a coherent diplomatic response alongside movements of the US Seventh Fleet. Submarine provided intelligence would have provided round-the-clock real-time data together with satellite and other overhead data sources. This raises one persistent question ever present when reliable and timely US and UK Intelligence is providing very clear warnings. Whatever the value of intelligence the US-UK Intelligence community, with full

Five Eyes support, can only go so far. Intelligence does not make policy or political decisions. Once highly reliable intelligence has been presented to the political leadership, then this critical role has been fulfilled. During the Cuban Missile Crisis, President Kennedy received explicit and reliable data from U-2 flights over Cuba. He acted accordingly, and the rest is history. By contrast, in the aftermath of the 9/11 attacks, the president of the United States and key advisors decided against strong US-UK Intelligence evidence that there were no weapons of mass destruction in Iraq (other than certain chemical and biological agents that had been transferred to Syria). Similarly in the UK, the British prime minister ignored not just the excellent scientific and technical intelligence that was presented to him by the British Joint Intelligence Committee (JIC) but also the strong assessment by no less than his chief of the British Defense Staff, Admiral Sir Michael Boyce that an invasion of Iraq was both illegal in terms of international law and was flying in the face of very sound and reliable intelligence. Prime Minister Blair chose to ignore the intelligence and the recommendations of his defense chief.

In the case of China, what were possible alternatives given the intelligence assessments? The United States, supported by its allies, could have signaled the Chinese well in advance that such moves would not be acceptable and implemented a major blockade with a powerful US Navy and Marine Corps force. This would not have been confrontational. This would have been the wise and accepted, in historical terms, of the deterrent value of maritime forces signaling that outright aggression will not work. Are their risks? Yes. However, the alternatives, if ignored, are even more risky. Deterrence works if executed in a timely manner with full force that is credible and clearly capable of protecting in a military sense the vital national interests of the United States, the United Kingdom, and their allies. The intelligence was solid. What the United States did in consequence by not reacting to the intelligence provided was to embolden the Chinese, to give them encouragement to be more aggressive.

The year 2022 was the one hundredth anniversary of the death of the British naval strategist, Sir Julian Corbett. In comparative terms, Corbett is the UK's equivalent to the United States' great nineteenth-century strategist Alfred Thayer Mahan (1840–1914, aged 74). The work of both these fine men, with strong historical references in their works, exemplifies in part the need to reassess, not necessarily in complete Mahan-Corbett terms, the roles of deterrence in modern strategy. Their joint concepts today can be supported by excellent intelligence sources and methods. However, unless intelligence is acted upon, the concepts of these two fine thinkers and strategists become redundant.

One definition of strategy is the use of power in all its forms in the pursuit of peace and the vital national interests of the United States, the United Kingdom, and their allies, and this entails the wise and unequivocally clear use of military power, coupled where appropriate with soft power and sanctions. The latter have to be measured and well thought through in terms of overall consequences. It has been argued that oil and gas sanctions on Russia have rebounded in ways that perhaps were not fully analyzed and anticipated. US and UK European allies faced a bleak winter after sanctions were imposed at a time when reliable US-UK Intelligence showed that Russia was finding means to circumvent sanctions by providing oil and gas supplies to several customers by effective backdoor means. These customers included China and India, who needed Russian oil in particular.

US-UK Intelligence has to provide timely data so that diplomacy may proceed hand-in-glove with military measures, though not in ways that provide belligerents with time to stall and prepare for outright aggression. In the current and future global security environment, many strategists argue in favor of a maritime strategy, closely interwoven with air and land power, as the answer for the United States, the United Kingdom, and their allies.

In 2014, Vladimir Putin was allowed to unilaterally take over the Crimea, in total violation of international law, and also shamefully ignoring the 1994 Budapest Memorandum that the United States, Russia, and the United Kingdom agreed to and "committed to respect the independence and sovereignty and the existing borders of Ukraine," and (most important) "to refrain from the threat or use of force" against Ukraine. The latter gave up the third-largest stockpile of nuclear weapons in return for this guarantee. In 2014, the United States did not "deter" Russia in the face of explicit aggression. The United States had the means but neither the will nor the political strength to do this. President Kennedy and the likes of Winston Churchill and Franklin Roosevelt may have been aghast if with us today. What did not happen in 2014 further emboldened Vladimir Putin and his coterie of sycophantic supporters.

The United States and its allies now face a situation in 2023 as a result of a failure to "deter." The US and the UK together could have taken proactive measures under the Budapest Memorandum to checkmate Putin. The intelligence was solid regarding Putin's intentions, force movements, and dispositions. The US and the UK, and other allies, provided Ukraine with considerable military support and training since 2014. This has been very effective. However, the United States in particular could have strengthened support and a united US-UK "deterrence posture" once US-UK Intelligence knew Putin's real intentions. It takes Kennedy, Roosevelt, and Churchill–type strength, courage, resilience, and clearness of purpose to do this. This issue will be addressed later regarding the current Taiwan situation.

One solution for resolving the Ukraine war may depend very much on finding a solution to the Crimea. Your author's recommendation is for the United States to lead in the United Nations in creating Crimea as a "Free State" under a UN Mandate with a United Nations High Commissioner and staff managing the Crimea as a

"Neutral Non Aligned Free State" under the above Mandate. Russia and Ukraine, and all other trading nations, would use the Crimea as a key entrepôt (ports of Evpatoria, Sevastopol, and Theodosia) and would have full and equal access to port facilities. Crimea would be managed as an independent economic entity with World Bank funding to jump-start its operations. This solution would prevent Putin from taking potentially drastic measures in the event of a Ukrainian military assault on the Crimea that may return it to its pre-2014 status as Ukrainian territory. Russia would have full access and zero control; similarly with the Ukraine. The specter of Russia resorting to the use of tactical nuclear weapons has to be avoided. The above is one solution, with Russia withdrawing from all occupied Ukrainian territory. All the above will require accurate and timely US-UK Intelligence, critical to ensure that the situation does not escalate, and Russia poses a threat to use tactical nuclear weapons.

In 2023, China is the most significant challenge. Let us review several key indisputable facts. China has moved from an army-centric to a maritime power, with global deployments, including the Mediterranean and Baltic. By both numbers and tonnage, the Chinese Navy is now the largest in the world, with nineteen major naval shipyards, compared with seven in the United States, and one of these is estimated to be about four times the size of Newport News Shipyard. Sustainability and resupply are being enhanced. Hypersonic anti-ship cruise missiles, Chinese air stations built in the South China Sea, and joint Chinese-Russian strategic patrols over the Sea of Japan reflect ever-growing capabilities. May 2022 witnessed a major Chinese carrier exercise that had apparent Taiwanese threat vectors. The August 4, 2022, major Chinese demonstration has been assessed as a possible step toward an invasion of Taiwan. In October 2022, the US secretary of state and the chief of naval operations, Admiral Michael Gilday, indicated that a Chinese invasion of Taiwan may be closer than thought. Timelines vary depending on which assessment may or may not be reliable. All the above has been supported by excellent US-UK Intelligence, supported by the other three Five Eyes and additional allies such as Japan and South Korea.

US-UK Intelligence can only be valuable up to a point where decision-makers have to make critical choices at the strategic and tactical levels. Your author's recommended solution is a US-led alliance-based maritime strategy with one primary objective: deterrence. The current Five Eyes, Quad (United States, Australia, India, and Japan), and other existing US unilateral and bilateral alliances need to be encapsulated in stronger and more cohesive round-the-clock interoperable and interchangeable maritime forces and 24/7 operations. In addition, the US Navy and Marine Corps should lead in creating an alliance-based common operational picture, with real- or near-real-time intelligence sharing, as appropriate. Indicators and warning (I & W) capabilities need to be expanded and shared with the necessary security safeguards.

At the center of the above alliance-based deterrence strategy is the great virtue of naval power, forward deployed presence. Allied submarine operations offer round-the-clock special capabilities with formidable firepower. Information warfare and deception are crucial capabilities that need to be part of the shared alliance inventory. The Chinese navy has vulnerabilities. These need to be exploited. At the center of all these requirements is sound, timely, and thoroughly secure intelligence.

Effective deterrence needs to be constantly signaled. It cannot be a series of stand-alone exercises, however significant. Rim of the Pacific (RIMPAC) 2022 included 26 nations, 38 ships, 4 submarines, more than 170 aircraft, and 25,000 personnel from June 29 to August 4. This was an outstanding exercise in and around the Hawaiian Islands and Southern California. What is recommended is taking a leaf from NATO's Cold War playbook and create a permanent "Standing Naval Force Pacific and Indian Ocean," and in parallel increasing the frequency of allied maritime exercises. The various alliance countries can join the ever-present and forward-deployed STANAVINDOPACOM force for exercises on a regular basis, in addition to major exercises such as RIMPAC. Supporting these operations has to be US-UK Intelligence, plus intelligence from the other Five Eyes and key allies. The sharing of intelligence via highly secure means is critical. We live in an information warfare age. Constant round-the-clock sharing of intelligence may determine outcomes. Submarine-derived intelligence will be especially timely and invaluable.

US Air Force and US Army operations need to be integrated with US Navy and US Marine Corps plans and operations. The excellent article, "Providing Stability and Deterrence: The US Army in INDOPACOM," by Dr. Carol Evans in *Parameters*, 2021, published by the US Army War College, provides a way ahead. Dr. Evans, director of the US Army's Strategic Studies Institute (SSI), advocates a powerful "Ring of Fire" concept for integrated joint services and allied operations in the INDOPACOM theater, with deterrence of China as the pivotal objective.[1]

A "deterrence"-based maritime strategy provides a viable and achievable way ahead to address the complexities of the threats that the United States, the UK, and their allies face. To do less may place the United States, the UK, and their key allies in serious jeopardy. The leadership of both the US and the UK is encouraged to reassess the "deterrence" posture across the myriad threats and to examine the timely implementation of a greatly enhanced forward-deployed alliance-based maritime strategy to the well-being and long-term security of the United States, the United Kingdom, and their allies.

With the above in mind, it is timely to address the benefits and pitfalls of current and future US-UK Intelligence in the above context, with

---

1   Dr. Carol Evans: Providing Stability and Deterrence: The US Army in INDOPACOM. *Parameters*, US Army War College Press, 2021.

special reference to the differentiating factors that both separate strategic planning and goals with the tactical and operational. Operation Biting and Operation Market Garden analogies have prodigious value to avert in East Asia the reproduction of possible past failures. US and UK Intelligence at all these levels will be vital in both maintaining peace while ensuring success in the worst eventualities of conflict over Taiwan.

CHAPTER 4

Strategic and Tactical and Operational Issues in East Asia and INDOPACOM: The Critical Role of Intelligence to Avoid Disaster

In spite of the decades since Operation Biting and Operation Market Garden, there is considerable relevance for today's threatening situation in East Asia. Operation Biting had considerable technical and tactical objectives. The recovery of the German radar was the objective. Market Garden, by contrast, was totally strategic in its objectives and planning. The primary strategic objective was to ensure a rapid advance into Germany and for US and British forces to reach Berlin before the Soviet Army. However, despite the courage and fighting skills of allied forces, culminating in the legendary stand at the Arnhem Bridge, rightly today named the John Frost Bridge in honor of the courageous leader of the defending British force that fought to the bitter end in the face of overwhelming odds from a German panzer division.

The poignancy of the difference between these two operations with reference to East Asia today and the whole Indo-Pacific theater is paramount.

The best strategic goals, formulated by experienced, well-trained and educated professionals, can come disastrously unstuck for lack of one key factor: timely, accurate, and implemented intelligence, and at every level.

In the previous chapter, we saw how a strategic objective of deterrence through a maritime strategy may deter China, one supported by an all-arms strategy involving naval, land, air, space, and marine forces, all united in one common operational plan to implement grand strategy.

What went wrong with Market Garden? The answer is quite simple. Critical intelligence was ignored.

The objective to seize nine bridges, employing US and British airborne forces (Market) and followed up with land forces including armor (Garden). It was the largest airborne operation of the war up to 1944. First, the topographical and environmental intelligence was poor to nonexistent. What the planners failed to recognize because intelligence was lacking was that not only was the main route for the land forces, Highway 69, just two lanes wide but also the lane on either side was soft to support heavy vehicles, particularly armored vehicles. The surrounding dikes along the road were also cluttered with tress. The planners did not recognize any of this, and that early fall was not the right time of year. The marshy terrain made any outflanking operations impossible.

The pincer movement planned by the supreme allied commander's staff was sound but built on zero appreciation of the terrain. The ground forces were also inadequate in terms of numbers and strength, consisting of XXX Corps of about five thousand vehicles plus bridging equipment and a large number of engineers who had to be transported, about nine thousand British "Sappers." The end result was that XXX Corps could not advance and seize the key bridges and particularly move quickly to the Arnhem Bridge, where the British paratroopers led by Frost were holding the bridge in the face of an overwhelming German panzer force.

All the above was in stark contrast to Operation Biting, where the environmental issues were supported by superb intelligence and planning. Tides, sea height, beach profiles, inland terrain, weather, and road profiles were all outstanding. No aspect was left unturned, and the intelligence was superb in all regards, accurate and timely. By contrast, the US 101st and 82nd and British First Airborne Divisions were badly let down by allied intelligence. The details about the German Ninth and Tenth SS Panzer Divisions were disastrously lacking. September 21, 1944, witnessed the surrender of Frost's men at Arnhem, with the British airborne division trapped west of the Arnhem Bridge. The Rhine was not crossed, and the allies did not succeed until March 1945. All hope of reaching Berlin and ending the war by Christmas 1944 vanished.

In 2023, US and British Intelligence combined has, together with additional Five Eyes and other allied sources and methods, outstanding capabilities. The lessons of Market Garden should be studied closely when reviewing the maritime deterrence strategy devised to contain China and prevent conflict, particularly in regard to Chinese constant saber rattling over Taiwan. What may appear to be a sound strategic plan has to be predicated on absolutely accurate and timely intelligence with the added contemporary complexities of cyber, hypersonic missiles and drones and a wide range of electronic warfare capabilities. Let us look at how the current overall commander of USINDOPACOM sees the current situation in the spring of 2023, in testimony on Capitol Hill in Washington, DC, to the key Congressional Committees of Record.

Admiral John Aquilino, United States Navy, the top Pacific

commander, made it patently clear that he assessed that the US and its allies are running out of time to match China's growing war machine. He presented at the unclassified level an assessment of the emerging threat from Beijing. Admiral Aquilino described China's rapidly growing navy, the spread of hundreds of silos under construction to house nuclear-armed ballistic missiles, and the doubling in production of fifth-generation stealth fighters.

What Admiral Aquilino described the "largest, fastest, most comprehensive military build-up" since the Second World War in both the "conventional and strategic nuclear domains." He showed that the Chinese president Xi was directing this buildup personally. Admiral Aquilino said the following to the US House of Representatives Armed Services Committee: "Conflict in the Indopacom area of operations is neither imminent nor inevitable. Nevertheless, we do not have the luxury of time, we must act now to maintain a free and open Indo-Pacific." The strategic partnership between President Xi and President Putin now has "no limits," Aquilino said, leading to the Russian transfer of highly enriched uranium to Beijing for developing weapons-grade plutonium. He presented evidence to illustrate the burgeoning relationship, later demonstrated for example by a Russian Tu-22M3 bomber flying over the Sea of Okhotsk and the Sea of Japan. The admiral's testimony gave detailed witness to the growing tensions between the superpowers, with Taiwan as the center point. President Xi and reliable open-source Chinese government policy statements have made it clear that China plans to bring Taiwan under Beijing's control.

Relations between Washington and Beijing are regularly exacerbated by a to and fro of military actions and exercises. The US will provide, for example, four hundred Harpoon anti-ship missiles to Taiwan. The Chinese respond accordingly: "The military liaison between the US and Taiwan and the arms sales by the US to Taiwan seriously violate the one-China policy and the three Sino-US joint communiqués," Wang Wenbin, a spokesman for the Chinese foreign ministry, said. However, China continues to build a formidable capability as Admiral Aquilino described and regularly makes threatening moves against Taiwan's sovereignty by entering its airspace with significant forces. The strategic situation is stressed further by the ambiguity of the United States' avowed position on Taiwan. Under the one-China policy, the US recognizes the People's Republic of China (PRC) as the sole legal government of China but only "acknowledges" the Chinese position that Taiwan is historically part of China, though a separate democratic country. The unofficial US relations with the Taipei government, underscored by visits by significant US officials and politicians, has a much more overt and direct relationship with Taiwan with the supply of arms to defend itself. President Biden has pledged on several occasions that the US would come to Taiwan's aid in the event of an invasion. Wang said the sale of Harpoons "severely harms China's sovereignty and security interests and seriously threatens the peace and stability in the Taiwan Strait." This situation calls out for diplomacy to soften the rhetoric. However, the reality at sea and on the ground calls for a US strategy that has to be thoroughly supported by absolutely first-class intelligence given the potential magnitude of possible conflict. Deterrence is quintessential. Xi Jinping and his spokespeople have made their position clear. Wang has warned that should Washington continue on the "wrong road of US-Taiwan collusion," China would "certainly take resolute and forceful measures to firmly defend its sovereignty and security interests." None of this is good. The Chinese media, all government controlled, is therefore reflecting Chinese Communist official policy. The *Global Times*, a party-run newspaper, has reported, for example, that US missiles are a "step of the so-called porcupine strategy to equip the island (Taiwan) to deter the Chinese forces, because the missiles could target China's amphibious landing fleet." The Chinese media overall characterizes US policy of "resisting reunification by force" as "playing with fire."

In this situation, intelligence is vital in ensuring that United States and allied strategy and its implementation are absolutely sound.

If deterrence is to work, intelligence will have to be painstakingly accurate and timely 24/7 and messaging with the Chinese leadership clear and unambiguous to avoid conflict. Admiral Aquilino made a significant comment in his testimony to the US House of Representatives Armed Services Committee: "Beijing publicly claims a preference for peaceful unification over conflict. However, its consistent pressure tactics and coercive behavior demonstrates a significant disconnect between their words and their deeds." He provided a serious warning that predicates constant vigilance and readiness. The warning signs have to be collected by US, British, and allied intelligence and coordinated with unprecedented timeliness. This point is reinforced by another key observation that Admiral Aquilino made regarding the developments in the People's Liberation Army's (PLA) rocket force. He informed the House Armed Services Committee that the PLA was actively and massively expanding its arsenal of conventional and nuclear missiles. He went to stress in his testimony that "this almost certainly includes a large number of hypersonic missiles, some of which may be nuclear-capable." He added, "Construction of silo fields across northern China, coupled with modern ballistic-missile submarines and the Xian H-6N nuclear-capable, air-to-air refueling bomber, underscore China's focus on developing a survivable nuclear triad." It can perhaps be argued that China is balancing the US-China nuclear triad of nuclear-powered ballistic missile submarines, land-based intercontinental ballistic missiles, and strategic bombers. However, when viewed against the total Chinese military buildup, particularly of its naval forces (the largest navy in the world), then this view may be perhaps naïve, even foolhardy. Admiral Aquilino's testimony was an accurate and stark warning for the western democracies to take notice and be prepared to deter Chinese aggression. His comment that the Beijing leadership was obfuscating "the scale of its nuclear force expansion" was hugely significant. He made it very clear that current estimates suggested that before the end of the decade, the Chinese military would "likely possess at least 1,000 deliverable nuclear warheads." The admiral added a poignant observation that "this larger arsenal could provide the PRC with new options before and during a crisis or conflict to leverage nuclear weapons for coercive purposes, including military provocations against US allies and partners in the region." He was clearly advising that he assessed that this was likely Chinese strategy in the event of the US trying to defend Taiwan in the event of a Chinese invasion.

One of Admiral Acquilino's observations resonated because he raised in many minds what the United States did in the 1980s to challenge the Soviet Union head-on. This was the "600 Ship Navy," a symbol that the United States and its allies would outclass the Soviet Union at sea. He informed the committee that the Chinese had added seventeen warships to its navy last year (2022), including four guided-missile cruisers, three destroyers, five frigates, two attack submarines, and a large amphibious assault ship. The admiral predicted that the People's Liberation Army Navy (Plan), currently with 350 "battle force ships," would increase in size to 440 by 2030. US and British Intelligence define such a force as aircraft carriers, submarines, surface combatants, amphibious warfare ships, combat logistics vessels, and support ships, such as at-sea refueling tankers and ammunition ships. He went on to stress that under current US Navy shipbuilding plans, the number of battle force ships would increase from 292 today to a maximum of 367 by 2052. When looking at the relative aircraft carrier fleets, the US Navy still has more carriers than China. The US has eleven compared with China's two that are operational and one new-generation carrier that was launched in 2022. He estimated that the PLA Navy may have five aircraft carriers by 2030.

Admiral Aquilino's very significant statement was that regarding a possible Chinese invasion of Taiwan. He stated that the Beijing has indicated that 2027 may be the target year for the PLA to deliver capabilities, "needed to counter the US military in the Indo-Pacific and project power across the globe." He added further details to support this about additional capabilities that he assessed were geared to this time frame. Fifth-generation J-20 "Mighty Dragon" stealth fighter production was being doubled. He estimated that 150 aircraft would become operational. Aquilino also stated that China was developing a jet-powered supersonic unmanned aircraft system (UAS or drone). This statement caught the committee's attention because of its implications for US, British, and allied aircraft carrier security and survivability. This raises the key point about the roles and missions of operational intelligence in the near term as well as the out years to say the mid-2030s. Ways and means, sources and methods need to be created to detect and defeat such threats and to make allied targets nontransparent. A new generation of electronic warfare systems will be required. This will be addressed in more detail in a later chapter. The Chinese are already expanding their intelligence, surveillance, and reconnaissance capabilities. China performed sixty-four successful space launches in 2022 and placed at least 160 satellites into orbit, expanding significantly Chinese ISR (intelligence, surveillance, and reconnaissance) capabilities. Admiral Aquilino made the telling point to the committee that this was compared with fifty-five space launches in 2021, a dramatic increase in 2022.

The commander of USINDOPACOM provided an unequivocal picture of growing Chinese capabilities. Intelligence is central to addressing the threats that he so eloquently described. We will look at how US-UK Intelligence can be better equipped to face these challenges in later chapters. For now, one critical thread that runs through this chapter is the dialogue between the strategic and the tactical-operational levels. Operations "Biting" and "Market Garden" serve as good insights all these decades later into the differences and how if the right actions are not taken it is possible for disaster to occur. To reinforce the point, there have been many examples where things have gone sadly and often tragically astray.

Two examples illustrate: When US forces in North Korea advanced toward the Yalu River in October 1950, Chinese forces counter attacked, fearing a US invasion of Chinese territory. These forces went largely undetected by the United Nations Command and General McArthur's US Staff. The Chinese destroyed all the bridges starting with the Chinese intervention at Dandong. The extraordinary leadership and valor of US Marine Corps units led by then lieutenant colonel Raymond G. Davis, commander of the First Battalion, Seventh Marines at the Battle of the Chosin Reservoir, saved the situation from disaster. The Medal of Honor winner saved key US Marine units from annihilation by overwhelming Chinese forces. On November 24, 1952, Pres. Harry S. Truman presented Davis with the Medal of Honor at the White House. The tactical and operational factors had been ignored by General McArthur and his staff as a result of a strategic goal to occupy North Korea and secure the border with China. Intelligence was poor to nonexistent regarding both Chinese reactions and intentions, together with assessment of their capabilities. The result is well known. North Korea today remains a communist dictatorship with nuclear weapons.

Strategic and tactical intelligence came into play in the disastrous decision in 2002–2003 to invade Iraq based on false and totally inaccurate intelligence regarding weapons of mass destruction inside Iraq. Although Saddam Hussein was a thoroughly bad person in many ways, not one Iraqi had been involved in the 9/11 attacks, which had in fact involved Saudi Arabian and Egyptian nationals. Iraq was also a bulwark against Iran, very much in US and allied interests. In the UK, the British chief of the Defense Staff, Admiral Sir Michael Boyce, made it clear to the British prime minister Anthony (Tony) Blair that the intelligence was clear that there were no weapons of mass destruction in Iraq and that an invasion would be in contravention of international law and the Geneva Conventions. He advised his prime minister not to go along with supporting a US invasion and to counsel Pres. George W. Bush and his advisors against such an attack.

The relevance for the current East Asia scenario is clear cut. It is critically essential to have absolutely reliable and timely intelligence about Chinese intentions, plans, and operations. This has to be at the strategic and tactical levels. Deterrence can only succeed if the right messages are transmitted to a potential threat and enemy. Negative consequences for the Chinese have to be apparent, self evident in all regards. The balance of the odds coming down against China have to be so apparent that the internal political risks for the leadership have to weighed against any possible gains from retaking Taiwan.

Traditional human intelligence (HUMINT), espionage by another name, may be limited in the tight-knit highly secure world where surveillance is a 24/7 occurrence, particularly for traditional means of connecting with Chinese nationals of consequence. All source communications intelligence, supported by the latest AI techniques, and satellite data across the spectrum will be vital, together with 24/7 intelligence monitoring of all and every aspect of the Chinese military machine. Differentiating a Chinese large military exercise from a real attack on Taiwan should be apparent if intelligence is thorough and timely. Real-time data is critical. All the key factors and capabilities can be gamed in advance with excellent AI tools to assess probabilities and what likelihood. Bayesian analysis techniques will interact with reliable data to explore ambiguities and unknowns. Log-likelihood theory will complement hard intelligence data. At the operational and tactical levels, US and British Intelligence, supported by the other Five Eyes, Japan, and other regional allies, have to ensure that US and allied countervailing forces can react in both timely and effective ways. A surprise attack cannot be allowed to occur. There has to be time for reaction both militarily and diplomatically.

Time and distances play heavily in the Taiwan scenario. Deterrence may only work if the correct balance of forces is present in theater, ready to demonstrate both presence and significant capability. Warning time for the Taiwanese goes hand in glove with the above. The ability for the Taiwanese to react quickly and effectively is paramount. This raises the question of the necessity for intelligence sharing across all nations involved in countervailing operations.

Interoperability and interchangeability will only work in a secure and reliable communications environment with highly effective counter cyber and jamming technologies. The ability to deceive the enemy while sustaining secure US, British, and allied communications is essential given current and emerging Chinese threat systems. Likewise, the ability to game the various options assessed as available to the Chinese provides a sound basis for understanding likely timelines and particularly warning factors.

What the Cold War called "I & W" pertains in a new format in East Asia. Indicators and warning have to be fully defined and understood. Like the signs and symptoms in the medical world for detecting and defining ill-health issues, so too in the national security world. They can be monitored and, together with game theory in traditional war games, may provide the US national leadership and INDOPACOM with adequate warning time. The major issue that needs to be addressed is the timeline of warnings that indicate Chinese aggressive intentions set against US and allied reaction times in terms of the deployment of US and allied forces. A new Standing Naval Force INDOPA may be one solution based on a combined US and allied force constantly in being at sea and able to react in a timely manner. Time and distance are critical factors. Should the Chinese plan and gamble on a fait accompli based on untimely allied reactions, then this scenario needs to be examined in fine detail to implement US and allied remedies.

CHAPTER 5

US-UK Intelligence Roles, Missions, and Operations in a Rapidly Changing World

The character, locations, and roles of US and British Intelligence, and their three Five Eyes partners and other allies, will change in this new era of conflict that has been defined by the Russian invasion of Ukraine and the many and varied challenges from China.

In certain scenarios, advanced weapons technology may often not be either enough or the correct response. Overwhelming kinetic force may not be the solution to complex political–military–theocratic and economic scenarios in which military power and the use of force can only be one component. In some scenarios, the very threat of the use of force, such as the Iranian oil tanker seizure situation in the Strait of Hormuz in July 2019, may indeed exacerbate it.

What should UK-US Intelligence capabilities look like for the next generation, and how should these two nations work together to help preserve both international order and the critical national self-interests of each country?

The sum of the parts within US-UK Intelligence is much greater than the individual units themselves. For examples, if we look at Bosnia, Kosovo, Sierra Leone, Libya, the Arab Spring, the major conflicts in Iraq and Afghanistan, plus Syria, the whole ISIS phenomena, and the current situation in Ukraine in very objective terms, we can see how this aggregation of capabilities yields advantages. These events tell us something about how the US and the UK should invest in intelligence and see the return on their investments. Let is look back on these events.

The Bosnian crisis in southeast Europe, 1992–1995, witnessed a wholesale humanitarian tragedy. The main protagonists were the Republic of Bosnia and Herzegovina, and Bosnian Serb and Bosnian Croat entities within that Republic, following the breakup of Yugoslavia and secessions of 1991. The conflict was a clash of ethnic and religious rivalries, overlain by the ambitions of individual leaders, particularly Slobodan Milosevic, the Serbian leader. The worst manifestations and atrocities occurred with the massacre (or ethnic cleansing) of the Bosnian Muslim and Croat population. US and UK combined intelligence reporting was thorough and accurate.

However, there was considerable negative political blowback as a result of US inaction during the unfolding crisis, so close to mainland Europe, and in spite of the mounting intelligence assessments.

The European Union was politically committed to deterring and countering any return to the very causes of European disharmony and bloodshed that had witnessed countless slaughter since the early Middle Ages. The intelligence provided led to the US and the UK and their European allies agreeing on intervention. The British government chose the Royal Navy as its symbol of commitment, sending HMS *Invincible, Illustrious*, and *Ark Royal* (the three light through-deck cruisers of Sea Harrier-Carriers) into the Adriatic, conducting sanctions enforcement. Early on in these operations, on April 16, 1994, one of the Royal Navy FA2 Sea Harriers was shot down by a surface-to-air missile fired from a Serbian launcher. Fortunately, the pilot escaped unharmed.

In addition to Royal Navy Sea Harriers, the UK also provided twelve Royal Air Force GR7s. It was some time before the US ramped up its direct involvement, with operations in Kosovo starting on March 24, 1999, with Operation Allied Force, which was NATO's bombing campaign to halt the internecine hostilities and ethnic slaughter. This in itself was a major milestone insofar as this was the very first time that NATO went to war. The targets of US Navy and Royal Navy strikes were the forces of Slobodan Milosevic. This conflict was also a first in that the Royal Navy SSN, HMS *Splendid*, fired Tomahawk missiles for the first time. Seven Sea HarrierFA2s provided airborne strike, in somewhat stark contrast to the high level of airborne strikes launched by the US Navy. UK-US Intelligence provided excellent intelligence that made these strikes effective. The sources and methods employed were across the span of state-of-the-art collection and analysis.

The UK supported an Australian-led operation to stabilize the situation in East Timor in 1999 by sending the destroyer HMS *Glasgow*, a Royal Marines Special Boat Section unit, and a three-hundred-strong Gurkha unit. Intelligence support was not just across UK–US-Australian boundaries, rather the total Five Eyes community.

Similarly, when the UK intervened in the civil war in Sierra Leone in 2000, with the deployment of HMS *Argyll* and HMS *Chatham*, the assault ship HMS *Ocean*, and the light Sea Harrier carrier HMS *Illustrious* with thirteen Sea Harriers on board, US-UK Intelligence network shifted into gear. The UK had the full support of US intelligence sources and methods. The agility and flexibility of US-UK Intelligence to support maritime expeditionary warfare operations became increasingly important. The combined expeditionary forces of the US and the UK plus the other five nations are compelling, and when given a legal international mandate, such as United Nations Security Council Resolution 1368, following the 9/11 attacks, the role of US-UK Intelligence to support these operations becomes evident. This capability is in addition to Article Four of NATO's Charter—that the member nations will assist one another in collective self-defense; an attack upon one is an attack upon all. In this context, US-UK Intelligence works together as always and, in addition, across NATO boundaries, with agreed intelligence passed to other non-Five Eyes nations based on the exigencies of the situation.

US-UK Intelligence was crucial from October 7, 2001, when the UK and US launched key attacks with naval aircraft and cruise missiles against Taliban and al-Qaeda training camps and their communications, and Five Eyes Special Forces played key roles on the ground. On November 16, 2001, the al-Qaeda leader, Mohammed Atef, was killed by a US air strike based on excellent intelligence. On the night of October 4, 2001, USS *Theodore Roosevelt* (with Carrier Air Wing One, CVW-1) launched the initial strikes against al-Qaeda from the northern Arabian Sea. It then spent 159 consecutive days at sea, with zero dependence on shore support, breaking the record longest underway period in the history of the US Navy since World War II. This was an extraordinary achievement and, most importantly, symbolic of the flexibility and sustainability of naval power. Without a constant 24/7 stream of good intelligence from US-UK Intelligence plus full Five Eyes support, its mission would have been constrained. Persistent forward-deployed presence during this vital period to destroy what was, in effect, the threat from a relatively small group of Islamic fundamentalists, that had rocked the civilized world, was sustained by round-the-clock US-UK Intelligence. We will not dwell on the decision by the US and the UK to invade Iraq in 2003. This was discussed earlier. The US House and Senate gave their approval (the Joint Resolution to Authorize the use of United States Armed Forces Against Iraq, October 2, 2002, and enacted October 16, 2002), and the House of Commons voted 412 in favor and 149 against on March 18, 2003, so, in effect, no one, save a few, is truly blameless regarding what many see in retrospect as strategic blunder. What is relevant here is that US-UK Intelligence made corrections to these missteps immediately thereafter. Intelligence does not make policy and determine grand strategy. It does not adjudicate on the rights and wrong of "regime change" for example. It is a support function. However, there are many dynamics at work in the US-UK Intelligence domain other than just providing what is hopefully the best actionable information.

The US and the UK, together with their three Five Eyes partners, have facilities in key locations around the globe. For example, the UK's Diego Garcia Island in the Indian Ocean and the UK sovereign base at Akrotiri in Cyprus proved invaluable for intelligence as well as military purposes. Intelligence infrastructure and five-way communications are paramount. The Australian facility at Pine Gap is of enormous importance, together with facilities in the UK itself at places like Menwith Hill in Yorkshire. However, good as these may be, and they are outstanding, the complexity of political-military-intelligence interactions often may cloud the enormous value that good intelligence provides.

This point became clear as the Iraq campaign was waged, with a whole new set of politically unanticipated problems arising, characterized by sectarian upheaval and violence. In more structured scenarios, successful outcomes are more predictable.

For example, US-UK Intelligence support to counter piracy operations in the Gulf of Aden and off Somalia can be measured in quantifiable terms. There were 197 pirate attacks in 2009, and, by 2013, there were just 13 attacks. At the time of writing, the problem has been surmounted if not eliminated, though there will always be pirates in certain regions who are desperate enough, like most criminals, to chance their arm against the odds.

What this again demonstrated was the total overwhelming

effectiveness of US-UK Intelligence support. As 2019, progressed it became clear that full support was required for the preservation of international maritime law in the Persian Gulf/Arabian Sea and the Strait of Hormuz and its approaches in the Gulf of Oman.

The seizure by Iran of the British tanker *Stena Impero* was described by British foreign secretary Jeremy Hunt as an act of piracy in the House of Commons on July 22, 2019. To provide escort protection, reliable real-time intelligence was required so that beneath the surface of diplomatic maneuver was a rock-solid input of current intelligence.

Humanitarian relief and evacuation of nationals and others from hot spots have always been key peacetime missions of the US and the UK. For example, the December 2004 tragic tsunami in South and Southeast Asia and the July 2006 Royal Navy evacuations from Lebanon during the Israeli-Hezbollah conflict required intelligence support. In January 2010 came the Haiti earthquake, and in November 2013 the devastating Typhoon Haiyan in the Philippines, all requiring a measure of intelligence support.

Among natural disasters came global political change with the "Arab Spring"—a series of anti-government protests and uprisings that spread across the Middle East in early 2011. The beginnings in Tunisia spread across the Middle East, to Egypt, Libya, Yemen, Syria, Bahrain, Kuwait, Lebanon, and Oman, while the governments of Morocco and Jordan preempted revolt by various constitutional reforms knowing that protest could and would escalate. There were protests elsewhere, including Saudi Arabia, Sudan, and Mauritania, but the center of change began on December 18, 2010, in Tunisia with the Tunisian Revolution. By mid-2012, the "spring" had faded to a "winter." By spring 2012, rulers had been forced out in Tunisia, Egypt, Libya, and Yemen. There were major civil uprisings in Bahrain and Syria. From a UK-US Intelligence perspective, the 2011 Libyan revolt required support. On February 26, 2011, the United Nations imposed UN Resolution 1970, an arms embargo, on Libya, together with a UN-mandated No Fly Zone, UN Resolution 1973. UK-US Intelligence provided support to Royal Navy Tomahawk strikes from the SSNs HMS *Triumph* and HMS *Turbulent* with similar strikes by US Navy surface ships in Operation Odyssey Dawn in March 2011. More than 112 Tomahawk cruise missiles attacked over twenty targets in the first assault: Libyan air-defense missile sites, early warning radar, and key communications facilities, mainly around and in Tripoli, Misratah, and Surt.

US-UK Intelligence brought a wealth of intelligence knowledge and experience to these operations, developed over a significant period from the beginning of the Cold War through to, for example, US operations in Lebanon in 1982–83, in Grenada in 1983, and in Panama in 1989. These operations, together with operations such as the Falklands, in Sierra Leone, and East Timor, build resilience into US-UK Intelligence coordination. Multi-intelligence sources and methods were used throughout these operations, with, for example, overhead IMINT complementing on-the-ground special SIGINT capabilities and HUMINT. By 2023, there is very little that the US-UK Intelligence team, plus full support from Canada, Australia, and New Zealand, has not faced.

In some instances, the US and the UK were powerless in spite of first-class intelligence. The 2008 Russian invasion of Georgia provoked no military response from the US or the West in general. In August 2013, the British House of Commons voted against intervention in the Syrian crisis and civil war, with a resounding withdrawal from concepts of "regime change" as a strategic objective of intervention. The US-UK Intelligence apparatus is outstanding, but its purpose is not to illicit or encourage political decision-making. For example, where there was excellent intelligence but no political response: India's invasion of East Pakistan in 1971 in support of Bangladesh secession invoked no response; similarly, the 1978–1979 invasion of Cambodia by Vietnam to destroy the very evil Khmer Rouge regime was simply observed; in 1978–1979, Tanzania intervened in Uganda against the equally evil regime of Idi Amin without a US-UK response. Perhaps tragically, the US and the UK, and the West as a whole, did not intervene in the terrible 1994 genocide in Rwanda. Shades of the Hungarian uprising and the invasion of Czechoslovakia by the Soviet Union began to emerge in another key location.

In August 1999, Vladimir Putin, today notorious because of the invasion of Ukraine, and a former Soviet KGB officer, became Boris Yeltsin's prime minister. Following the Second Chechnya War, Putin became president of Russia. In August 2008, Putin launched the invasion of Georgia, a sovereign state, against international norms and the collective positions of the US and the UK. The occupation of the Crimea by Russia gained more attention. What all this shows is that the US and the UK have picked their interventions.

Intelligence has been in a support role, and only that. In fact, in the thirty-three years from 1990 to 2023, most of the interventions globally have been under the auspices and mandates of the United Nations. This observation somewhat undermines the often-misleading notion that the UN remains moribund in the face of challenge. In the early part of the period, between 1989 and 2013, the United Nations directed and supported a total of fifty-three documented peacekeeping operations, with the US and the UK supporting these actions.

One arena where there has not been so much political differences, rather the nuances of diplomatic position taking between the US and the UK and the other three member nations of the Five Eyes, is in regard to the United Nations Convention on the Law of the Sea (UNCLOS). This became effective on November 16, 1994, with sixty nations signing the treaty. At the time of writing, 166 countries and the European Union as a whole have joined the convention. International lawyers tend to debate and agree to disagree whether the convention has in effect codified what is commonly accepted as customary international law as embodied in prior case law.

The United Nations has no role in implementing the convention. Authorities such as the International Maritime Organization, the International Whaling Commission, and the International Seabed Authority (established by the UN Convention) do play very active participatory roles. The United States is a nonparty to the UNCLOS.

The US did participate in the prior conference on UNCLOS from 1973 to 1982, and the subsequent negotiations and modifications to the treaty from 1990 to 1994.

In essence, UNCLOS is a law of the sea. It defines rights and responsibilities of nations in the use of the world's oceans, delineates maritime business guidelines, environmental issues, and, most significantly, it lays down code for the management of marine natural resources. There is a strong legal intellectual movement in the US in support of the US Congress ratifying and the president signing the UNCLOS respectively. Much of the argument has devolved from the current situation with China in the South and East China Seas.

US and UK combined intelligence has been significant in nuclear weapons agreements.

Both Iran and North Korea have challenged the West in the development of their nuclear weapons programs, and in the case of Iran in monitoring their program in light of the 2015 agreement in Lausanne, Switzerland, between Iran and the P5 + 1, and the EU—namely, the permanent members of the United Nations Security Council: the United States, the United Kingdom, Russia, France, and China, plus Germany, and the European Union. On July 14, 2015, the Joint Comprehensive Plan of Action (JCPOA) was announced.

On May 8, 2018, the United States president Donald Trump announced that the United States was withdrawing from the agreement. The specificity was extremely well defined as to what Iran would do to enjoy lifting of sanctions, with the IAEA (International

Atomic Energy Authority) providing the in-country monitoring of Iran's compliance. Both the secretary general of the United Nations, Ban Ki-moon, and the director general of the IAEA, Yukiya Amano, welcomed the agreement. The role of US-UK Intelligence is to supply ideally first-class actionable intelligence. In addition to the work of the IAEA inspectors, all of whom are regarded as highly competent by their peers in the nuclear weapons inspection community, there has been separate and independent intelligence operations by the US and the UK and the Five Eyes as a whole on a collective basis. There have been no official political pronouncements from the UK, Canada, Australia, or New Zealand political leadership that there is evidence that Iran has violated the agreement. These member countries plus the United States will have employed and coordinated multiple sources and methods to ensure that Iran has not been cheating on the agreement. When the product of these sources and methods is aggregated with the direct in-country work of the IAEA inspectors, the probability that Iran is cheating on the agreement is extremely low. The risks for Iran of losing the economic benefits of the agreement are tremendous. This illustrates perhaps better than no other contemporary case in the past five years where intelligence can only go so far. At the time of writing in 2023, Iran is showing unequivocally that it may well transgress. Negotiations via Saudi Arabia are active. The end result remains open-ended with some likelihood that Iran will make negative moves in its acquisition of a nuclear capability. US-UK Intelligence is today vital in this regard. The ability to intervene without kinetic force may rest with advanced US-UK electronic intelligence means.

It is rather like the old equine adage, "You may lead a horse to water, but it may not drink." It is never the role of intelligence to directly influence policy. However, conversely, it is always possible, as we saw in the case of the invasion of Iraq, that intelligence can be used by politicians to justify their policies and actions, even when that intelligence is skewed.

US-UK Intelligence in Iran clearly watches, listens, looks, samples, and follows the discreet paths of the Iranian supply chain. Rather like an analogue with the current Chinese maritime buildup, there is a detailed and very observable supply chain that enables a country such as Iran to assemble the infrastructure for developing nuclear capabilities, whether for energy purposes or for weaponry. A country such as Iran, with a GDP in 2017 of US$387,611 million (twenty-ninth in the global GDP league table in 2017), lying in GDP terms between the state of Indiana, with a GDP of US$361,732 million and the state of Maryland with a GDP of US$397,815 million, cannot on its own produce all the key components for a nuclear weapons program.

In 2017, Maryland was the fifteenth US state in GDP, and Indiana was the sixteenth US state in GDP.3 (CIA World Factbook). This data puts Iranian national assets and wealth in the proper context, somewhat like the economic status of Russia. The further imposition of US sanctions has undoubtedly reduced Iran's current GDP from 2020 onward. Various other countries have to be compliant in aiding, and in the past, abetting Iran, a country that can be seen from the above data is not wealthy. Similarly, intellectual capital is required of a high order. Atomic weapons scientists and technologist do not grow on trees. They have to be trained and acquire all the necessary skill sets to manage and develop a nuclear weapons program. Every part and component of a nuclear weapons system is understood by the scientific and technical intelligence community within US-UK Intelligence with specialist support, for example, in the case of the United States, the national laboratories, such as Los Alamos, Lawrence Livermore, and Oak Ridge, where key technical staff are part and parcel of the technical intelligence community. The same is true in the United Kingdom, the other nuclear weapons power within the Five Eyes. The movement of key components and intellectual property are targets for US-UK Intelligence. This process also indicates who else is compliant with Iran, perhaps more often for financial gain than simply just political allegiance and position taking in the politics of the Middle East. They, too, are watched, listened to, and closely monitored to establish the technical dependencies and relationships between key individuals. An Iranian nuclear scientist can try to hide from exposure to US-UK surveillance, but this is an extremely difficult task, and the more key people try to hide, the more they become vulnerable to exposure, and their collaboration with second and third parties becomes more and more exposed. One highly competent, knowledgeable, and experienced defector or émigré can yield so much intelligence that a whole hierarchy can be well understood.

A former MI6 HUMINT operation will illustrate just one of multiple ways of gaining access. This operation entered the public domain in November 2010 as a result of a report in the UK's *Guardian* newspaper by Richard Norton-Taylor, the lead staff reporter. This illustrates certain trade craft capabilities of US-UK Intelligence, and the Five Eyes as a whole.

MI6 employed two businessmen from a Coventry, UK-based machine tool company, Matrix Churchill, and another company, Ordtec, to spy on Saddam Hussein's nuclear weapons program. The operation only became public knowledge because two key executives, Paul Henderson of Matrix Churchill and John Paul Grecian of Ordtec, were inadvertently accused of breaching various UK trade embargoes on Iraq. One part of the UK government that was not in the know did not communicate with another part, the intelligence community that naturally wished to keep its deeply buried program well away from the purview of regular British civil service trade overseers. Both men were actually put on trial at the Old Bailey in London. Both men were later exonerated and well compensated by the British government. What sadly became exposed was the key fact that MI6 had gained inside access by allowing a British company to sell components to Saddam Hussein's program. MI6 gained thereby access to much of what was transpiring in Baghdad.

Today, US-UK Intelligence keeps a constant close watch on "who, what, and wherefrom" as far as the global movement of nuclear-related materials, components, and brainpower are concerned. The same applies to non-weapon-related radionuclide materials, such cobalt-60 and strontium-90 that if used inappropriately can, for example, be combined with various types of high explosives to make a "dirty bomb."

In the digital microwave communications era, US-UK Intelligence has to contend with the complexities of the electronic spillover from microwave towers, particularly of largely unencrypted communications, to sweep up vast volumes of communications. Satellites become crucial in this mission, and at the analysis end of the business are highly sophisticated key word search engines sifting the wheat from the chaff. The latter requires constant software upgrades plus the added challenge of multiple dialects in the key languages of interest. The Cray computers of the 1970s are today dinosaurs in comparison with what US-UK Intelligence requires to analyze the vast amount of real-time traffic.

North Korea has presented much more of a challenge for US-UK Intelligence and the Five Eyes than Iran at one level. The reasons are well known, particularly as North Korea has been a closed society with no access of note, and for those who have been visitors from the West, always running the risk of arrest and imprisonment. The usual North Korean excuse for such arrests has been espionage. Space becomes very significant regarding North Korea in the absence of HUMINT, very much akin to the Soviet Union during the Cold War and certainly true of China today, where western attachés, for example, are not permitted to visit certain key military sites inside mainland China.

It is impossible to hide nuclear construction sites from satellites; similarly, with the North Korean missile facilities and launch sites. Modern commercial satellites are highly capable systems, and imagery from these is available for the world to see, together, for example, with Chinese military construction sites on islands and atolls in the South China Sea. Facilities cannot be hidden. However, detailed technical plans and status are less easy to acquire but are nonetheless available to good scientific and technical intelligence analysis. North Korean missile telemetry gives away much valuable information that cannot be hidden. Even with mobile launchers and attempts to conceal and camouflage launch systems, both US national and commercial systems can see such platforms.

The US National Geospatial Agency is most likely ahead of any other non-Five Eyes agency in supporting collection by the US NRO (National Reconnaissance Office) in terms of processing and presentational techniques and technology. Underground facilities and bunkers are naturally a problem for satellite surveillance, but even these are open to imaging during construction. US-UK Intelligence has a wealth of historical knowledge and expertise in collecting against and analyzing nuclear weapons programs that go as far back to the early days of the Soviet programs and the first Soviet nuclear detonation on August 29, 1949, at the Semipalatinsk nuclear test site in what is modern-day Kazakhstan. Technical collection against air burst and underground nuclear tests is extremely well developed. MASINT, or Measurement and Signature Intelligence, is not as new as may appear. The generic title covers multiple domains that have been developed over many decades since World War II. These domains include Radar Intelligence (RADINT), Acoustic Intelligence (ACINT), Nuclear Intelligence (NUCINT), Radio Frequency and Electromagnetic Pulse Intelligence (RF/EMPINT), Electro-Optical Intelligence (ELECTRO-OPINT), Laser Intelligence (LASINT), Materials Intelligence, and various forms of Radiation Intelligence (RINT). These unclassified domains show the extent to which US-UK specialist technical intelligence collection has developed. Along with the science and technology underpinning these developments, the US and UK have developed specialist clandestine collection ways and means to measure just where in the development cycle, for example, a Soviet nuclear weapons program was. Nothing has changed today with Putin's Russia.

Decades of experience have been brought to bear on current Iranian and North Korean nuclear systems. An a priori knowledge base is essential for accomplishing all the above. This applies particularly to both the United States and the United Kingdom in their development of both nuclear weapons and nuclear submarine and submarine-launched missile technology, the latter being shared with the United Kingdom by the United States as a result of the agreement signed in December 1962 between President Kennedy and Prime Minister Macmillan. The 2023 nuclear submarine building program for Australia with the US and the UK is a continuation of that process in the face of the urgent need to increase nuclear-powered attack submarines' numbers and presence in the INDOPACOM theater of operations.

A major part of the US-UK nuclear weapons intelligence posture has been indicators and warning (I & W), applying to the 24/7 watch for a possible nuclear weapons launch by any non-UK-US country, and particularly one of the defined "rogue" nations. I & W capabilities require multi-intelligence sources and methods.

Clearly, one of the most worrisome scenarios is a possible accidental launch as a result of a system failure, a cyberpenetration and attack, or a rogue group taking over a launch site together with all the necessary command and control facilities.

An accidental missile launch that does not contain a nuclear warhead is a most challenging scenario for very clear reasons. Unannounced test launches have a high priority and require 24/7 watch systems to differentiate a test launch from an attack. The Japanese government has, for example, naturally been deeply concerned about North Korean ballistic missile launches passing over Japanese territory.

In these situations, every source and every method comes into play, particularly if the threat nation employs various deception techniques.

The above illustrates perhaps more than anything the fundamental role of US-UK Intelligence with their Five Eyes partners in maintaining global peace and security and keeping international order on an even keel.

Pres. Donald Trump's meeting with Kim Jong Un of North Korea in Singapore on Tuesday, June 12, 2018, was the first time a US president met with a sitting North Korean leader, in an attempt to begin negotiations for North Korea to begin denuclearization of its nuclear weapons program. The US president met with a man that has been a dictator who has authorized the execution and imprisonment of all who opposed him or offered any form of challenge to his dictatorship. The rocky road ahead, from June 12, 2018, onward, was analyzed almost into paralysis by the world's media. Every political commentator throughout the globe had their version of what may or may not have transpired in Singapore in terms of likely outcomes. This was followed on June 30, 2019, by the Trump-Kim meeting at the Demilitarized Zone (DMZ) in Korea, followed by President Trump entering North Korea. World media speculation again abounded. One aspect is most certain in the uncertain world that followed June 12, 2018, and June 30, 2019—US-UK and the Five Eyes intelligence community will be ever vigilant, employing not just the sentinels in space but also all and every one of the sources and methods described above to monitor North Korean moves.

The microwave and digital revolution has had a dramatic impact on US-UK Intelligence.

The technical order of the Cold War was changed significantly by the microwave and digital revolution, together with the vastness of contemporary communications in terms of volumes of voice, data, and imagery passing via undersea cables and space. US-UK communications systems have to be both well defended as well as retaining the ability to penetrate threat communications across the spectrum. Cyberattacks have changed the parameters of not just intelligence sources and methods but also those very sources and methods themselves. Threat systems have figured out that the one key way to penetrate the Five Eyes intelligence bastion is in the development and acquisition stages and through cyberattacks. By these means, threats to the Five Eyes can understand in advance what systems are being developed.

Penetration of the US-UK industrial base is the key to these operations. This is well illustrated by an article that appeared in the *Washington Post* on June 8, 2018, by Ellen Nakashima and Paul Sonne. This article described how China had hacked into "a Navy contractor and secured a trove of highly sensitive data on submarine warfare" in January and February 2018. According to the article, the *Washington Post* agreed to "withhold certain details about the compromised missile project at the request of the Navy, which argued that their release could harm national security."

What this illustrates is a major change in the rules of the game.

Protection of vital US-UK and Five Eyes systems from cyberattack is crucial, together with protection of space assets and in particular GPS satellites and the infrastructure that support them. GPS is not just the means and end for an almost endless list of military and intelligence systems; it is the ways and the means for multiple global applications across every sector of human activity, and not simply the obvious ones related to our daily use of GPS mapping and location finding. GPS underpins the global financial system. Dependable commercial satellite systems are part of the way of life of the global economy. Detecting and countering threats to these systems by the US and UK have now risen very high on the list of intelligence missions.

We can look back to the 1880s and the age of Blinker Hall and his father to the communications transformation of the twenty-first century. During this period, one aspect of the intelligence process has not changed. This is open-source material, or simply what our fellow human beings write. Within open sources is a wealth of intelligence that relates to, for example, the likely intentions of nation states. It is very easy to neglect this valuable source of information. The amount of valuable information in open sources is simply prodigious.

On Thursday, May 17, 2018, Capt. James E. Fanell, US Navy (retired), a former director of intelligence and information operations, US Pacific Fleet, gave a lengthy and detailed statement to the US House of Representatives Permanent Select Committee on Intelligence (HPSCI), with specific reference to China's worldwide military expansion. Captain Fanell's statement was entitled "China's Global Naval Strategy and Expanding Force Structure: A Pathway to Hegemony." His statement drew heavily on reliable Chinese open sources, what the Chinese have indeed told us about their future plans and expansion not just in Asia but also beyond. The outer island chain expansion policy has been followed in Chinese literature by Captain Fanell and his former staff. When these open-source writings are coupled with what the Chinese have actually done, together with other intelligence sources and methods, a highly reliable intelligence picture emerges.

Listening and reading is invaluable, and this applies across the board of foreign societies, not just key leaders. This encompasses scientific and technical journals and a whole range of foreign technical, political, and economic press and journal sources, together with official governmental statements and speeches. As Captain Fanell wisely demonstrated in great detail, "What the Chinese have said they plan to do, they have indeed done." The open-source approach may be sometimes neglected.

For example, the foreign and Five Eyes nations' open-source literature is regularly addressing the issue of undersea communications cable vulnerability and reports of foreign undersea intrusions on vital undersea nodes. This is clearly a serious issue and one that cannot be ignored by not just the Five Eyes intelligence community but also the combined political leadership of each member nation.

The world has changed so dramatically in geopolitical terms since 9/11, and in technical terms, there has been a revolution in digital and microwave technologies.

The disparities with the twentieth century are enormous. US-UK Intelligence must not lose, institutionally, culturally, technically, and operationally, some of the key achievements of the twentieth century. The last thing that the US and the UK need to do in the world today is lose the knowledge and experience base that may still be relevant in spite of the dramatic changes that we have examined. Reinvention of the wheel is a costly experience.

On February 27, 1984, Denis Healey, member of Parliament in the UK House of Commons and former minister of defense in the 1960s, made the following observation: "GCHQ has been by far the most valuable source of intelligence for the British government ever since it began operating at Bletchley during the last war. British skills in interception and code breaking are unique and highly valued by our allies. GCHQ has been a key element in our relationship with the United States for more than forty years." Denis Healey's words were turned into bricks and mortar twelve years later when, between 1996 and 2003, the plans were laid and construction began and was completed for the new GCHQ complex near Cheltenham, England.

The grand old men of GC & CS, such as Hugh Foss, Dilly Knox, Comm. Alastair Denniston, Comm. Edward Travis, and the early leaders of SIS, such as Commander Mansfield Cumming (the original "C") and Hugh "Quex" Sinclair, would have been duly proud of the new edifice, the "Doughnut," called such because of its doughnut-like shape, that emerged in the English countryside. It is salutary to reflect that on October 21, 1941, four great stalwarts of Bletchley Park, Hugh Alexander, Stuart Milner Barry, Gordon Welchman, and the inimitable Alan Turing took it upon themselves, without any approval or the knowledge of higher authority, to write to Winston Churchill directly asking for more resources for Bletchley Park.

Such was the change from the dark days of October 1941 to the brighter post–Cold War days of the 1990s, with the postwar record of GCHQ and its American and Five Eyes cousins in Canada, Australia, and New Zealand, standing as a record of successful cooperation.

Winston Churchill saw the incredible value of Bletchley and made the necessary investment immediately. We can reflect on Prof. Max Newman and Tommy Flowers at the Post Office Research Facility, at Dollis Hill, building the first electronic computer "Colossus" for Bletchley Park. The great cooperation between the United Kingdom and the United States exemplified in the January 1941 agreement to share the Magic data with the UK, a quid pro quo for UK Enigma data. In September 1942, the deputy director of Bletchley, Comm. Edward Travis, and the head of the Naval Section, Frank Birch, traveled to Washington, DC, to conclude the "Holden Agreement" that initiated full and total UK-US cooperation and integration on German naval traffic, of which Enigma was a critical component. This was further expanded in 1944. In May 1943, the UK-US BRUSA Agreement expanded cooperation to German Army and Air Force SIGINT traffic. In 1945, Winston Churchill is reputed to have told King George VI that Enigma's product, Ultra, won the war, according to Gustav Bertrand, the French military intelligence officer who played a key role in deciphering Enigma in the 1930s.

After 1945, nothing changed. UK-US cooperation continued in full, with the VENONA Project a great example of successful joint penetration of Soviet KGB message traffic. The latter led to the pinpointing of the British spies Donald MacLean, Guy Burgess,

John Cairncross, and the notorious Kim Philby, who caused massive damage to MI6 operations. The British atom spy Klaus Fuchs was similarly detected. As part of the growing involvement and cooperation with Australia, the KGB Moscow-Canberra cable traffic was read in almost real time by GCHQ. The British First Sea Lord, admiral of the fleet Andrew Browne Cunningham, First Viscount Cunningham (nicknamed "ABC"), wrote in his diary on November 21, 1945, "Much discussion about 100 percent cooperation with the USA about SIGINT. Decided that less than 100 per cent cooperation was not worth having." Admiral Cunningham's words sum up aptly the state of play that has persisted within US-UK Intelligence and the Five Eyes after World War II through to our time.

All was not rosy during this period. For example, when North Korea invaded South Korea on Sunday, June 25, 1950, both the US and the UK were taken by surprise. Similarly, when the Chinese entered the Korean War in October 1950, both nations were surprised. In 1956, both GCHQ and NSA had failed to predict the Soviet invasion of Hungary. President Truman was so unimpressed with intelligence's performance that, in 1952, he had ordered the classified "Project K" that created the National Security Agency (NSA) at Fort Meade, Maryland. Similarly, in the UK, there was disquiet over "our intelligence about Soviet development of atomic weapons is very scanty." On August 21, 1968, the Soviet Union's land forces invaded Czechoslovakia to suppress the "Prague Spring" led by Dubcek. In spite of warnings from highly reliable sources on the ground showing quite clearly that the Soviets and their Warsaw Pact allies were not just preparing but also actually moving toward the Czech border with the clear intention of invasion, the British Joint Intelligence Committee in London failed miserably in its assessment to provide clear direction to the prime minister and then to the Five Eyes nations and the NATO allies. There was intense criticism of the Cabinet Office staff by the British Ministry of Defence.

The British BRIXMIS team in East Germany gave very loud and

clear warnings of an impending invasion. The CIA performed no better. After this debacle, there was a power shift in London from the Cabinet Office to the Defence Intelligence Staff.

The British Ministry of Defence had its own considerable panoply of collection and analysis assets as the post-Czech invasion period progressed, through into the 1970s and today. On a more positive note, US-UK and Five Eyes SIGINT was forced by circumstances to become ever more critical as tensions erupted in the Middle East, after a gap following the 1967 June War. Egypt and Syria launched what appeared to be a surprise attack on Israel on October 6, 1973, beginning what became known as the Yom Kippur War. Shortly thereafter, Turkey invaded Cyprus. Some analysts and historians have ranked this surprise attack as an intelligence failure by the West, not dissimilar to the Japanese attack on Pearl Harbor and even Hitler's invasion of Russia. The evidence is by no means all in on this issue, even forty-seven years after the event, given the need to still maintain the key sanctity of various Five Eyes sources and methods.

The country that was undoubtedly most surprised was Israel. In effect, the attack was a preemptive invasion. There were repercussions in both Washington and London over the timely analysis and distribution of what was, in retrospect, clear evidence of Syrian and Egyptian plans and preparations to attack Israel. In a not dissimilar vein, there was similar disquiet in the corridors of power on both sides of the Atlantic after the February 1979 fall of the Shah of Iran. UK and US SIGINT, out of locations such as Cyprus and Turkey where there were clear collection sites, had not been asleep at the switch, and nor had MI6 and the CIA, together with other collateral sources and methods. There was simply very little that the Western powers could do to change the dynamics on the ground in Iran of a successful revolution.

The failures in the UK in the spring of 1982 as Argentina invaded the Falkland Islands have been analyzed in copious books, but suffice to say that all the evidence existed that the dictator Gen. Leopoldo Galtieri and his cohorts Admiral Jorge Anyana and air force general Lami Dozo were planning to invade. The resignation of the British foreign secretary Lord Carrington says it all in terms of the political failure to take action as the situation worsened. What these failures brought home to the political leaders of the US and the UK was that SIGINT and the other key sources and methods had worked admirably. What had failed was analysis and coordination, and in some cases listening to experts lower down in the bureaucratic chain and process, and then addressing what political options were open. As a result of these lessons learned, the leaders of the free world found themselves increasingly dependent on SIGINT intercepts for timely and accurate intelligence. Once the realities of the Argentinean invasion sunk in within the Whitehall bureaucracy, the intelligence community was able to find innovative ways to counter capability discrepancies. For example, the Norwegians intercepted Soviet satellite data containing information on the movement and tracks of Argentinean naval assets. This crucial data was passed to their British ally and fellow NATO member. Also, by contrast, it should be noted that the earlier invasion of Afghanistan by the Soviet Union in 1979 was matched by outstanding prior invasion of SIGINT within US-UK Intelligence. When the British marched into Port Stanley on June 15, 1982, and the Argentinean forces surrendered, the lion's share of intelligence had been by far provided by Five Eyes SIGINT from multiple sources.

The Royal Air Force's NIMROD flights from Ascension Island and operations of specially equipped Nimrod SIGINT aircraft from Punta Arenas in Chile were not significant in the bigger SIGINT picture. Other sources and methods from the Five Eyes SIGINT community dominated. The initial UK SIGINT failures are highlighted by the key fact that it was not until Wednesday, March 31, 1982, that the JIC in London had incontrovertible SIGINT of an impending invasion that then took place on Friday, April 2, 1982. After this major lesson learned, the GCHQ director, Brian Tovey, committed to investing in a dedicated UK GCHQ SIGINT satellite capability. This was long overdue to complement the extensive US space network.

The US had become somewhat leery of the UK's commitment to the classical intelligence agreements when Britain joined the European Economic Community (EEC), the forerunner to the European Union (EU) in 1972. There were some blips on the screen between the two nations during the Kissinger years, but these amounted to nothing in the long term, with Mach 3 SR-71 flights and other even more sensitive operations being conducted from the UK with full US participation. US facilities at Chicksands in Bedfordshire, and at Edsel in Scotland, performed legendary feats at the height of the Cold War, the former tracking Soviet Air Force operations and the latter a US Navy Security Group special communications facility. Highly sensitive UK-US programs were being executed well outside public purview. Kissinger seems to have been sensitive to what the Europeans may do in the future, particularly if the British assisted them in improving their intelligence-collection capabilities. This was a somewhat narrow view of countries that were major NATO allies, irrespective of the French position. Some historians have made much of Henry Kissinger's apparent antagonism toward the UK over intelligence matters. The undeniable fact is that not only were the agreements rock-solid agreements, indeed inviolate treaties, but also the institutional daily round-the-clock connectivity and personnel exchanges between GCHQ and NSA, the CIA and MI6; and the Canadian, Australian, and New Zealand intelligence equivalent organizations, rendered Kissinger's protestations ineffective. Any symbolic acts by Henry Kissinger were seen by the permanent staffs within US-UK Intelligence and the Five Eyes as a whole as just one man's somewhat irascible temperament at a time when his president was on the slippery slope toward resignation.

The addition of Canada, Australia, and New Zealand to the special UK-US relationship brought added strength in multiple ways. In

Hong Kong alone, the US, UK, and Australia worked round the clock to run SIGINT operations, agent running, and interrogating Chinese defectors. In the 1950s and 1960s, as the new post–World War II order solidified, the US rapidly came to realize the significance of Hong Kong as a critical overseas intelligence center, together with multiple other locations that were British, Australian, Canadian, and New Zealand territories. The Australians' SIGINT targets included China, Indonesia, and Vietnam. In the 1960s, the British and the Australians worked hand in glove in combined SIGINT operations during the Indonesian Confrontation. These operations laid the foundations for the development of special tactics, techniques, and procedures (TTPs) for applying near or real-time SIGINT in support of Special Forces, particularly the British Special Air Service (SAS), Royal Marines Special Boat Service (SBS), and the Australian SAS.

Many of these TTPs have been expanded and applied since, in multiple operations and locations, including operations against the Irish Republican Army (IRA) in Northern Ireland. Nowhere was the Cold War hotter than in Berlin where the US and the UK worked side by side to break into Soviet communications. The tapping of the underground landlines that was so vital for Soviet communications was vulnerable as it was not encrypted. The Soviets considered it invulnerable as it was "underground." Tunneling as a source of intelligence from underground cables and moving agents across closely guarded, often impassable boundaries and fortifications, such as the Berlin Wall, has been a most effective way to avoid detection.

In the case of the Berlin Wall communications tunnel, it was only exposed to the Soviets by the treachery of the British spy George Blake, who, in 1956, as an MI6/SIS officer, betrayed the program to his Soviet controllers. However, data gleaned from this one source before Blake's treachery was prolific, including information on Soviet KGB and GRU personnel and operations. Similarly, undersea communications cables, as Blinker Hall had demonstrated so effectively before the outbreak of war in 1914, were equally vulnerable to highly complex operations. US-UK Intelligence and the Five Eyes as a whole cooperated fully in military airborne reconnaissance and clandestine high-altitude photo reconnaissance and SIGINT and ELINT collection.

Much has been written about the aftereffects of the 1960 shoot down of the U-2spy plane piloted by Francis Gary Powers and the subsequent US dependence on satellite SIGINT. The US launched its first SIGINT satellite in 1960, in fact not that long after Powers was shot down. However, the use of highly specialist aircraft by the Five Eyes persists to this day. In fact, the U-2 program gained new life. The US SR-71 Blackbird spy plane performed admirably until it became technically obsolete, as well as not cost effective. However, during its life, it operated at a moment's notice from key sites such as RAF station Mildenhall in the UK. Since 1960, US-UK Intelligence have had multiple aircraft types performing sensitive SIGINT and ELINT operations. Aircraft, like ships and submarines, can gain access in ways and times that satellites cannot. Because of their orbits and constellation programming and footprints, satellites cannot always be in the right place at the right time, nor can they carry various types of highly specialized intelligence collection equipment that cannot be housed in satellites, and also satellites cannot carry personnel for collection operations. The RAF Nimrod RI aircraft, for example, operated out of many different bases around the globe to provide critical SIGINT. RAF station Sharjah in Oman and clandestine sites in Iran before the fall of the Shah were also used to launch covert flights. Such flights were necessary either when satellite data was unavailable or the nature of the collection mission predicated an aircraft, not a satellite.

Specialist aircraft, supplemented now by unmanned aerial vehicles and drones, are still key elements of US-UK Intelligence collection inventory. The attacks on the USS *Liberty* and the USS *Pueblo* dented US-UK Intelligence's confidence in spy ships; however, the submarine persists as a critical component of the covert and clandestine collection of the most sensitive intelligence. The only truly dead spot in all these years before the breakup of the Soviet Union, and the digital and communications revolution of the twenty-first century, was probably the Suez crisis of 1956, a sad blemish on another wise outstanding record of cooperation. On October 29, 1956, the British prime minister Anthony Eden ordered the launch of Operation Musketeer to capture the Suez Canal from the Nasser regime in Egypt. British SIGINT played a crucial role in this operation. Eden decided to share neither his plans nor GCHQ SIGINT with President Eisenhower in the United States. Eden made a fateful mistake by not consulting and working with Eisenhower in the resolution of Nasser's takeover of the Suez Canal. The positive aspects are that lessons were learned, and the intelligence sharing that had persisted during and after World War II was soon back in fine fettle. Harmony had only temporarily been ruffled.

Has there been a "Poor Relations Syndrome"? There has never been what might possibly be construed as a "Poor Relations Syndrome" between the US on one hand and the UK and the other members of the Five Eyes family on the other, Canada, Australia, and New Zealand, based on massive US investment in intelligence compared with the other four nations. In spite of the irascibility of Henry Kissinger mentioned earlier, one critical aspect of the US-UK Intelligence relationship that the sum of the individual parts is much greater than the individual national capabilities. This is the sustaining mantra of the relationship, joined together in the dark days of World War II and sustained during the Cold War to our times. Like a well-knit family that may occasionally have an issue, US-UK Intelligence remains solid.

As we look back on this from the modern era, we have to ask ourselves, "Have we forgotten the past at the expense of being absorbed with the present?" Technological advances have certainly changed the physical collection environment, but are the challenges and innovations of the past being lost in the noise of contemporary technical change?

Landlines are just as important today as they were when buried under Berlin at the height of the Cold War. Similarly, undersea cables, with fiber optic cables today carrying per millisecond more data internationally than is possible to comprehend in terms of conventional numbers, are as vulnerable and exploitable today as when Blinker Hall ordered the cutting of the German undersea cable in 1914. Mail was an eighteen-century means of interception, predated by the Tudor and Stuart periods in the UK that had the British monarchy's agents locating and tracking couriers of undesirable nations, such as Spain and France, and intercepting the written word. Drugs today are increasingly being transferred and sold by mail to reduce the interception of drug dealers, street peddlers, and their higher-up drug lords.

Mail has new roles in the US-UK Intelligence world, and it will require new technologies to detect and track mail, together with their senders and receivers. The more the criminal community and foreign intelligence agencies become fearful of email and cell phone intercepts, the more reliance will be made of former means, including, for example, "word of mouth," via couriers. Detecting and tracking the latter will require additional technological expertise. Old-fashioned code systems, long used by the British and other European nations to communicate with their agents overseas, have a new life in deeply buried couriers' identities.

Uncovering money laundering schemes by terrorist and other criminal elements is prima facie a task for highly sophisticated contemporary computer networks, achievable in a global economic and banking network where trillions of dollars are transferred daily. Clandestine or covert arms deals have to be paid for across borders.

Russian weapons bought by Iran, for example, for Hezbollah, however much hidden in the murky world of burying identities and shipments, have to be paid for at key points. Russian Mafia and oligarchic controllers want their money. Identifying and stopping those payments are vital. By the same token, transfer evasion by covertly shipping large cash sums (in the tens of millions of US dollars or equivalent) have to be located and tracked. There is nothing new here. The British Navy and its merchantmen regularly intercepted and effectively stole the equivalent of billions of dollars' worth of gold from the Spanish in particular.

Intercepting terrorist and criminal groups' cash payments is critical, together with state-sponsored money laundering and clandestine shipments to fund arms, agents, and other activities, such as communications centers and propaganda machines.

Cyber hackers and criminals have to be paid. Locating, tracking, and intercepting their funds is paramount as more conventional international bank transfers are derailed.

Deception is as old as the hills in terms of intelligence practice. The art of deception can be easily lost in the haze of trillions of bits of intercepted communications, video, and other data. The brilliance of the "Double-Cross System" that was masterminded by the British in World War II has been lost in the noise of contemporary communications cleverness. Controlled and extremely well-designed false information can be created and passed by multiple channels, and not just the obvious modern media tools. Data mining and analysis enables perpetrators, such as the attacks on the US election in 2016, to determine whom to hit with information, indeed propaganda, to persuade and influence.

On a larger scale, the tragedy at Pearl Harbor had its recompense with the brilliance of the American code breakers at the battle of Midway, the key turning point in the Pacific war. Technology can sometimes blur the vision of the art of the possible, as if only sheer technology itself is the answer. Asking the critical question, "What do we want to achieve?" is crucial before marching down the all-expensive technological path. By the same token, US-UK Intelligence needs to be ever vigilant about what possible adversaries may do in this domain to deceive and cajole the allies into fateful states of mind that pronounce "all is well." For example, can Iran and North Korea execute workarounds to deceive the allies over arms-control issues?

Diplomacy can suddenly become moribund in the face of sudden recognition that friendly nations have been duped.

Both Germany and Japan were skillful in evading their arms programs in the 1930s, so that by the time the Chamberlain government woke up and the prime minister headed to Munich to try to negotiate with Hitler, Neville Chamberlain was very much in the situation that Winston Churchill so aptly described on becoming prime minister: "You cannot negotiate with a tiger when your head is in its mouth." The Soviet acquiescence over nuclear arms control was deeply investigated by US-UK Intelligence to ensure that American negotiators were truly talking with well-intentioned opposite numbers, and not being drawn into the tiger's mouth, to quote Winston Churchill.

The MAD (Mutual Assured Destruction) doctrine was working, and both sides were indeed acting in total good faith to the benefit of global security from nuclear warfare.

US-UK Intelligence and the Five Eyes all collectively participate in the management of and use of the international maritime Automatic Identification System (AIS), an outstanding piece of modern communications and data architecture that is managed by the IMO (International Maritime Organization), a specialist agency of the United Nations responsible for regulating shipping, with headquarters in London. Its antecedent organization (Inter-Government Maritime Consultative Organization) was founded in Geneva on March 17, 1948, with changes in organizational structure occurring in 1959 and 1982. There are currently 174 member states and three associate members.

IMO has a comprehensive full-time staff and UN secretariat. Its headquarters are located on the Albert Embankment in London. The secretaries general of IMO have been international. All members have ratified the Convention on the International Maritime Organization. The three associate members are the Faroe Islands, Hong Kong, and Macao. Most nonmembers are landlocked, except for the Federated States of Micronesia and Nauru, which are island nations in the Pacific Ocean. IMO controls approximately sixty legal instruments binding on member nations. Secretaries general of IMO have come from the UK, Denmark, France, India, Canada, Greece, Japan, and South Korea.

IMO has multiple technical and safety committees and many more subcommittees.

Its work and organization are far too voluminous to describe here. AIS is an outstanding service and capability of IMO, used extensively by the Five Eyes to augment information on the identity and precise movement of all merchant ships of member nations. Information includes current speed and direction, together with details on port of departure, intended arrival port, cargo, technical details of each ship, all passed in real time to any other AIS ship that must have an AIS/GPS receiver/transmitter. AIS helps guarantee safety at sea, particularly collision avoidance. AIS ships now rely heavily on AIS as a key addition to radar as well as the mark one eyeball. AIS data is provided by a constellation of commercial satellites in or very near real time.

My sailboat that has been ported in Annapolis, Maryland, for many years has an AIS integrated with the navigation systems and GPS display. I can examine detailed information on all AIS fitted shipping within any area of navigational concern. Rogue ships that are mandated to be fitted with AIS, because of their size, and are not transmitting AIS data, even when fitted with AIS, become clear targets for surveillance and tracking. Such ships are marked as possible vessels with noncommercial intent, including possible piracy, gun running, drug and human trafficking, and acting as an intelligence gatherer. Such rogue ships may then be tracked by other covert means. If such ships are transmitting on AIS and are on the rogue ship list, then they will be watched by the Five Eyes. This was impossible in the pre–commercial satellite years when the US National Reconnaissance Office and the Soviet Union, followed later by the Chinese, and indeed the British with their SIGINT satellites, dominated satellite intelligence. Today, IMO-controlled satellite data and multiple other commercial systems provide outstanding imagery. There is nothing that the Chinese can hide from such commercial satellites on the reefs and atolls in the South China Sea and the disputed Paracel and Spratly Islands.

Anyone with a laptop computer or similar device can look at commercial data of Chinese military installations in the South China Sea.

US-UK Intelligence has a golden opportunity to transcend the nature of hitherto highly classified government satellite imagery by combining commercial satellite data and, where and when necessary, releasing this for public consumption in those circumstances where it is in the public interest to raise awareness of unfriendly and threatening acts by those who intend to disrupt the international order. This can apply to all manner of situations, not just the more ominous scenarios, such as a possible Chinese threat to Taiwan and, at worst, preparation for and execution of a covert invasion plan.

Very little can be hidden from commercial satellites today. As the 2020s progress, such data will become even better. Public knowledge and awareness are better served if information is shared by US-UK Intelligence and the Five Eyes in a responsible agreed manner, rather than commercial satellite companies and private individuals pointing out worrisome data. This applies equally to other issues— for example, IMO concerns for ships depositing trash in coastal and international waters, illegal fishing and overfishing, and contraband of many kinds. Assistance to local national law enforcement agencies and coast guards can only do good. On a more insidious level, international hackers, both state and non-state sponsored, together with criminal gangs and mafia-sponsored entities, have penetrated global maritime companies with serious financial effects.

This is achieved by disrupting key maritime terminal operations and the detailed workings of large-scale companies such as Maersk. Ships' physical equipment has been hacked, causing, for example, dangerous effects on Ro-Ro ships' ballasting systems. Cybersecurity in the maritime domain has to be of key national interest to the Five Eyes as well as IMO members.

The same cyber threats apply to offshore oil and gas rigs and, most of all, to the huge oil and gas merchant ships that are the life blood of the Western and Asian nations. Economic disruption can occur therefore without sinking a single ship, reemphasizing the concept of the defense of maritime trade. This type of cyberattack is also a form of both blockade and embargo if it prevents the free passage of ships and goods. Mining may be unnecessary in the Straits of Hormuz, for example, if effective cyberattacks can leave port handling systems in disarray and the actual working machinery spaces and navigation systems of ships out of control and dysfunctional. A most insidious threat is to the actual electronic charts on which all modern ships, with very limited crews because of extensive automation, rely for their navigation. Penetration of these systems, particularly the GPS data itself, can be potentially catastrophic particularly when ships are on autopilot. In 2019, I was given a briefing and demonstration of the latest unclassified commercial technology.

After the demonstration, I held a small highly capable GPS disruption device that can operate within a limited but nonetheless effective range of ships and other key locations and assets. This also applies to airfields and the effects on aircraft systems.

GPS signals are very vulnerable because of the nature of their transmission modes.

The threat to seaborne trade has taken on not just new meaning in the twenty-first century but also a whole new complexion of threats. US-UK Intelligence and the Five Eyes will need to consolidate their capabilities in the defense of maritime trade, the lifeblood of the world.

The one area of international business that has a direct financial interest and security concern in these realms is maritime insurance. Shipping insurance can come at a high price when the risks increase to a global insurance company such as Lloyds of London, founded in 1686 by Edward Lloyd. Lloyds is not an insurance company as such. It is a corporate body governed by the Lloyds Act of 1871 and other acts of the British Parliament. Lloyds is a group of financial backers grouped in "syndicates" that come together to "spread risk." These are the famous Lloyds underwriters. They can be both individuals and corporations. In 2017, the annual value was 33.6 billion pounds sterling according to published annual reports.

The relevance of this is that Lloyds List Intelligence is an extremely capable maritime intelligence service. The database alone is extraordinarily detailed, up-to-date with real-time data, and provides detailed insight into global shipping and commercial maritime operations. US-UK Intelligence has an ever-present interest in its data and data sources. In the event of a crisis in, for example, the Persian Gulf (Arabian Sea) situation involving Iran in 2019 and threats to merchant shipping, Lloyds can have a major impact insofar as insurance rates may immediately rise, or Lloyds may forbid transit through various sea areas to mitigate risk. Ships that ignore such restrictions may proceed at their own risk without insurance, a huge risk for, say, a one-hundred-thousand-to-five-hundred-thousand-ton oil tanker. In the current environment, risks from cyberattacks are equally if not more threatening than, for example, clandestine mining. The interface between the US and the UK, and the Five Eyes as a whole, and their respective navies, and Lloyds' data is therefore an enduring capability.

Shifting away from modern electronics and cyber warfare, we should likely rethink lessons learned from both World War II and the early postwar years when the British and their Commonwealth allies within the Five Eyes successfully practiced unconventional warfare, infiltration, and espionage that was different from what may be described as organized special warfare forces. This refers not to covert CIA-type agents or SEAL Team Six–type operatives, or MI6 agent runners, or any of the several cadres of US Special Forces units (Green Berets, Rangers), or by comparison with the former Soviet Union, Russian Spetsnaz. The Five Eyes institutionally have forgotten how British SOE (Special Operations Executive) recruited, trained, and operated in Nazi-occupied Europe during World War II. The institutional memory has been lost, and much of it resides in the British National Archives and some highly important written narratives by operatives who are long gone, a very salutary thought.

The US Office of Strategic Services (OSS), founded by William Joseph "Wild Bill" Donovan, predecessor to the CIA, never really caught up with the British SOE, mainly because the US joined the European war later, effectively not until well into1942. US-UK Intelligence may wish to reevaluate why and how SOE was so successful, not just in following Winston Churchill's explicit order to "set Europe ablaze" but also in the extremely subtle, deceptive, and capable ways in which SOE operatives, many of whom were not at all the typical Special Forces and MI6 types, were so successful in clandestinely disrupting the Nazi occupation. The SOE operative used many subtler means than just kinetic attacks, with a whole range of penetration skills that have been lost in the passage of time. This is not just about deep cover and identity obscuration. It is about a whole range of cultural, linguistic, technical, and psychological knowledge-based skills that are not easily imbibed in the specialist schools run today by CIA, MI6, and their sister organizations in Canada, Australia, and New Zealand. The types of people involved were indeed very special and extremely capable. Women made excellent SOE operatives. The SOE people were different, the skill sets were different, and the modus operandi was different from classical agent running and HUMINT operations.

In the modern era, various media sources play well to the latter-day SOE trainee and operative, supported by the most covert communications capabilities. Take one scenario: we have observed earlier that without nuclear weapons and a large cyberattack force, the Putin regime supported by the Russian oligarchs and Mafia would be nothing in the great international scheme of things. With a GDP less than the state of California, the state of Russia is poor and relies on energy exports for its lifeblood. Nuclear weapons and cyber capabilities make Russia a serious threat to global stability. Agent running in Russia belongs, in my opinion, to a bygone age, unless, of course, a Russian citizen decides of their own free will to come over. In the latter situation, an SOE-type asset is the best in situ handler. Russia, China, North Korea, Iran, and several less worrisome nations have intensive national security and counterintelligence organizations, an army of dedicated and loyal specialists supported by thousands of minions, and, in the case of Russia and China, targeting not just foreign nationals but indigenous disaffection and opposition. Classical CIA-type operations using diplomatic cover are more and more in the moribund category. Regular diplomatic contacts, observation on the ground, photography, and electronic eavesdropping are much more productive than seducing nationals to give away secrets. The SOE-type operative is a different person and will be far more effective in this new world order and, most of all, in terms of personal security and survivability, is almost guaranteed not to be detected and arrested, interrogated, tortured, and murdered.

US-UK Intelligence may need to collectively analyze this requirement and rethink the past. There are within these overarching capabilities skill sets that must be left only to the day of reckoning, when it is critical for their use. The new Hitlers and the Waffen-SS are with us but in different forms. There are still brutal dictatorships, but they cannot be addressed by kinetic force unless they first do things that require only one response. Much more subtle, safer, and over time far more effective techniques and procedures are required from people with different skill sets than the traditional CIA and MI6 recruit of the past. All the above refers not to the SOE operatives who were indeed committed to kinetic operations in fulfillment of Winston Churchill's directive, such as sabotage, assassination of gestapo leaders such as Geheime Staatspolizei, and amassing weapons in readiness for the liberation of Europe. It refers to the much more complex tasks of total insinuation and infiltration and total undetected acceptance in society for long-term intelligence gathering and warning and indicators, none of which involve high-risk agent recruitment or exposure to counterintelligence operations.

Tagging, tracking, and locating technologies and concepts of operation became paramount in the pre- and post-9/11 eras. Knowing where the threat was is one thing; being able to continuously monitor it was another. The large Joint Stars USAF aircraft (a converted Boeing 707) is able to track a vast number of mobile ground targets and relay the data, but it has endurance limitations in terms of both fuel and crew. The large UAVs such as Global Hawk have considerable range and endurance and successor systems in a stealthy mode can provide persistent round-the-clock data to complement satellite IMINT, ELINT, and SIGINT systems. I worked both ends of this problem as a program lead after the first Gulf War ended in 1991 until very recently (acquiring data and then distributing it in a timely fashion), and a key achievement of the team that I have worked with was the operational introduction of integrating all the above and many other tactical and theater sensor systems into a single multi-intelligence collection and distribution system in virtual real time, a huge leap forward compared with the situation in the First Gulf War. We gained operational experience and developed CONOPS (Concepts of Operation) for users by rigorous and realistic FBEs (Fleet Battle Experiments) and LOEs (Limited Objective Experiments), using very realistic threats played by SEAL teams. The unclassified title Distributed Common Ground Station (DCGS) eventually entered the lexicon many years later, providing an unclassified insight into what we achieved.

Behind the sensor systems, HUMINT reporting, and clever integration and distribution technologies lay answers to major problems when either intelligence data was too scant or the data was overwhelming. How could one make reliable decisions from disparate and often confusing data? "How do you know what you don't know?" to coin a well-known intelligence adage. How can you make sound decisions from imprecise data when traditional statistical means based on well-used probability theory cannot apply? I worked with teams that employed advanced Bayesian log-likelihood mathematical techniques that enabled us to sort the wheat from the chaff.

My colleagues Carl "Tony" Barlow and Dr. Theodore "Ted" Kadota are exemplars of solving almost intractable intelligence problems using unique applications of Bayes's original theory. Thomas Bayes was an English statistician, philosopher, and Presbyterian minister, 1701–1761, educated at Edinburgh University, and one of those incredible unknown geniuses during his lifetime. His notes and key theory were published after his death by Richard Price. Bayes's work enabled my colleagues and me to resolve several major problems for US Intelligence. These problems involved, for example, locating and tracking sensitive targets in complex physical environments.

Targets included materials and equipment as well as people.

Operational fieldwork instilled in me the need to always bear in mind the operative on the ground, often in difficult and dangerous circumstances, and to provide the best means of secure undetectable communication and the best real-time data. Weather comprises a vast array of information. To couple terrain data with weather and the other "Multi INTS" referred to earlier became an imperative. Weather, compromising both meteorological and oceanographic data, is not as easy to access and provide in formats that fit the operational needs of those on the ground, or, for example, a SEAL team being launched from a submarine at night in difficult sea conditions. A colleague, Jay Rosenthal, came up with a perfect scientific solution. As a distinguished former Navy METOC specialist, Jay worked with us to integrate the complexities of ocean, land, and air weather with three-dimensional terrain data provided by the National Geospatial Agency and overlain with all the "INTS" that are relevant for any particular location, scenario, and operational intelligence requirement, a huge step forward for clandestine operatives and Special Forces.

Targeting is a very generic term in the intelligence community. It has many and varied connotations depending on the scenario. Most readers may link targeting to a kinetic solution, placing a Tomahawk missile from a submarine or a Hellfire missile from, say, a Predator UAV on a terrorist target. This is correct, but it may also vary to include an electronic target such as an individual's computer in an another country, a highly technical R & D program in a less friendly nation, an individual or group that is laundering money, running drugs, or is engaged in human trafficking, and, more recently, for example, attacking the election infrastructure in the United States. These are all targets and require different collection techniques.

The legendary CIA operative Theodore "Ted" Shackley (1927–2002), known to all operatives in the CIA Directorate of Operations as the "Blond Ghost," had enormous clandestine experience before becoming the deputy director of the CIA's Directorate of Operations (the "DO," today, in 2023, the National Clandestine Service), second in command, in other words, for all covert operations. When Admiral Stansfield Turner became director of the CIA in 1979 in the Carter administration, he cleaned house in the DO, arguing that clandestine operations had a poor track record and NSA provided better intelligence. Shackley was relieved with many others, and he retired in 1979. The Reagan administration took a different view under its new director, William J. Casey (director from January 1981 to January 1987), and clandestine operations were reborn, though many key personnel had either retired, left, or found reemployment in other parts of the US government. Shackley did retire, but he never really left. He contacted me to visit him in his Rosslyn office, in Arlington, and asked me to perform a covert operation for the agency on behalf of the president in a country I cannot name for obvious reasons.

The reason was most sensitive, and there were major risks. I fulfilled the mission and was duly remunerated and thanked, but only after I had narrowly escaped and spent several days in a foreign hospital, not in the target country, recovering from a poisoning attempt on my life. The information I collected went straight to the Oval Office. What this shows is that very occasionally, HUMINT is invaluable when all the other myriad collection systems just cannot do the job in a timely manner.

But this is rare.

Special Support to SUBPAC (Submarine Forces, US Pacific Fleet) was always one of the most enjoyable and rewarding professionally, with output that made a difference to keeping the United States on top in the Pacific region in what at the time was just the emergence of a resurgent China and its PLAN (People's Liberation Army Navy). Submarines are not ubiquitous, and the US Pacific Fleet has naturally a finite number of nuclear-powered attack submarines forward deployed, on station, at any moment in time. The team that I led provided best means to optimize deployments and to ensure that in the likelihood of rising tension or, worst case, hostilities, that the Pacific Command could obtain the optimum military utility from these incredibly capable platforms.

I have alluded to the disparate value of HUMINT. However, this can be complemented by invaluable "open sources," whether political statements, highly technical foreign reports on new and innovative technologies, economic and logistics intelligence, or internet-based source material of a myriad kind, all of which may be linked to more often than not government-collected unclassified information such as customs' data (those entering and leaving the UK and US, where did they come from, where are they going, did they take circuitous routes, false or legal passports, and so on), fingerprint and eye scan data, video collection in real time, airline and ship passenger information, and the analysis of internet metadata that yields much about individuals as well as technical information. There are multiple key open-source databases, such as the Lloyds of London insurance database and ship movements, with cargo and end user data, that complement global AIS data.

All of these types of information colleagues used to link with HUMINT as well as highly classified SIGINT, MASINT, and ELINT. The compounding of all this information often constituted pure gold when run through the discreet sieves of UK-US computer systems, and we as teams analyzed discreet data sets of interest from the above types of sources.

New and innovative quantum computing techniques will permit the deciphering of vast amounts of real-time information that my generation could not handle because of sheer volume and complexity. At a more tactical level, the US Special Operations Command, for example, is developing smartphone apps for operatives that will permit the real-time collection, transmission, and distribution of biometric data, such as fingerprints, ruggedized to cope with austere locations and challenging temperatures, humidity, and scenarios, and where covertness is at a premium.

My generation had similar capabilities, all to be supplanted with the march of technology and innovation in the digital era.

The Walker spy ring in the United States gave away vast amounts of invaluable intelligence to the Soviet Union. The team that I led in the UK, and then followed up with in various initiatives when I came back to the United States as an immigrant, stayed ahead of Soviet programs. The latter was achieved by both outstanding collection and very capable analysis of data, thereby enabling the UK-US to, for example, figure out how to counter Soviet improvements in acoustics, nonacoustics, noise quieting, and command, control, and communications. It is my very best assessment that in the early days of any major confrontation (short of any kind of nuclear escalation) with the Soviet Union and its Warsaw Pact allies, the UK-US team, with its NATO allies and those in Asia, would have disabled Soviet capabilities. In my opinion, from a purely intelligence collection (sources and methods) perspective, GCHQ and NSA produced during this fifty-year period the most valuable of all intelligence on a consistent basis. Neither MI6 nor the CIA's DO was in the same league. However, the CIA's analytical organization was outstanding, as have been several of the services' intelligence organizations such as the National Maritime Intelligence Center (NMIC) and what was once the Foreign Technology Division of the US Air Force at Wright Patterson Air Force Base in Dayton, Ohio.

In the 2020s, the new generation of MI6 and CIA personnel will have to be "data geeks" as much as luring foreign nationals over clandestine meetings to betray their nations' secrets. "Walk-ins" and sources "turned" after multiple encounters may still yield valuable information, but it is equally likely that it will be highly fashionable and operationally cost effective to be termed with the slang sobriquet "geek," as much as someone who just turned an important source. The analysis of data may become far more significant than the endless endeavor to find the perfect agent to betray their country. However, one cautionary note is that the likes of Kim Philby in the UK and Aldrich Ames in the US betrayed a whole network of UK-US agents, respectively. One bad apple can indeed ruin the whole barrel. "Insider threats" are just as dangerous in any intelligence organization, whether it is a HUMINT or SIGINT collector, or any other. My experience of dealing with HUMINT operations, and the analysis of such intelligence, can be hugely lucrative, but it is very random, not consistent, and therefore does not have the overall efficacy of the other combined "INTs."

Indicators and warning (I & W) is a much-underrated UK-US intelligence function. In the digital era, I & W is just as critical as it was during the Cold War to alert the political leadership to not just a rising threat but also the very serious likelihood of kinetic confrontation or the possibility of cyber penetration, whether it is election interference, infrastructure attack across a whole range of vulnerabilities, or the disruption of vital national security capabilities. I & W will have to be addressed in a concerted highly integrated way across all domains by the US Directorate of National Intelligence and the British Joint Intelligence Committee and their key customers in their National Security Councils, the White House, and 10 Downing Street.

I still regard as the golden thread of collection and analysis over the past decades since World War II the relentless and highly classified combined and individual intelligence operations executed by the US Navy and the Royal Navy, during and after World War II. They still stand as a beacon and testament to their illustrious forebears such as Admiral "Blinker" Hall, Royal Navy, and Capt. Joseph Rochefort, United States Navy, both pivotal war winners.

Chapter 6

Key That Will Unlock the Door for Future US-UK Intelligence in an Age of Rapid Technical Change: People and Innovation

The world events since September 11, 2001, have shaken the resolve of many nations, particularly within NATO, where member nations have witnessed and become somewhat disenchanted with out-of-area operations and commitments to operations that have gone sadly and strategically out of kilter. Iraq, Afghanistan, and Libya come immediately to mind, and each of these emphasizes, above all, the lack of wide-ranging strategic thinking not just about the how and what but also the why. For example, vast cultural differences and huge sectarian rifts that have spanned the centuries within the Moslem world, with their critical ethnic, religious, and regional affinities, were largely ignored in a somewhat heedless and headlong dash to seek reprisal for the events of 9/11, for what initially was a small terrorist organization, manned largely by Saudi nationals, not Iraqis or Iranians, with limited funds and resources. Lessons learned from the past, if applied judiciously, may prove invaluable. The institutional memory of the Five Eyes community has at times been blunted by the sheer passage of time and generation changes during which technical and operational tradecraft were not passed on. What will be required is something bigger than just UK-US extended bilateral agreements, but "A Five Eyes Cooperative Strategy for 21st Century Intelligence Collection and Analysis," supported by all agencies and their political leadership. The combined strength of Five Eyes intelligence has to be a formidable instrument of strategic power in the service of the security of the collective nations.

This predicates the need for a "Shared Five Eyes Intelligence Vision."

Intelligence is only valuable to the user if it is superior to normal open-source information, and that provides both clear benefits for decision-makers and advantages in terms of insight into and knowledge of the particular subject matter. Ultimately, the "game of intelligence," as played out, for instance, during the Cold War by the various HUMINT services of the main international protagonists, is not relevant unless there is real hard-core information emanating from that process. Pitting one secret intelligence service against another may be the subject of spy fiction, but it is irrelevant to the essence of providing actionable, accurate, and timely classified information of real value.

We have already seen that the pace and quality of technological change has accelerated drastically in the last decade. US-UK Intelligence and the Five Eyes governments have tended to be behind the curve in responding to technological change, with outmoded contracting systems and timelines from R & D phases to initial operational capability (IOC) woefully slow and ponderous, with the result that the commercial, nondefense intelligence world is far more ahead of the technical game because of the ability to innovate quickly and effectively. Small start-up incubator companies have become the name of the commercial game not just in Silicon Valley but also across the whole Five Eyes industrial and scientific base. Five Eyes governments have tried to step up the pace but have not succeeded to date, with post-DARPA-esque organizations such as the United States DIU (Defense Innovation Unit) failing to deliver for a host of bureaucratic, funding, and political reasons. We noted earlier that large defense and aerospace companies with massive multiyear contracts that seriously influence their bottom lines and annual shareholder returns are chastened by the possibility of small start-ups that can well negate the value of the very programs that are their financial lifeblood. This aspect is a problem that has to be addressed. There are solutions for all parties. For example, the more systems of whatever technical nature are open architecture, with the ability to introduce major innovative changes without starting from scratch. In this environment, radical innovations can be quickly implemented without the costly multiyear cycle of typical procurements within the defense and intelligence sectors. Intelligence has a massive technical component.

All US-UK Intelligence and Five Eyes key agencies that both cost most in annual budgets and employ most people are at the leading edge of technology. They live and breathe and, one may conjecture, possibly die in the future by being one or more steps ahead technologically than the threat. To fall behind is to fail. At the heart of this issue is, simply, people, and very smart people. US-UK Intelligence will have to increasingly search for, recruit, and train the next generation, and, most of all, allow for innovation to occur at the grass roots, just as the pressures and exigencies of war and survival forced the British to recruit the finest minds to Bletchley Park, SOE, and the Double-Cross System. Across the Five Eyes community, there will need to be a "Brains Trust" of the best and the brightest to keep the community ahead. Greater cooperation and sharing will become more critical within closely guarded compartmented programs, very much along the lines of the US Navy–Royal Navy special intelligence collection and analysis programs. The nonmilitary customers' requirements of the Five Eyes may on the surface look very different from those of the military services, but on close inspection, there is in fact considerable similarity and overlap, where, in the twenty-first century, the digital communications revolution affects, for instance, foreign policy decision-making that overlap with understanding and countering threat weapon systems. The intelligence products, and uses to which they are put, may be different, but the essence of the collection sources, methods, and analysis may be very similar in an increasingly artificial intelligence-oriented world in which data sources bear no resemblance to the days of the Cold War. This will require a restructuring of US-UK Intelligence and the Five Eyes intelligence education and training, requiring experts with proven successful track records to design and implement courses that inspire innovation.

US-UK Intelligence in 2023 is now in a "Brave New World of Next Generation Technologies." The "5G" international technical race has been running for some time. The companies that will win this race will have unprecedented commercial power, and therefore, from an intelligence perspective, it is critical that both the US and the UK and their Five Eyes partners are 100 percent not just well informed but also planning how they will interact with what will be a further revolution in global telecommunications.

For those not well versed in telecommunications, you may ask what is 5G and what will be its impact? 5G is a disruptive technology that will make current use of our cell phones and other digital telecommunications devices look like dinosaurs, because they will in fact be dinosaurs. They will be the fifth generation of systems.

5G devices will be at least one hundred times faster than what you have today in 2023. They will use ultralow energy, will have extreme broadband (your data rates will boggle the mind), high reliability, flawless mobility (where and when you use), with ultralow latency, and deep coverage globally, and, most of all, low cost. Latency is where battery life is extended without affecting performance, and data is processed at much higher rates. There is therefore a technical challenge to achieve increased processing power while conserving energy. Whoever comes out on top in this race will have a huge commercial gain.

From an intelligence perspective understanding and knowing the technical complexities, and exploitation of 5G systems and the global telecommunications architectures that will support it is paramount. It will require the best of the best in technical intelligence know-how to exploit. Who then are the key players?

They may be divided, for convenience's sake, into "Big Boys" and "Little Boys." The former are the top telecommunications carriers and manufacturers: Huawei, ZTE, Ericsson, Nokia, and Samsung. The latter are Deutsche Telecom, Sprint, Orange, SK Telecom, Korea Telecom, T-Mobile, AT&T, Verizon, and US Cellular. There may be others that join the race in due course. It is a strategic imperative that the Five Eyes anticipate every technical dimension of this race and who does what, where, and how. The exploitation strategy must be designed and implemented well in advance of these systems and the telecommunications architectures of the main players reaching the global marketplace.

The question of what the next generation after 5G will look like is a strategic issue for US-UK Intelligence and the Five Eyes to address, anticipate, and plan for. One of the characteristics of Five Eyes intelligence and procurement systems has been the linear extrapolation of technology, rather than innovative step changes. The natural business cycle between Five Eyes contractors and their government agencies has been to improve on the last system. This makes absolute sense at one level. If you can make an intelligence collection system or an analytical tool better than this makes absolute sense. The downside is that the whole technical and procurement system tends toward conservative change. DARPA in the US has a history to a certain extent of avoiding this pitfall and supporting leading-edge, even over-the-top, high-risk, innovation. However, even DARPA programs have life spans that are extraordinarily lengthy before they eventually transition to a real-world application, so that in many cases they are no longer innovative and may indeed be costly dinosaurs. I worked on one highly classified DARPA program that was years in the gestation, and although its output was technically innovative, by the time it could be integrated as an operational system, it had lost its edge and was excessively costly. The science behind it was outstanding, but the US government simply could not convert to an operational system in the right timeline. Winston Churchill had a simple phrase when he issued a direct order saying make something happen immediately: "Action This Day!" It may seem antiquated to reinvent this particular Churchillian aphorism, but on close inspection, it really is not. Catastrophic cyberattacks will require in the coming decades the same degree of instant action, anticipating and mitigating the threats by well-prepared and rapidly implemented counterstrokes.

The latter is what may be termed the "Golden Eggs" syndrome. In other words, for the Five Eyes to have in their intelligence basket a whole collection of golden eggs that not just have anticipated the threats' challenges but also have at the ready effective means to counter and deceptively negate the enemy's capabilities by highly secure covert means.

This resilience is essential for US-UK Intelligence and the Five Eyes in the coming generation. It will take cooperation and the willingness to share intellectual property in the most secure ways. The vetting of participants must be rigorous, and new security systems to obviate the worst kind of internal treachery must be in place. The latter requires a whole new systems and technology base. For example, if another Edward Snowden began to interrogate highly classified data and then download to thumb drives, new systems would not only immediately alert, track, and interrogate such actions but also prevent access in the first place by the most rigorous AI applications. If system denial comes up on the screen, then the user will have to justify access to a superior.

We know that the ocean floor in 2016 had about three hundred major transoceanic submarine cables carrying approximately $4 trillion worth of banking, commercial, and personal transactions of one sort or another, in addition to about 95 percent of the world's voice and internet traffic.1 In 2020, these numbers have increased exponentially, and from an intelligence perspective, 95 percent of the world's key data and communications pass through undersea fiber-optic cables. An examination of who laid these cables, who owns them, who operates and maintains them clearly raises key questions about their intelligence value. Shades of Blinker Hall? Well, yes is the simple answer. Much of the data, voice, and imagery will be heavily encrypted and passing in discreet transmission modes. In those cables, together with space-based communications systems, landline systems, and microwave tower-based transmissions lay intelligence nuggets. The sheer volume of traffic alone is a great technical challenge for Five Eyes intelligence. It will require the most sophisticated AI tools to interrogate such data, provided the Five Eyes can collectively retrieve data in a timely manner. If we reexamine how quickly and efficiently Blinker Hall's team intercepted and decrypted the Zimmermann Telegram and then compare the similar tasks of the 2020s and beyond, it will be appreciated just how things have changed and the intellectual challenge ahead. The good news is that what human beings invent, design, engineer, and implement can likewise be understood and countered. The inventiveness and intellectual prowess of the Five Eyes will have to be married to new forms of deception and technical artfulness that is sustained by highly resilient systems.

Internally, US-UK Intelligence and the Five Eyes as a whole will require more and more backups, and across-the-board power sources and power distribution protection, communications resiliency, discreet standalone cyber detection systems, and ways to mitigate threat access by clever use of new electronic deception tools. Classical Cold War electronic jamming will seem old hat compared to the demands of ensuring GPS systems and transmissions survivability and durability as the 2020s pass into the 2030s. Surprises are never welcome in the Five Eyes intelligence community, whether it is warnings and indicators against, for example, a Chinese surprise attack against Taiwan, or new and insidious ways for threat nations and their surrogates to undermine the Five Eyes and their allies and friendly nations in maintaining critical infrastructure and, in the case of the military, the resupply and transport of military personnel and equipment in a timely and effective way to threat areas.

The worst-case technological surprise scenario is likely to come from the realm of quantum-resistant cryptography, a domain in which US-UK Intelligence and the Five Eyes must pool their brain power and resources to avoid a bombshell-like impact on communications, security, and the ability of the Five Eyes to remain electronically dominant. Encryption is vital for US-UK Intelligence and the Five Eyes for internal security, and, conversely, the ability to break others' encryption is the other side of the coin. There is a current concern that high-capacity quantum computers will be able to break the most sophisticated current encryptions, presenting unacceptable vulnerabilities from a Five Eyes perspective.

The current sophisticated human-created algorithms that supposedly are randomly generated numbers, but in fact are not, will be solvable by quantum computers.

The latter are a step change in technology, using photons, neutrons, protons, and electrons to execute hugely sophisticated calculations versus ones and zeros. Quantum computers will be the new supercomputers of the 2030s and beyond. US-UK Intelligence must ensure that this critical pillar of information security, encryption, is not undermined, and, at the same time, a lead must be made in striking out technically against adversaries using that very capability. The goal will be for the Five Eyes as a whole to create mutual technology that will be "quantum resistant" while exploiting the capability to decrypt others' transmissions.

New forms of technical deception can provide bulwarks against invasive attacks on all forms of civilian, military, political, and commercial infrastructure and operations.

The great strength of the Five Eyes is the natural distribution of its many and varied global intelligence assets. Sharing data has to be top of the list, underscored by personnel exchanges, and with highly compartmented security arrangements. The most significant differentiator of the 2020s from the post–World War II era is that the civilian world in peacetime is as equally vulnerable to a wide range of electronic attack that was not technically possible earlier. Individuals, banks, the international financial structure, transport, and all other forms of critical infrastructure from power and water supply to communications and the media are subject to state-sponsored cyberattacks, and those of state-sponsored surrogates, criminal organizations, and malicious hackers.

Next-generation technologies have to be not only anticipated and worked on in terms of basic R & D by the collective Five Eyes but also ahead in both capability and timescale of not just current threats but also those predicted over the next ten to twenty years. US-UK Intelligence and the Five Eyes are challenged in both the civilian and military sectors. These encompass anti-access, area-denial weapons and nonkinetic systems, cyber warfare, and the wider electronic warfare spectrum, together with what are now a vast range of information threats, and a range of asymmetric threats. The latter cover not just the Five Eyes military but also their civilian populations and those of their allies and friendly nations with whom they trade. ISIS is not at all dead.

It is proliferating in Africa and Asia in unprecedented ways. In themselves, the advanced technologies under review, such as big data analytics, artificial intelligence, autonomous systems, robotics, directed energy, hypersonic, biotechnology, and advanced space and airborne surveillance systems and sensors (including drones, UAVs, and UCASs), are not enough. US-UK Intelligence and the Five Eyes will have to integrate these technologies into tactical and strategic operational systems across the breadth and depth of all Five Eyes countries in the most highly secure and compartmented ways with internal threat security systems of the highest order. In this process, one aspect is uppermost. Cooperation is essential.

No one country can monopolize crucial technology. We witnessed how intelligence sharing in World War II helped save the day. To support these developments, the Five Eyes will have to develop together the necessary planning and training for joint implementation. The bottom line is that these developments must be shown to impact decision-making to justify overall Five Eyes intelligence investment.

Education within the Five Eyes intelligence community is critical, with both the scientific and technical intelligence directorates working alongside operational intelligence personnel, to ensure that not just the most effective programs are pursued but also the training courses are designed on an across-the-board basis so that American, British, Canadian, Australian, and New Zealand personnel share training under a common umbrella. We know from past experience that the camaraderie and cross fertilization of ideas between the nations' intelligence communities yield huge dividends. It is recommended that civilians and military personnel are mixed so that there is mutual exposure to threats, needs, and solutions, together with the incubation of new tradecraft, sources, methods, and analysis. The Five Eyes can collectively develop from this process new intelligence doctrine and operational plans, and commit these to policy agreements as add-ons to existing agreements, and kept highly secure. The above is predicated, as always, on good visionary leadership.

Historically, the lead nation in terms of investment and global sources and methods has been the United States. However, for the above to be successful, the United States will have to be open and sharing within strict compartmented intelligence parameters. In parallel, each of the Five Eyes' military schools and war colleges should be drawn into this process, both in terms of inputs and also training and education.

There has to be more dialogue between these five communities. Intelligence training schools and the war colleges need more synergism. We have learned since World War II that nothing encourages this more than personnel exchange programs, so that not just ideas and information are exchanged and developed but also, most of all, personal relationships are developed that can be bedrock for the rest of people's careers. The benefits in a crisis are legion. I remember well at the height of the Cold War regularly picking up the secure phone and calling my opposite numbers in each of the Five Eyes nations and almost daily on some occasions leaving my office to visit various intelligence personnel in either the London embassies or in various UK exchange locations. We never, ever failed and, in the words of Admiral William McRaven, formerly commander of Naval Special Warfare and commander of Special Operations Command, spoken at the University of Texas Class of 2014 Commencement Ceremony in June 2014, "We never, ever, rang the Bell!" We stood together in the spirit of US-UK Intelligence and Five Eyes cooperation, and although at times we may not always have agreed on whatever, we never stopped working together in the spirit of total committed cooperation.

Russia has used social media disinformation to attack the western media and sow doubt and dissension among all levels of society from intellectual elites to the less educated. This divisiveness strategy is difficult to measure in terms of overall effects, but the intelligence objectives are clear cut—namely, to create political and social divisions within and between the key democracies. Disinformation is a formidable weapon in the deception armory. Scare tactics using false information confuse and dissemble otherwise stable and fair-minded people. The Kremlin has directly driven these tactics. Its goals are to shape public opinion over a wide range of events, issues, and policies.

These include, for example, the 2016 US election, BREXIT, the Khashoggi murder, the downing with Russian missiles of flight MH-17, the poisoning of the Skripals in Salisbury, England, chemical attacks by the Assad regime in Syria, Russia's de facto invasions of eastern Ukraine, and the illegal annexation of the Crimea, and many other social media disinformation campaigns. The Five Eyes has extraordinary talent to not just counter these attacks but also turn them around against the Russian regime. US-UK Intelligence and the Five Eyes have enormous potential capabilities to counter using, for one unclassified example, AI. The opposition will use AI as much as the Five Eyes. The latter have to be many steps ahead all the time. Project Maven in the US was under contract in two months, and a capability was delivered in six months.2 Maven (also known as Algorithmic Warfare Cross Functional Team) uses advanced secure AI algorithms to analyze in real time key data from multiple sources and methods. Vladimir Putin fully understands AI's value. Speaking in 2017, he said, "It comes with colossal opportunities, but also threats that are difficult to predict. Whoever becomes the leader in this sphere will become the ruler of theworld."3 US-UK Intelligence and the Five Eyes need to be way ahead all the time as Putin's Foundation for Advanced Studies (a DARPA-like equivalent) seeks equivalency and terrorists use social network mapping, AI-enabled drones, and social engineering attacks to both recruit and undermine stable populations. Counterterrorism intelligence within the UK-US and wider Five Eyes community will need to concentrate joint resources in identifying in real time and eliminating from the worldwide web such terrorist material. Radicalization and extremism are growing, not diminishing. US-UK Intelligence and the Five Eyes will have to collectively extend current public-private technical partnerships to stay ahead of the threat and undermine it before it has effect. Similarly, with international hostage taking and kidnapping, where UK-US Intelligence can use AI-based systems and technology to detect, locate, track, and eliminate criminal and politically inspired hostage and kidnap entities.

On the military side, it will be possible using AI-based technologies with various discreet advanced sensors and guidance systems to use lethal autonomous weapons by the Five Eyes nations and their key allies in real-time situations against terrorist targets, in ways that were impossible with earlier systems like Hellfire missiles on various UAVs, such as Reaper and Global Hawk. The ability to process massive amounts of discreet intelligence data and make accurate real-time decisions beyond normal human operating speeds will change the rules of the game in the counterterrorist fight. The US National Cyber Strategy and the US Defense Department's Cyber Strategy, released in September 2018, call for defense of the homeland, to protect American prosperity, deter, detect, and punish malicious actors, and with allies push for an "open, interoperable, reliable, and secure internet," and also protect US space assets simultaneously. Russia and China are clearly identified as adversaries, with China "eroding US military overmatch and is persistently exfiltrating sensitive information from the US public and private sector." In a contested public, private, and military-political cyberspace environment, the Five Eyes clearly need to be not just one step ahead but also many, so that high-level policy documents such as the one quoted above have real flesh on the bones of what are somewhat obvious goals to even the less knowledgeable layperson. Five Eyes collaboration is paramount. The US cannot go it alone, and, most pleasingly, the Pentagon has stated its objective to "strengthen the capacity of allies and partners and increase DOD's ability to leverage its partners' unique skills, resources, capabilities, and perspectives." At one level, this may be seen by the Five Eyes community as US patronage. However, given the strong historic bonds, the younger generation in the US Department of Defense, with little or no knowledge of the Five Eyes' historic record, will need to be both educated and inducted into the Five Eyes community.

One key solution lies in the huge historic bedrock experience of UK-US Intelligence in deception. Deception helped win World War II and certainly shortened it and, in the assessment made by Sir Harry

Hinsley, the official historian of British intelligence in World War II, may have shortened the war with the combined strengths of Enigma and the Magic by as much as two years. Cyberspace offers myriad ways for the Five Eyes to cooperatively outthink, outmaneuver, and overwhelm both peer level threats and also low-level terrorist groups and criminal hackers and their paymasters. Classification naturally prohibits disclosure. Suffice to say that the US and the UK together with the other three Five Eyes nations have enormous resources and intellectual pedigree to outflank any of the threats referenced earlier.

Reaching a major conflict zone, staying there successfully and accomplishing various missions, is now not as easy as it was even ten years ago in 2010. To sustain persistent forward presence, say, in the Pacific and particularly the South China Sea and adjacent sea areas, the US has the weapons and overall force structure to accomplish various missions laid down in national strategic plans in the event of various threat scenarios. However, intelligence shows that peer military adversaries could attempt to block, interrupt, and, worst case, kinetically challenge US presence and intervention. In this increasingly complex environment, Deception, with a very big *D*, becomes essential. The threat must never know what it doesn't know and be made to believe a whole host of conflicting informational aspects, while denied, deceived, and disrupted by the most subtle and egregious means. The threat must have zero knowledge of what the Five Eyes are both doing and could expand as situations deteriorate. Various silver bullets need to be preserved for the ultimate threats, kept under the most secure wraps until needed. Winston Churchill and Franklin Roosevelt, and their key top military commanders, are excellent role models in this regard. They preserved and protected their most secret deception plans and technologies and only employed them when the timing was just right.

The Five Eyes have the brains, the technology, the cultural and social adhesiveness, plus the binding agreements of decades to work against several adversaries who have nothing like the cohesiveness of the Five Eyes. In parallel to the big "D" are other technological advances, from robotic operating systems on the land, the sea surface, underwater, and in the air, with unmanned systems, embedded and mobile sensors enhanced by onboard data processing systems, with AI dominant, so that operators are assisted in decision-making functions, rather than being overwhelmed by saturated information. The Five Eyes can empower commanders with critical decision-making information, coupled with advances in AI-focused space-based systems that provide resiliency in contested environments so that Five Eyes space-based communications remain secure and intact. All the above will need integration with planned advances in high-energy lasers, hypersonic vehicles and weapons, and the hypersonic propulsion systems that carry them. In due course, the Five Eyes will have the ability to challenge most threats in ways that were inconceivable less than a decade ago. The problems that have been very eruditely analyzed by Jonathan Ward in his paper "Sino-Indian Competition in the Maritime Domain,"4 may hopefully not come to pass if all the above becomes increasingly clear to peer competitors, as a major deterrent to aggressive action that may precipitate crisis. The wise words of former US Navy secretary Richard Danzig may indeed come to pass, that "promoting innovation and enhancing lethality should become a higher priority than acquiring additional ships."5 *Time* magazine in its June 4, 2018, edition discussed and analyzed various intelligence-related aspects with then director of national intelligence Dan Coats. The article indicated that Director Coats, with a background on the US Senate Select Intelligence Committee, and ambassador to Germany, 2001–2005, has solid credentials but caveated that he may not be able to convince his president of the value of the US intelligence community's intelligence assessments over issues, for example, relating to Iranian nuclear weapon development compliance.

In this environment, US-UK Intelligence becomes ever more critical as a collective mouthpiece of intelligence credibility, standing firm on well-reasoned analysis based on thorough and accurate sources and methods. In this context, US-UK Intelligence and its political oversight and leadership assume a new dimensional role. This became self-evident in August 2019 with the resignation of Director Coats, followed shortly afterward by his principal deputy director, Susan M. Gordon, emphasizing that good unvarnished non–politically oriented intelligence can only serve the national interest if there is independence from political influence, a hugely different concept from political oversight.

What has evolved from the above discussion is the need for an overall Five Eyes "Grand Strategy" based on one key notion that intelligence is a dynamic living process and is never static. A biannual "summit" of all the key players from all the Five Eyes intelligence departments and agencies could take place rotationally in each of the five capitals. During the intervening two years, working groups and round tables from the many and varied specialist intelligence communities can work on the issues of the day and those predicted in the future and deliver the most important issues for resolution at the summit. Regularity of meetings is essential in an era when the nature of all the threats that we have addressed, and many that none of us can ever foresee or anticipate, demands meetings of the minds. Such summits can agree on threats, consolidate solutions, and initiate joint technology and operational cooperation, with the necessary planning and budgets. The summit members can have their best national advisors present, with one key objective of agreeing on the next phase in the technological revolution and its impact on intelligence collection and analysis. From a security perspective, the Five Eyes summit will need to compartmentalize special programs and lay down security guidelines. In the wider security context, it is important that the Five Eyes have agreed ways to uniformly address the insider threat, to mitigate the worst of internal treachery. The Five Eyes should not be hesitant in sharing systems and technology that undermine those who betray the Five Eyes internally. Given good compartmentalization, it does not follow that one bad apple will ruin the whole barrel, but, nonetheless, one bad apple can create enormous damage. We saw historically what Philby did in the UK and the Walkers in the US.

One increasingly strategic issue that such summits must face is the civilian-commercial world interface with government. Cyber threats to every level of society and activity and attacks on critical commercial intellectual property and defense and security technology require new approaches to educating and training the Five Eyes public and businesses in countering these pervasive threats. Exfiltration of intellectual property is a massive economic and security threat. This applies to not just cyberthreats but also physical and personnel security.

Part of the summit process will likely be a domain that is neglected at least from the public's perspective. This is economic intelligence. We tend to concentrate so much on all the other "INTs" and the many threats that confront us that we can easily forget many of the global economic issues that may well be transformed into threat scenarios. Most are aware of the impact of oil and gas issues that have driven foreign and commercial policies for decades and how protection of oil and gas flow to the economies of the democracies has been paramount. None of this will change.

However, other equally pervasive economic issues may constitute compelling threats in the future. Water rights and water supply issues may become more and more serious. An analysis of all the critical minerals that make up electronic components and whole systems, such as vehicles and aircraft, let alone domestic products, reveals the delicate international economic balance regarding which countries have which minerals and their commercial destinations. In the twenty-first century, the global economic heartland may well be predicated on what minerals are needed for which industries and products and their location and supply chain.

For these summits to be successful and indeed for the whole Five Eyes community to be successful for the foreseeable future, we must have a clear and well-articulated statement of what "Five Eyes Strategy" is. Grand intelligence strategy is not about "how" and "what" all these various entities do and their fine products. It is, very simply, "why" they do what they do at any moment in time. The "what" and "how" come later, as implementation. There is one overriding element that determines the "why." These are the vital national interests of each of the Five Eyes and their combined collective interests. These interests drive the "why." They drive the Five Eyes intelligence community machinery that will provide the vital security for modern society now and for the foreseeable future.

Without clear definitions of what these vital national interests are, and indeed these will change over time as the global situation changes in its many and varied forms, the great historic intelligence traditions of US-UK Intelligence and the Five Eyes as a whole will be grasping at straws. On August 10, 1941, Winston Churchill and Franklin Roosevelt met on board HMS *Prince of Wales* in Placentia Bay, off Newfoundland. The president had sailed from Washington, DC, in USS *Augusta*. At that meeting, these two great men agreed on one fundamental thing, grand strategy to defeat Nazism, and this strategy was predicated on one key basic tenet, the vital national interests of the United Kingdom and the United States. The Five Eyes will have to continuously address the changing global scene and adjust their intelligence operations, technology, sources, methods, and analysis to those vital national interests defined by their political leadership.

The history of US-UK Intelligence is an incredible history of cooperation and dedication.

The heart and soul of US-UK Intelligence is at the working level, the intelligence specialists from the United States, the United Kingdom, Canada, Australia, and New Zealand that have greatly served this extraordinary community. They have and will continue to serve with great distinction. I have been hugely privileged over a fifty-year period to have participated in this great community, my roles minuscule as they were in the truly great scheme of things, but like all of us who lived and worked in this community during this turbulent and challenging fifty years, the sum of all the efforts, dedication, hard work, and sacrifice of everyone made a massive difference. I really believe that this international intelligence community reflects and represents the core strengths and values of these five great democracies, epitomizing the ability of every country to stay the course, not to waiver, and be steadfastly consistent and loyal in the darkest hours as well as the bright moments of triumph.

The essence of US-UK Intelligence and the Five Eyes as a whole is an "enduring culture."

What occurred within US-UK Intelligence that was conveyed to the Five Eyes community as a whole, in retrospect, is quite remarkable.

Governments for the past seventy-eight years since 1945 have come and gone, but US-UK Intelligence and the Five Eyes have survived without any serious threat to their existence. There have been challenges, but, on the whole, the abiding professional loyalty that has bound the large number of individuals together, past and present, is emblematic of something much deeper and more sustainable than political change. At one level, the Five Eyes have defined the strength of the values and commitment that underpin the essence of each nation's sense of democracy and freedom in a very uncertain world.

There have been political variances within the Five Eyes political hierarchies over issues associated with, for example, the Suez campaign by the British and the war in Vietnam by the United States, but none of these issues have ever undermined the bedrock relationships. The Five Eyes stood together when North Korea invaded South Korea on June 25, 1950, and fought alongside each other, sharing intelligence, until the war ended on July 27, 1953, with an armistice agreement. The UK fought a successful counterinsurgency campaign in Malaysia and received maximum support from its Commonwealth Five Eyes members. The British supported the US clandestinely in East Asia during the Vietnam War, and the US came headlong in support of the British in the 1982 Falklands campaign. Whatever the political differences over the Middle East foreign policies of the US and Britain, with the other three nations tending to play out their international political roles via the United Nations, the intelligence process based on the core relationships at the working level has endured.

The future of US-UK Intelligence and the Five Eyes as a whole is in the hands of a new generation that supplants me and all the wonderful dedicated people that I have been privileged to know and work with in US-UK Intelligence and the Five Eyes over the past fifty plus years. I am confident that they will continue the great work and traditions. The bonds that will continue to bind them together were created by several generations that began during the dark days of World War II. They will go on, and they will endure.

The photograph below should remind us all of the bonds created by two great leaders when the world was totally challenged.

The Great Tradition That Will Endure
United States and British Intelligence
Providing Abiding Security in an Uncertain
and Challenging World

Winston Churchill, Franklin D. Roosevelt, Admiral Stark, and Admiral King on board HMS *Prince of Wales* in Placentia Bay off Newfoundland, August 10, 1941.

The relationships that were established at this momentous meeting have endured for the past eighty-two years. In the new era, the spirit of Franklin Roosevelt and Winston Churchill will live on in a fine new generation of United States and British Intelligence personnel. Let no one threaten this critical relationship as the US and the UK, the Five Eyes as a whole, and their allies face the changes of the twenty-first century.

Appendix A

Current and Emerging Threats

The growing power of China and the development of what is clearly a "Grand Maritime Strategy" will play out in support of not just China's Belt and Road policy but also China's overall strategic national security goals. This will affect not just US-UK Intelligence and the Five Eyes as a whole but also increasingly their unilateral, bilateral, and multilateral relations with India, a crucial nation in the Indo-Pacific region. China's key policy statement issued in July 2019, "In the New Era" (issued by the State Council Information Office of the People's Republic of China), makes it abundantly clear where China is headed, with the Chinese navy becoming the centerpiece and instrument of China's power and influence.

Insider Threats

The years since 9/11 have seen the development of "insider threats" to not just the United States and the United Kingdom but also all the main democratic nations in the West. This has come through the march of technology and for which new paradigms and technologies will be required in the post-2023 period to counter those who wish to penetrate the daily lives of individuals, businesses, and governments by electronic means. However, there is also the enduring factor of the more traditional insider threat posed by classical traitors and spies, and also those who betray sensitive and classified information in the name of the public good, and the protection of privacy.

New forms of propaganda, subliminal opinion forming, and disinformation are now commonplace in the digital era when so much information can be accumulated by the very nature of the internet and its vast information-gathering capabilities.

The large internet providers' huge data collection engines, analysis, and storage capacity know as much about each subscriber, user, or customer as the governments of the countries in which they are located. Advertising and commercial transactions are drivers and the offshoots of this massive amount of data. The concept of privacy is moot when all of us as individuals make daily selections on the internet for news, products, and information searches that both define us and characterize our needs, likes, and dislikes. We are then naturally targeted by commercial entities, having provided a very detailed profile of our lifestyles, likes and dislikes at myriad different levels, including political persuasion.

Classic spies gave away highly classified information on UK-US Intelligence operations and personnel. Some gave away valuable technical information. The British GCHQ spy Geoffrey Prime was not unlike the Walkers in the United States, giving away extremely sensitive navy operational and technical intelligence. Prime betrayed data on UK-US efforts to track Soviet strategic submarines and various means by which the US Navy and Royal Navy used SIGINT and SOSUS. The year 1985 became the "Year of the Spy" in the United States. Ronald Pelton was exposed at the National Security Agency; the Walker spy ring was broken up; at the CIA, Edward Lee Howard was caught spying, and, in November 1985, Jonathan Pollard was arrested for spying for the Israeli Mossad. After 1985, Aldrich Ames was exposed at the CIA, and Robert Hanssen at the FBI, both giving critical information on CIA HUMINT operations and counterintelligence operations to the Soviet Union. Much later, the case of Edward Snowden, who copied and leaked classified information from NSA. He did this, so he claimed, in the name of "Liberty versus Security," exposing several key global surveillance programs run by NSA and the Five Eyes, with cooperation from various telecommunications companies and European governments. Many of these spies' modus operandi could have been penetrated not by just better physical security checks and vetting procedures, in addition to covert review of bank accounts and personal communications, but also, and very importantly, better and sophisticated monitoring of access to computer data. There are very good tools available with real-time checks for not just regular access to sensitive data but also unwarranted and out-of-hours computer access, and certainly the removal of data via a thumb drive, disc, and hard copy printer and reproduction. Programs can immediately alert security personnel to unusual and/or out of routine access. For example, anyone accessing US-UK Intelligence data using a thumb drive should sound an alarm immediately if there is no prior approval for such action.

The current threat situation in 2023 is more insidious than the above type of espionage threats. The internet poses the greatest challenge to US-UK Intelligence since the dawn of SIGINT. The cooperation of the Five Eyes and their trusted allies in a concerted technical and operational effort to develop new ways to cope with the overwhelming amount of data transmitted every millisecond on the internet is paramount. No one country can claim dominance, and certainly all the brain power and skills of New Zealand, Canada, Australia, the UK, and the US are required. Cyberattacks have and will continue to take multiple forms. Long before the current wave of cyberattacks, there had been, for example in the 1990s, attacks on the New Zealand power grid in Auckland and the London banking system. In parallel, companies began to provide privacy protection via encryption technologies fairly early on. The renowned PEP (Pretty Good Privacy) 1993 case in the United States is an exemplar of the march of commercial innovation that complicated Five Eyes'

SIGINT operations. The American Phil Zimmermann provided the public worldwide with "Public Key Cryptography," and the case against him by the US government failed miserably.

As the British government was investing in building the "Doughnut" to house GCHQ in the late 1990s, at the time the largest construction program in both the UK and Europe, both GCHQ and NSA were increasingly facing the daunting challenge of intercepting unprecedented volumes of data that even with the most advanced "keyword" searches could not keep up in situations where, for example, likely targets were using coded words in Pashtu, Farsi, and multiple obscure dialects, making life extremely challenging for the dedicated Five Eyes listeners and analysts.

Traffic analysis became the order of the day as a quick and easy way to attempt to isolate threat data. In light of this observation, it becomes clear that the US and UK governments, in their urgent need to protect their citizens and those of their closest allies from burgeoning terrorism, faced the challenge of "liberty versus security," in the vernacular of the debate over the mass trawling of personal data from the internet and phone calls. In retrospect, it is very easy to discern that the US and UK were up against intractable odds, with terrorist groups changing their cell phones and SIM cards regularly, often every few days, and transmitting in worded codes and dialects.

At the operational intelligence level in the field, these challenges were faced overtime very effectively by robust and highly intelligent tactical SIGINT systems, such as those used in Afghanistan. None of these systems depended on NSA- or GCHQ-derived data, unlike, for example, in earlier years when United States Air Force targets against Serbia were derived directly from GCHQ and NSA data.

There was no highly reliable SIGINT that, for example, confirmed or denied the existence, location, and possible types of WMD in Iraq in 2003. The head of the United Nations investigative team in Iraq,

Hans Blix, kept his team on the ball looking for hidden WMD. Data mining and using "Voice Prints," or the recordings of likely suspects for matching with vast amounts of intercepted communications, were still in their infancy. Drone technology was barely off the ground in 2003. In fact, as late as 2010, countries such as the UK did not have any effective drones for surveillance and reconnaissance. All this has changed rapidly with the Ukraine war witnessing the unprecedented use of drone technology.

Computer Innovations and Their Impact on Intelligence

The revolutionary Cray supercomputers1, first designed in 1972 by Seymour Cray, were subsequently supplanted by a series of massive parallel computers built by a large number of companies in the 1980s. However, by 2000, Cray was the only remaining supercomputing provider in the Western market, with its one rival, NEC Corporation. Ordinary mainframe computers were still very much the order of the day at most large corporate and US-UK intelligence centers. Cray went into Chapter 11 bankruptcy in March 1995, and in February 1996, Cray Research merged with Silicon Graphics (SGI). SGI's Cray Research Business Unit was subsequently sold to Tera Computing Company in March 2000. In April 2008, Cray and Intel joined to collaborate on future computing systems. By 2009, they produced the fastest computer in the world for the National Center for Computational Sciences at the Oak Ridge National Laboratories. Fast forwarding to October 2017, Cray, together with partner Microsoft Azure, brought supercomputing to "the cloud" and, in the same year, built two new Cray CS-Storm systems for artificial intelligence workloads, and on April 18, 2018, Cray announced the development of the most advanced processors to the Cray CS500 product line. Cray continues to make more revolutionary advances. The 2020s will witness limitless advances that will make the great innovations of the 1970–2000 timeframe seem like computing dinosaurs.

By its very nature, the US and the UK and their Five Eyes partners from the turn of the century onward have faced an uphill battle of keeping up with the march of technology. Private commercial companies have been far ahead of the UK-US governments in innovation and introduction to the commercial marketplace. A company such as Google is ahead of the game compared with NSA, GCHQ, and the Canadian, Australian, and New Zealand equivalents. Part of the problem is the very nature of the acquisition and contracting culture, particularly in the UK and US, with regimes that are slow and ponderous and not quick to adjust to changing technological circumstances. Added to this procurement plight is the inability to deal with vibrant and innovative startups with often critical disruptive technology that may challenge the secure multiyear contracts of large companies whose products are, in effect, already obsolete. This critical problem will have to be faced by the US and the UK, and in particular the United States Departments of Defense and Homeland Security, plus their intelligence agencies, as the 2020s progress. On Thursday, July 7, 2005, the UK had its tragic and devastating wake-up call with the suicide bomber attacks in Central London. This was the deadliest attack on British soil, and by British nationals, since World War II. This presented GCHQ with the need to rethink its total surveillance strategy. The worrisome thing is that between 2005 and today, the pace and scale of technological change has been greater than could ever have been anticipated. The ability to process data has to be accompanied by advanced decision aids that convert vast amounts of information to relatively tiny amounts of critically important actionable intelligence that will enable decision-makers to be ahead of the threat.

Intelligence and Drugs

There is a heroin-opioid epidemic in the United States, and to a lesser extent in the UK. Heroin is a highly addictive drug processed from morphine, a naturally occurring substance from the seed pod of poppy plant varieties. When sold as a drug, it appears as a white or brownish powder. Opium is refined to make morphine and then further refined, with various additives (some extraordinarily destructive to the body) into different forms of "street heroin." Opioids act on the human opioid receptors and have similar effects to morphine, in essence painkillers. Opioids have legitimate medical applications regularly prescribed by medical practitioners. Some experts claim that less professional practitioners either overprescribe or unnecessarily prescribe opioids instead of using other therapies— the pill-popping syndrome. Used nonmedically without proper control, they produce euphoric effects like an illegal drug. Excessive use leads to dependence, withdrawal symptoms, and, particularly when combined with other depressant drugs, results in death from respiratory failure. By 2020, a combination of recreational use, addiction, and overprescription, plus illicit inexpensive heroin, has led to millions of Americans, young and old, dependent and dying in large numbers.

Narcan is the brand name for naloxone and is used medically; indeed, it is vital for paramedics in US rescue squads to block the effects of opioid overdose. Rescue squads and emergency rooms administer intravenously and by injection. Often, multiple doses are required to save the patient. If a US rescue squad runs out of Narcan, this becomes a critical situation for a patient in need of urgent life support.

By the time a unit arrives at an emergency room, it may be too late. In the US, West Virginia, for example, has a nationally excessively high addiction rate. West Virginia rescue squad units often have to attend the same victims, indeed whole families, on more than one occasion during a twenty-four-hour period. The overall impact of this is not good if rescue units are not available for trauma cases (traffic accidents and so on) and medical emergencies (heart attack, stroke, emergency childbirth, and so on).

Heroin arrives in the US and the other nations via a discreet distribution chain.

Breaking that chain and arresting the criminals who make millions at the top end of this chain, and more modest sums at the bottom ends, and preventing distribution to our vulnerable fellow citizens are clear US-UK operational intelligence objectives. The drug cartels that manage and operate the initial distribution depend on international shipping, in addition to the fast-speed Caribbean shipments and small submarine operations that have been documented in the media. US-UK tracking of drug shipments requires multi-intelligence sources and methods. The tracking of rogue ships is not new to US-UK Intelligence. Each of the nations contributes to a 24/7 global tracking network relying on satellite intercepts, SIGINT, AIS (Automatic Identification System)-related data, and key HUMINT at places such as production sites and ports of embarkation. The heroin routes can be monitored from poppy fields to port delivery. Drug forensics permit obtaining the details of specific batches of the heroin's origin. Breaking into the money chain is as important as tracking illicit international shipping. The laundering of international drug money requires intensive analysis of offshore accounts, covert cover-up schemes to hide drug operations and payments, and at the lower level the ways and means by which drug pusher suspects' financials can be accessed. This requires the most intensive US-UK cooperation from ship tracking to financial analysis. Coast guards, or their equivalents, are important in the final stages of ship transits once vessels enter territorial waters, to board and search suspect vessels. The US Coast Guard Foundation Calendar states, "Every day the Coast Guard screens an average of 360 merchant ships for potential risks before they arrive in US ports," and, "Each day, vigilant Coast Guard patrols prevent over 1,000 pounds of illegal drugs from reaching our communities." In international waters, the navies of the US and the UK, their Five Eyes partners, and their close allies can legally board and search suspect vessels. The additive materials used in the manufacture of heroin, particularly the more virulent varieties, are well known, and their manufacture and distribution to locations where the "mixing" takes place can be traced. This process requires the involvement of multiple national agencies beside the traditional intelligence agencies of US-UK Intelligence.

In tracking heroin from poppy fields to street "pushers" requires drug enforcement agencies, local and federal/central government law enforcement agencies, sheriff departments, and customs authorities. The law enforcement task is further complicated by heroin distribution via mail, as opposed to by hand. Data "Fusion Centers" that combine the resources of both the intelligence agencies and law enforcement agencies at all levels (federal/government to local) with specialist drug enforcement agencies are crucial in the fight against heroin and other drugs' distribution. The same problems exist with breaking into drug cartels' communications that exist with terrorist organizations where awareness has made the bad guys much more resilient and cunning in their communications evasion and deception techniques.

If there was a single weak point in the distribution chain, it is in the shipping/transport process, whatever form that takes. The big cartels want to make major shipments, not dribs and drabs over protracted periods, because of the loss of revenue. Shipment delays to avoid and confuse interception require more complex planning and execution. A chain with a weak link is vulnerable, and as the 2020s progress, more and more effort will be required in this interception phase based on good intelligence of the total system, not just one part. Knowledge of where and when shipments will be made, and their ports of embarkation, are crucial datapoints. Corruption will be an ongoing problem, particularly in the law enforcement side of counterdrug operations. The best US-UK Intelligence can be thwarted by corrupt law enforcement and customs officials turning a blind eye to shipments and distribution. This will continue to require stricter vetting procedures and in the case of discreet high-level classified intelligence, not only restricting access to limited need-to-know personnel but also providing the type of computer and data security discussed earlier. In the digital era, it is possible to not just restrict access but also know what, when, and how each individual had access to data, and what uses were made of data. Counterintelligence can focus quite intensively on data paths and usage, particularly timing and other associations with highly specific data sets.

Artificial intelligence techniques, combined with, for example, advanced Bayesian mathematics employing the most sophisticated log-likelihood theory applications, can be used to analyze large real-time intelligence data sets in ways that were impossible for individual analysts striving to not just make sense of massive amounts of data but also deliver answers for users in very constrained timelines.

Today, relatively simple AI applications can make the intelligence analyst's job faster, less stressful, and vitally more productive. AI can quickly visually recognize people across international boundaries, recognize speech, and instantly translate the most daunting languages and dialects, while executing sophisticated tasks allied to machines processing data from a vast amount of accumulated experience and learning built into the AI systems that will then adjust to new changing inputs in or near real time. Machines can therefore demonstrate intelligence when the computer copies or mimics human cognitive functions that we all normally associate with how we learn and solve problems. The evolutionary algorithms are however created by human beings, not in any way self-generated by the machine, a popular misconception. If the machine and the operator can work together as if the machine is another human being, then the machine has passed the "Turing Test," developed by the famous Bletchley Park code breaker Alan Turing in 1950. AI is progressing by leaps and bounds and will undoubtedly add an extraordinary dimension to US-UK Intelligence, which at the time of writing in 2023 is almost impossible to predict. One fact does undoubtedly remain. Alan Turing was a genius. US-UK Intelligence requires more like him to revolutionize the intelligence process. Finding them is the challenge, but they are out there in the bright new generation of computer scientists and mathematicians.

Global Terrorism, Human Trafficking, Piracy, Illicit Arms Transfers, and Money Laundering

Global terrorism, human trafficking, piracy, gun running, illicit arms transfers, and the associated money laundering with these activities have ushered in new challenges for US-UK Intelligence, not dissimilar to international drug trafficking. The common thread that runs through all these operations is money. They all require the acquisition, transfer, and dispersal of funds to function. "Following the money" is an appropriate adage. The other common thread, with the possible exception of human trafficking, is weaponry. Weapons are required for these operations to function. Money and weapons are the lifeblood of these evil activities.

Preventing and/or disrupting the flow is a key goal. A multisource intelligence approach is required. Added to this mix is the crucial task of locating and tracking the means and methods of transnational recruitment and training, particularly in the terrorist domain, and in those other domains that are more of an international criminal nature where individuals are lured in, corrupted, or wittingly join the ranks, trained, and paid for their wrongdoing. The means are as important therefore as the individuals, and knowing the nature and dimensions of these means is paramount for successful intelligence operations in the future.

Since 9/11, cooperation has been the order of the day. Long gone are the days when, for instance, in the 1980s an NSA director, Lt. Gen. William Odom, US Army, decided to cut off NSA intelligence flow to New Zealand because of New Zealand's ban on US nuclear warships and submarines entering New Zealand ports.

This was short-lived, with GCHQ and the Australians supplying the New Zealand GCSB (Government Communications Security Bureau) with SIGINT and other intelligence. In fact, NSA working personnel surreptitiously worked around Odom's ban, such is the core strength and relationships within the Five Eyes. Nothing in the future, and particularly the whims and fancies of political change within each of the Five member states, should jeopardize the continuum of Five Eyes 24/7working cooperation.

Arms dealers and the middlemen, who operate in the shadows, often acting sub rosa for governments, are key targets since they mastermind the deals and transfers of funds to those who provide and those who receive weapons. Israel's operations and arms deals with Russia and Iran, in light of contemporary international relations, are eye-openers. What they provide is a template for thwarting arms deals that are clearly and unambiguously dangerous for the global order. This requires close collaboration rather than unilateral dealings. The sort of operations that CIA officers such as the legendary, perhaps infamous, James Jesus Angleton (1917–1987) ran at the CIA in the early Cold War decades with little or no cooperation with the other Five Eyes is perhaps an object lesson in how to both create a certain amount of chaos and, more important, seriously jeopardize the joint collection, analysis, and sharing of Five Eyes intelligence.

The key motivation driving both illicit and clandestine arms deals and the appalling consequences of human trafficking is money. However, out-of-control covert intelligence operations without proper oversight can and has led to disastrous political repercussions. The Iran-Contra affair illustrates this well. The intersection of intelligence as an arm of political policy is clearly a most troubling scenario. As the 2020s progress, the US and the UK, together with the other three Five Eyes, will have to pool their total resources. Based on a complete review of standalone clandestine intelligence operations since 1947 by the United States, it is recommended that unless there are overwhelming reasons for a standalone US covert intelligence operation, then the Five Eyes should work together in collaboratively tracking money, people, and weapons. This covers not only 24/7 electronic and other means of exchanging data but also the constant interaction of Five

Eyes personnel not just through the various personnel exchange programs but also through constant meetings.

The March 11, 2004, Atocha railway station bombings in Madrid, Spain, with 192 killed and approximately 2,000 people injured, showed that in tracking the al-Qaeda terrorist cell involved, there had been insufficient close working relations between the various European intelligence and law enforcement agencies. The bombings were the deadliest terrorist attacks carried out in the history of Spain and Western Europe. Close working-level meetings between the agencies may well have improved considerably the Spanish understanding and interpretation of the available intelligence data. As the 2020s progress, more and more close working meetings will be required to address not just weapon and human trafficking but also the wider strategic intelligence issues.

The end games for both illicit and illegal arms deals, weapons movements, and human trafficking are well understood—the motivation, the locations, the customers, and the likely possible routes. Take for example the AR-15 and AK-47 Kalashnikov weapons that are used extensively on the global markets, both legally and illegally.

Like almost every weapon, including those weapons that are manufactured ostensibly for official government military purposes, US-UK Intelligence knows where they are manufactured, both overtly and covertly. Tracking their sale and distribution is an art and a science of modern intelligence operations. The political context is the art, and the science involves the myriad technical intelligence sources and methods to track their movements and end users. Large weapons present an easier profile—tanks and armored personnel carriers are easier to track than Uzi submachine guns or RPGs (rocket-propelled grenades). Part of the problem is that nation states indulge in clandestine arms deals. Corrupt money deals often underlay the reasons for purchase, with paybacks for the key top people in the process, with hard cash passing between the principals, not via international banking. International relationships are not always what they appear to be. Today, it may seem a total disconnect that major Western European countries and Israel were major arms suppliers to Iran and that countries that could not necessarily go direct to the arms manufacturer or middlemen would use surrogates.

In the early days of the Cold War, Israel was a major source of intelligence on the Soviet Union because of the large number of Jews still in Russia and other Soviet states, and the backward and forward of Russian Jews, while at the same time that Israel was collecting intelligence, it was also buying arms from eastern bloc sources, particularly Czechoslovakia, with the full knowledge of their Soviet masters. This apparent symbiosis is likely to continue, and US-UK Intelligence will have to not just work much more closely together in tracking and inhibiting weapon and human trafficking but also be open about mutual political agendas. Outstanding intelligence organizations are communities of very talented and mostly hugely ethical people serving common purposes of protecting critical national interests.

The United States in particular may have to adjust some of its modus operandi in terms of greater transparency and sharing, though all under total security.

Money laundering tends to accompany terrorist weapons and explosives purchases, drug cartels, human trafficking, piracy financials, and gun running, together with more opaque weapons procurements. The technological edge can defeat these operations.

In addition to the types of technologies that we have already discussed, new technologies will augment the massive search and analysis engines being developed for both GCHQ and NSA, with technology sharing with the Canadians, the Australians, and the New Zealanders. Two examples will suffice: artificial intelligence (AI) can add to the sources and methods mix in hitherto unexplored domains, particularly when using a holistic approach to, say, gun running and arms transfers with very clever cognitive tools, which will automatically provide the sort of warnings and indicators that lead to interception, arrest, and seizure. Similarly, shared drone technology will enhance Five Eyes surveillance with stealth, improved power to density propulsion systems that will extend range and endurance, and ever-increasing sophisticated SIGINT and IMINT payloads with real-time low probability of intercept data links.

These new techniques will be added to the classical armory of SIGINT, IMINT, HUMINT, GEOINT, ACINT, and MASINT in all their myriad forms, and used in a fully integrated way so that the speed and accuracy of initial detection and location are enhanced.

Drones are here to stay. The Ukraine war has made this manifest. The more sophisticated stealthy covert drones with long endurance and highly capable sensors will augment the more lightweight tactical drones in adding to the SIGINT, ELINT, ELECTRO-OPINT/ INFRA-RED, and IMINT capabilities of airborne and space systems, whose whereabouts are often known by the threat. Drones are very versatile and, in money terms, hugely cost effective. They can be launched from ships and submarines, from friendly territories using surrogates, and not-so-friendly nations clandestinely. They can self-destruct in the worst scenarios. Locating and tracking portside activities using drones can become both more efficient and less risky than employing covert human operatives.

Paramount in this technological leap forward still remains the key collective strengths of the US and UK Intelligence, the Five Eyes as a whole and their key allies. In my fifty years of intelligence experience, there can be no hiding vital information that is of mutual benefit. For example, Canada may not have the same historic and current SIGINT organization of the British at GCHQ and the Americans at NSA, but the Canadians have a vast network through their embassies that augment their traditional CSE covert collection operations. The same applies to the Australians and New Zealanders. The sum of all parts will be more and more crucial as we move into the second quarter of the twenty-first century.

The combined navies of the US and the UK and their allies represent a prodigious round-the-clock forward-deployed presence to counter the international trade in illicit arms. These navies are complemented by the navies of friendly and allied powers. The Five Eyes share data with and through the US National Maritime Intelligence Center(NMIC) and the associated echelons in the other four countries. Locating and tracking rogue ships transporting illicit arms is today a hallmark of the Five Eyes navies. For example: on March 28, 2016, USS *Sirocco* intercepted a dhow in the Arabian Sea and confiscated 1,500 AK-47s, 200 RPGs, and 21 .50-caliber machine guns (these are manufactured by several nations including the Russians and Chinese); on August 27, 2018, USS *Jason Dunham* tracked and intercepted a stateless dhow(not flying a national flag) in international waters in the Gulf of Aden off the coast of Yemen. Aerial surveillance showed the crew throwing packages of AK-47s into a skiff. The following day, August 28, 2018, USS *Jason Dunham* boarded and seized the weapons that included more than 1,000 AK-47s. The above illustrates countless at-sea operations. Five Eyes shared intelligence and cooperation with other friendly navies has paid serious dividends.

Intelligence and the Middle East: Will the Past Be Prologue?

It is not the purpose here to reexamine the intelligence failures that occurred prior to and after the invasion of Iraq. These issues have been addressed by many authors, and much of the product is axiomatic. From a US-UK Intelligence perspective, however, there remains one key overriding issue. This is the separation of individual single-state policy (i.e., the policies of the United States and the United Kingdom) from both individual state-sponsored intelligence collection and analysis from collective Five Eyes intelligence collection and analysis. This is an important issue, and it involves total Five Eyes agreements and also the separate bilateral and multilateral intelligence agreements and intelligence exchanges that exist between the Five Eyes nations. The United States has, for example, pursued different policies in the Middle East from the other four nations, sometimes contentiously, with disagreement, as is clear from Five Eyes ambassadorial statements and votes in the United Nations. As has been stated several times, intelligence products, particularly key assessments from the various Five Eyes Joint Intelligence Committees, or their equivalent, should not be subject to any form of political pressure or influence. Intelligence's role is to provide the highest-quality unvarnished information for policymakers without any skewing of data to support either national policy or the political motives or intentions of political parties and national leadership. Intelligence should be at arm's length. It is never the role of intelligence to make policy. In this regard, US-UK Intelligence and the Five Eyes therefore hold collectively the moral high ground. The intelligence agencies and departments of the Five Eyes have an ethical standard to maintain, insofar as they cannot be swayed in their assessments by political exigencies, notwithstanding that there may at times be disagreement or varying interpretations of intelligence data. The latter is a different issue and can be a sign of a healthy, vibrant, and professional organization. As the 2020s progress, it is crucial that the cohesiveness of US-UK Intelligence and the Five Eyes as a whole endures and adheres in spite of national political policy differences to the above ethical considerations.

US-UK Intelligence has known one enduring fact since the 1950s and the consequences of the 1967 June War that has led to many contentions ever since. This is the need for intelligence collectors and analysts to truly know and understand the Middle East in detail, from every dimension, and not just in terms of classical political and international relations and diplomacy as practiced in the West but also in terms of the deep history, culture, political origins and developments since World War II; religions, economies, educational systems, traditions, family structure and community organization; diverse languages and dialects, and the origins of current and likely future political alignments and intentions—both internally, regionally, and internationally. Without that knowledge and experience, US-UK Intelligence can, potentially, be clutching at straws in spite of the very best intelligence collection systems. There has to be greater awareness of the various shifts in all these variables as many external international players, some at total odds with US-UK interests, seek to pursue their national self-interests in what is likely the most conflicted region in the world, and one from which can emit the worst of consequences. History and culture come together in abundant strength in the Middle East. Understanding these is a prerequisite.

The aftermath of the occupation-invasion of Iraq in 2003 was clearly not adequately assessed prior to military operations, a huge lesson in itself. At the core of this issue most likely lay a fundamental lack of understanding of the history and culture of the Middle East. The latter were not fully understood and factored into decision-making in the White House. Herewith lay a potential recipe for strategic disaster. We must have collective understanding not just of why we are where we are today in the Middle East but also of the systemic underpinnings that are driving regional politics in ways that no one in Washington would have predicted in 2001.

Over the past twenty-two years, there have been many academic analyses and intelligence assessments regarding the rise of ISIS and its apparent successes. Interpretations have varied, in some cases quite significantly. Some researchers have attributed responsibility to Washington, while the others have seen al-Qaeda in Iraq (AQI) as the driving force behind the emergence and growth of ISIS. The overall fallout of these varying views is that it is a far more difficult and complex process to comprehend what caused the emergence of ISIS in 2006 and its claims to be a state. Despite various US political pronouncements, ISIS today, in 2023, is far from eliminated.

Although it has suffered serious military defeats and many of its leaders have been eliminated, it has a most unfortunate ability to regenerate and garner more supporters. ISIS has been declared defeated on several occasions only to reappear. The internet plays a role in the ISIS recruitment process, and although US-UK Intelligence very successfully tracks much of this, there remains the challenge of countering the recruitment process, training, and the supply of weapons.

Syria and Iraq lie at a geostrategic crossroads, where the Sunni and the Shi'a worlds intersect. From the south to the north, there is the main Sunni line, from the Gulf countries to Turkey. The Shi'a area stretches from the east to the west and consists primarily of Iran and Hezbollah. Syria and Iraq have mixed populations, and until the beginning of the twentieth century, both these countries had secular regimes, with mixed populations of Sunni and Shi'a communities coexisting in similar economic and sociopolitical conditions.

The role of ideology and doctrine in the Middle East should never be underestimated.

The struggle between Shi'a and Sunni Muslims has not ceased since the seventh century. The ruling regime, whether Sunni or Shi'a, is what determines outcomes, irrespective of population and Moslem demographics—Bahrain, for example, is a Sunni state, though it has a Shi'a majority. This key overlay should drive both intelligence collection and analysis.

ISIS appeared just after the Iraq parliamentary elections of 2005, initially in January. The Shi'ites obtained the overwhelming majority in the National Assembly.

In January 2005, the two main Shi'a parties obtained 180 seats (the Kurds receiving 75 seats, the rest 20). These results led to a wave of criticism, and the elections were repeated. In spite of an increasing number of Sunni votes, the Shi'a United Iraqi Alliance got 128 seats out of 275 (Kurds 53, the Sunnis altogether 58).

The civil war began, as the Sunni population would not acknowledge the legitimacy of the elections. The main role was played by terrorist groups that had evolved from breakup of the Iraqi army and what became AQI, and later ISIS.

In June 2005, Washington began a "Together Forward" operation, which finished in October. Immediately after that, ISIS appeared. This precipitated a reaction by those in Iraq not disposed to the US occupation, uniting them in a common purpose, to challenge the United States. ISIS consisted of some elements of the terrorist groups defeated in the civil war, including AQI, and other subdivisions and generals of Saddam Hussein's army. Though distinct entities, these groups displayed similarities. They combined to fight a common enemy, the Americans, and their aim was to expel the US from Iraq. What is much more important to observe is that they are all Sunnis. The very name of a new group, Islamic State of Iraq, marked a key common and unifying claim: to create a Sunni state by a Sunni political elite. To ignore this crucial fact is to blindside Five Eyes intelligence operations and assessments.

Sponsorship from the Gulf countries helped them to join together. ISIS's early emergence therefore is not directly related to the Washington government, to AQI, or to economic factors such as poverty, but rather support from the Gulf and, in particular, from Saudi Arabia and Qatar. Saudi Arabia has always claimed to be an indisputable leader between the Sunni communities and is a Sunni regional leader.

Although Qatar had intensified its connections with European countries to increase its GDP, Qatar still needed to have a Sunni key relationship to the north.

Syria was ruled by the Alawi kin and showed political affinity for Iran, and Iraq had a strictly secular regime and a Shi'a majority in population. As a consequence, the Gulf countries such as Qatar felt a strong need for a separate Sunni state. If these fundamental facts are ignored, it is clearly possible for US-UK Intelligence and the Five Eyes as a whole to go astray in making assessments.

The First Gulf War, Iraq, August 1990

The invasion of Kuwait by Saddam Hussein, August 2–4, 1990, eliminated a chance for the US and its allies to cooperate with his regime, while good relations between the Assad family and the Iranian government opened the door to challenges to US influence. Readers should bear in mind one key aspect that a former head of the Israeli Mossad, Efraim Halevy, points out in his book *Man in the Shadows*: "The beginning of our journey in this book took us to Baghdad and to the key player, Saddam Hussein—confronting the Shiite revolutionary hurricane emanating from Iran. Hussein was then the savior of the modern Arab world and the vital interests of the United States in the region." The tragic irony that the Mossad chief points out underscores a crucial fact that, much as Saddam Hussein was a well-proven extremely evil man in many ways, he was the regional bulwark against Iran and indeed the dire enemy of an emergent threat from al-Qaeda. Much earlier in his book, Halevy points out that it was Saudi Arabia, not in any shape or form Iraq, that supported Moslem extremism and provided most of the manpower for the 9/11 attacks.8

Moderate Arab leaders had always indicated to the West that Hussein, bad person that he was, provided the best defense against both Iran and Islamic extremism.

Halevy, toward the end of his book, makes a significant statement regarding WMD, and particularly the nuclear element, that Islamic extremists are much more likely to use WMD, including nuclear weapons, and, by implication when revisiting his assessment of Hussein and Iraq, pose far more of a threat than ever Hussein did.

Halevy shows how moderate and loyal allies of the West, such as King Hussein of Jordan, followed a position of neutrality and a tilt toward Iraq in 1991 and the First Gulf War because he realized that Saddam Hussein kept the region safe from Iranian intrusion and a Shi'ite resurgence. Halevy states regarding Hezbollah, "However, it has one more characteristic that distinguished it from Khammas and Al Qaeda: It is the Shiite movement allied with Iran . . . in these respects Hezbollah will have to renounce much more than Khammas if it wishes its dreams of respectability to come true."10 These quotes from a distinguished former Mossad chief show an analysis of the region that was tragically either forgotten, ignored, or never appreciated in the first instance, in the headlong haste to invade Iraq.

After the invasion, the political instability created in Iraq, particularly from 2006, allowed a Sunni organization with a clear political course to gain momentum toward, potentially, the creation of its own state. The Sunni state lying between the Gulf and Turkey had to facilitate laying a gas pipeline from Qatar to Europe and also divide the Shi'a geopolitical and theocratic space into two unconnected parts. This view of a new Sunni state also solved the Saudi problem of political leadership. Syria, primarily agrarian, and Iraq, an oil producer, would not challenge Saudi and Gulf state economic supremacy. It is important to recall that ISIS had been waiting near the Syrian-Iraqi borders and began its expansion in 2013–2014. Why did it wait so long to act? The answer is that ISIS could not establish itself solidly in the Sunni territories of Iraq, as it would have to face surrounding forces, both the Shi'as of southern Iraq and neighboring countries, and the Kurds. Also, it could not connect directly to Turkey, or any sea, so from a strategic viewpoint, ISIS, while solely in Iraq, had strategic limitations. However, ISIS saw an opportunity in Syria.

When the Western intervention in Syria began, after two years of civil war, when all conflicting parties and the population became exhausted, ISIS crossed the border and interfered in the war. ISIS needed support from the local population.

The idea of a caliphate was created to win over peoples in the newly controlled territories. Syria became therefore a critical factor in ISIS's survival and possible growth.

In retrospect, it is clear that the main aim of ISIS was in fact to establish a state, a serious challenge for the West, the region, and the US-UK Intelligence apparatus, and one that had to be internally stable and could in fact be used by the Gulf countries as a bridge between them and the West. The early success of ISIS militarily can be explained not by military superiority but rather the total fatigue of Syria and Iraq caused by civil disorders and external intervention by Russia and the West, and occasional incursions by Israeli air strikes. However, this very scenario also militated in the other direction, preventing ISIS from gaining stable control in a hugely volatile environment that remains to this day. The chief political-military objective of the United States and the United Kingdom has been to contain and at best eliminate ISIS in Syria, while creating an environment in which the Assad regime will negotiate. The latter has been exacerbated by Russian support for the Assad regime and the very complexity of the ethnic-political-religious diversity that divides Syria. By the spring of 2019, ISIS had suffered major military defeats in Syria. The question remains about the future of the remaining ISIS fighters and their families and supporters in Syria. Will they disperse, and if so, where to? Will they be integrated? Will they be interned in camps? The situation is still ambivalent. Moreover, what will happen to the many foreign nationals who were fighting for the defeated ISIS in Syria? These people remain in transit. Will their countries of origin accept them back and attempt cultural rehabilitation? In some cases, countries of origin may charge returning ISIS fighters with terrorist offenses.

For those ISIS supporters who are not Syrian nationals, what is their economic and social future? Time has shown too that ISIS regenerates. It is crucial, naturally, that this is not allowed to occur. Intelligence is crucial in this process of identifying where and how such regeneration is occurring.

We know that the so-called domestic strategy of ISIS was centered on creating a state, a propagandist tool if unrealistic. ISIS has never tried to break into Shi'a territories, and in both Iraq and Syria, they have claimed to want to control only Sunni lands. They have, however, tried to capture some parts of Kurdistan to reach the Turkish border. ISIS's direct territorial control strategy, most likely a pipe dream, appears to have been the basis for developing a caliphate ideology that would allow Syrians and Iraqis to tolerate their loss of sovereignty and influence, by creating a theocratic self-identity as an Umar-like11 caliphate. Fortunately, none of this has been achieved, while the current situation in Syria remains volatile, unpredictable, with massive dislocation, intense suffering, and a massive refugee problem for Jordan in particular. From an intelligence perspective, it is important to place ISIS within the much bigger Islamic framework outside of current state structures. ISIS has been criticized severely for direct violations of sharia law by various groups within Islam. However, none of the key theologians or religious leaders have dared yet to publish fatwa against the ISIS regime. The Moslem intelligentsia, within the religious leadership, has come out in direct criticism in light of ISIS atrocities of massive proportions. The latter has been exemplified by the violent treatment of non-Muslim women. Intelligence can provide data that will show how to ideologically target those populations and communities most vulnerable to ISIS recruitment propaganda by using well-constructed counterpropaganda, employing all the subtleties of dialect and local culture.

Prior to the mid-2010s, ISIS could claim some success by creating state-like institutions. The ISIS regime has provided in areas where they have or had controlled electricity, water, and facilitated building schools and hospitals, roads, and mosques.

US-UK Intelligence collection has and remains important in the ways in which ISIS seeks to control perception of itself, and especially where ISIS wishes to be perceived by the local populations as an organization that tends to do best for its people. ISIS would like to have itself perceived by its grassroots followers, and those who are caught innocently in the turmoil of theocratic cross fire, as the political conjunction of the material and spiritual, in fulfillment of its people's needs for stability.

As the 2020s progress, the US and the UK in particular will need to exploit more effectively ISIS technical and theocratic vulnerabilities in coercing populations and particularly paramilitary recruits to its ranks. There is a requirement for a more sophisticated approach to media interactions by US-UK Intelligence, far more capable than, for example, the Voice of America, during the Cold War. As we observed above, dealing with ISIS propaganda and recruitment requires detailed sophisticated insight into local cultures and dialects. One key ISIS vulnerability is open to penetration: the reality and the perception that ISIS has spiraled into atrocity after atrocity, driven by an evil creed of violence and mayhem, has now been clearly seen for what it is in Syria. This provides US-UK Intelligence with an open door to influence those who are vulnerable, threatened, and have some hope of being saved from ISIS oppression if the West stays engaged militarily, particularly with the presence of US-UK Special Forces in non-Assad-controlled enclaves. The latter are political-military decisions but should be underscored by sound intelligence that indicates where and how the most effective counter-ISIS propaganda and recruitment tools and funds can be employed.

One area where UK-US Intelligence intervention can be most efficacious in the 2020s is in the countering of ISIS recruitment of professionals, such as scientists, administrators, engineers, technologists, and economists, to manage ISIS-controlled industry, agriculture, and trade wherever it appears and that is clearly under ISIS direct control. For example, ISIS was able, with external financial support from the other Sunni-dominated states in the region, to operate the dam on the Assad Lake, a thermal power plant near Aleppo, petroleum enterprises, and claims by ISIS that it issues its own currency. Future ISIS-related critical infrastructure and logistics can be thwarted by UK-US Intelligence operations in conjunction with political-military-diplomatic actions. Many ISIS specialists and consultants have come from Western countries. US-UK Intelligence and the Five Eyes as a whole have the means to identify such people, isolate them, and dissuade them from association with a terrorist organization, a serious crime in Western states, and certainly in the Five Eyes countries.

UK-US Intelligence will also have to divert energy to collection and analysis of internal ISIS perspectives and self-assessments as ISIS continues to face internal problems. These are difficult to gauge unless serious programs are initiated to both assess and then disrupt ISIS internal theocratic propaganda and its core organization, especially funding, weapon supplies, and recruitment media. HUMINT has a serious role in this process, and collaborative operations with non–Five Eyes collectors will be important. If internal dissent is created within ISIS, then it may lose most of its territorial ambitions under pressure from regional forces. Jordan, for example, joined the Kurds and independent elements in Syria and Iraq in their struggle.

Sowing disagreements between ISIS's leaders is potentially as valuable as alienating them in drone strikes and other kinetic means. To date, neither Saudi Arabia nor Qatar has been able to control ISIS leaders. The creation of rifts by the Five Eyes community together with pressure from both the West, the United Nations, and the Sunni Islamic states could aggregate to undermine the ISIS leadership, and ultimately lead to its capitulation.

ISIS's main objective to conjoin the Sunni space will have been undermined if, in the 2020s, well-organized and coordinated Western opposition with regional allies contains ISIS's spread. ISIS's "future map" of the 2010s will look like a pipe dream.

If the right things are executed, it is very unlikely that ISIS will be able to have a major support base beyond Syria and Iraq. However, if the Five Eyes intelligence infrastructure does not maintain a major intelligence collection and assessment capability in this key region in support of national policies, then the future will remain ambiguous.

If ISIS regenerates a foothold of any kind in Syria, it is very unlikely to make inroads in the face of Pres. Bashar al-Assad's forces, supported by the Russian Army, Special Forces, and Air Force, arms supply, and other covert Russian operations.

The main aim of the Bashar al-Assad regime has been to exterminate local radical terrorist groups and to stabilize the remaining territories, and then to recover the economy in the context of a lost Euphrates. All this remains to be seen. The Syrian scenario is further complicated by relations between Syria and Israel, and their primary supporters and military benefactors, Russia and the United States respectively.

US-UK Intelligence, the Five Eyes, and their Western allies need to exploit relations between ISIS, Saudi Arabia, and Qatar. ISIS atrocities and a clear divergence from fundamental Moslem teaching can polarize opposition to ISIS, leaving the Islamists isolated and surrounded, facing a demise akin to those twentieth-century tyrannies that sought to impose their will by brutal suppression and atrocities. ISIS will have hopefully masterminded its own downfall by brutally violating all the norms of human conduct and indeed the very essence of the prophet's words. Cruelty, inhumanity, and sheer violent atrocity have no place in the civilized world, and the UK and US should play their key intelligence roles in ensuring that ISIS reaps the whirlwind of its own making. The Five Eyes, together with political initiatives by the United States, the United Kingdom, Jordan, and their allies in the Middle East and Europe, have a clear moral and "just war" mandate to destroy the backbone of ISIS that has masterminded atrocities.

At the end of World War II, the US pursued one of the most far-seeing strategies to turn around a country that had perpetrated the worst kind of atrocities and war crimes in history. This model, the reverse of the Versailles Treaty model, signed on June 28, 1919, was created by George Marshall and the American leadership. Once ISIS is defeated, indeed obliterated, the extraordinarily demanding challenge will be for the US and its allies to find just and equitable ways to resolve the complexities of the Sunni-Shi'a territorial and theocratic space. It will require immense humanity to steer through the vastly troubled waters of Sunni and Shi'a rivalries and centuries of theocratic divergence. This is at the very heart of the issues in the Middle East.

The lost opportunity after the Iraq intervention-invasion to separate Sunni, Shi'a, and Kurd into defined geographic and theocratic political territories may have been lost, resulting in an ancient sectarian divide that then engaged in bloody conflict, but all things are possible in the Middle East, and US-UK Intelligence will have a critical role in supplying highly reliable intelligence to frame what will have to be new and innovative diplomatic initiatives.

The Israel-Palestinian Challenge

During his presidency (2009–2017), Barack Obama proclaimed that he wished to see Israel return to the pre-1967 June War boundaries in accordance with United Nations Security Council Resolution 242, passed at the end of the 1967 June War. President Obama argued that this was a critical prerequisite to begin a truly long-term solution to the Israel-Palestinian situation. His administration's position rested on the fundamental UN concept embodied in Resolution

242 that Israel took land that was not Israel's by force and that to meet Palestinian rights to nationhood and wider Arab demands, that the Golan Heights and the West Bank be restored to their lawful owners. These were strident demands and were in keeping with United Nation's resolutions. It should be noted that according to the Department of Peace and Conflict Research in Uppsala, Sweden, Israel has been sanctioned in forty-five resolutions by the UN Human Rights Council for various violations regarding the Palestinian situation. Much earlier, between 1967 (shortly after the end of the 1967 June War) and 1989, the UN Security Council adopted 131 resolutions directly addressing the Arab-Israeli conflict. What this demonstrates is the need for constant accurate UK-US Intelligence across all domains affecting the ongoing Israel-Palestinian situation. This is complicated by the United States' unique relationship with Israel, making an already complex situation for the other four nations of the Five Eyes intelligence agencies even more sensitive. The United Nations General Assembly has adopted a number of resolutions stating that the United States' relationship with Israel encourages Israeli expansionist policies, particularly in the West Bank.

This complicates life for the UK, Canadian, Australian, and New Zealand intelligence agencies and the political systems that they support individually and collectively. For example, the Ninth Emergency Session of the UN General Assembly was convened at the request of the UN Security Council because the United States refused to adopt sanctions against Israel. The US has tended to follow what became called the "Negroponte Doctrine" (after John Negroponte, US ambassador to the United Nations, September 2001–June 2004) that opposes any Security Council resolutions that criticize or sanction Israel without also denouncing militant Palestinian activities by Hamas and Hezbollah. Collecting and analyzing impartial intelligence in this environment becomes demanding not so much because of the sources and methods involved but because of relationships within the Five Eyes that are driven by the national foreign policies of each of the individual countries. For example, at the same time that the Five Eyes are tracking illicit arms transfers from Iran to Hamas and Hezbollah, they also have to keep close watch on Israeli covert operations in the United States and the other Five Eyes countries for conducting both classical espionage and also intellectual property penetration and collection, particularly of sensitive military technology or other commercial technology that Israel deems desirable for sustaining and expanding its economy. There are inherent conflicts in this complex scenario, particularly in even more conflicting scenarios where, for instance, Israeli military intelligence and clandestine service (the Mossad) may from time to time provide timely and valuable intelligence. For example, the latter may include Iranian sanction violations, covert arms shipments, and Russian-Syrian operations. The overall situation since the 1967 June War has been exacerbated more recently by more proactive US policies in favor of Israel and the Trump administration's withdrawal of substantial aid to the Palestinians.

The move of the US Embassy from Tel Aviv to Jerusalem also caused friction within the Five Eyes political-diplomatic community. The Trump administration's announcement on March 25, 2019, to support Israel's claims to permanent sovereignty and possession of the Golan Heights drew global anger. The fallout remains to be seen. Syria's ally, Russia, will likely not stand by and do nothing, with an extant UN resolution in their favor that may give both countries legitimacy in a range of possible options. Obama had already used this resolution as a basis for Israel returning territory occupied since the 1967 June War. This situation is a potential tinderbox waiting to be ignited by perhaps reckless adventurism by all the key protagonists.

However, US-UK Intelligence has to remain aloof in the future from such differences and produce unvarnished and impartial intelligence reports.

President Netanyahu of Israel reacted vehemently to several Obama White House statements, stressing to multiple international audiences that in any two-state solution to the Israeli-Palestinian situation, Israel must have what he defines as "defensible boundaries." He saw a return to the 1967 status quo as giving up territory that is vital for Israel's survival in the event of various military and economic scenarios.

His opposite number, President Abbas, and several US secretaries of state have fully understood the reasons for his declarations. However, many independent international relations specialists on Middle East affairs have stated that if the peace process is ever to enter a substantively new era from the prior decades, and if the Palestinians are indeed ever to accede, as Israel did, to become a nation state within the community of nations, clearly more has to happen than declarations, whether rhetorical or otherwise.

The UN Resolution 242

There has been considerable analysis over the years since 1967 of the intent of the wording of Resolution 242, drafted by the then British ambassador to the United Nations Lord Caradon. The resolution is to most lawyers and international specialists quite explicit, precise, and well worded with no ambiguity. However, the wording that has caused most analysis is the section of the resolution that says, in affirmation of Article 2 of the UN Charter, the United Nations Security Council affirms: "Termination of all claims or states of belligerency and respect for and acknowledgment of the sovereignty, territorial integrity and political independence of every state in the area and their right to live in peace within secure and recognized boundaries free from threats or acts of force." Within this section, the words that cause most disagreement are "rights to live in peace within secure and recognized boundaries." The Israelis and President Netanyahu have been explicit in stating that any redrawing of the pre-1967 June War boundaries, now essentially the West Bank of the Jordan River and the Golan Heights, since Israel has withdrawn from the Sinai, must be so that Israel can be secure. The latter has been defined by President Netanyahu as being "defensible boundaries." To most military and US-UK Intelligence personnel, this phrase has significant and very definable connotations.

In looking back briefly to the 1960s, the Middle East was a critical part of the Cold War standoff and a hot bed for playing out the international rivalries between the United States and the Soviet Union. Israel felt naturally threatened and surrounded by potential belligerents that were encouraged and supported by Moscow. By June 1967, the situation reached boiling point. The sudden preemptive strikes made by Israel to seize territory from Egypt, Syria, and Jordan to extend its boundaries and create defensive barriers were extremely successful. Israel's actions precipitated a crisis that all but plunged the United States into a conflict with the Soviet Union. This could have occurred if Israel advanced beyond the Golan Heights toward Damascus, followed by Soviet intervention. Very well-documented research has shown how the Soviet Union would have launched forces against Israel if they had continued in their march toward Damascus from the Golan Heights. The world has changed with the demise of the Soviet Union and, in its aftermath, have emerged equally compelling threats to Middle East stability, not least the rise of Iran and the emergence of several parties and groups that espouse terrorism as a vehicle for achieving political goals.

Other state and non-state players have become either directly or indirectly involved through the supply of arms, training, and other equipment.

It is very easy to forget that terrorism is not a recent phenomenon. It has been a vehicle for change in the Middle East since World War II. Pres. Menachem Begin of Israel was a member of Irgun, an organization dubbed by the international community as a violent and extremist terrorist organization and described by David Ben-Gurion, national founder and first prime minister of the state of Israel, as the "enemy of the Jewish people." Begin saw himself as a freedom fighter, not a terrorist.

It is easy to forget that in the Middle East, the past is often prologue. Hamas and Hezbollah pursue political goals often by unacceptable violent means, most often dubbed terrorist acts by the international community. Such factions cite the same principles in working for the creation of an independent Palestinian state that the postwar Israeli "terrorists" cited to justify their violent actions in seeking the creation of the independent state of Israel. It is very easy to lose this perspective, while at the same time condemning, as the international community should indeed do, any acts of terrorism, whatever the goal. In 1977, Menachem Begin, the man born a Russian Jew and persecuted by both the Nazis and the Soviets, became prime minister of Israel. Begin was responsible for the peace treaty with Anwar Sadat of Egypt that returned the Sinai to Egypt and which led to both men winning the Nobel Peace Prize. What this demonstrates is that all things are possible, even though in 1946, Begin had led the bombing of the King David Hotel in Jerusalem, and in March 1952 the attempt on the life of Chancellor Konrad Adenauer of West Germany. UK-US Intelligence has to operate within this hugely complex historic backdrop, providing intelligence that will help both maintain Middle East stability and provide the warnings and indicators that certain events may precipitate potentially catastrophic consequences that may impact the global peace and economy.

Intelligence and Politics: The Clear Need for Separation

Today, the Sunni Islamist group Hamas that has run the Gaza portion of the Palestinian Territories, and Hezbollah, the Shi'a Muslim militant group and political party in Lebanon, appear very much like how Irgun looked in 1942 when it split from the Haganah, launching from 1944 to 1948 a campaign against the British in Palestine. On May 14, 1948, the state of Israel was created. The relevance and poignancy are clear: Israel was fundamentally born out of terrorism. The key for UK-US Intelligence is to have collection systems in place today that will help in providing accurate information to guide international policies to prevent the spread of terrorism, while clearly finding a solution to the above policy dilemmas. Some analysts see the answer perhaps lying with Jordan and Israel, supported by the United States and its key allies. However, the ever more volatile situation in Syria, aided and abetted by Russia, adds another regional complexity, plus the ongoing crisis in Yemen, and a range of Saudi-led activities and operations that have caused discord not just within the United Nations but also within the Five Eyes foreign policy elites, both inside and outside their current governments. US-UK Intelligence community has to remain aloof from controversy to perform effectively. Moreover, the US and UK have to choose their intelligence allies not just wisely but also with continuous circumspection based on the detailed exigencies of a particular scenario.

The 2018 book *Rise and Kill: The Secret History of Israel's Targeted Assassinations* (Random House, New York) by Ronen Bergman shows how decades of covert Israeli assassination operations, mainly by the Mossad, pre- and post-independence in 1948, may appear to have temporary short-term gains but in the long term fail to address the ultimate key strategic considerations, particularly a solution to the Israel-Palestinian territorial dilemma. This is the root cause perhaps of all Israel's problems that galvanize the international community, other than perhaps the United States, against its policies and operations, while the advanced democracies equally condemn the continuous bloodshed by both sides' clandestine and terrorist forces.

President Netanyahu's strategic concerns for the "defensive boundaries" of Israel are clearly demarcated by geography; the distance between key locations in Israel and the West Bank are on the order of six to nine miles, with a huge concentration of the Israeli population on the coastal strip where most of Israel's commercial and industrial life resides. His perfectly reasonable concern is that the West Bank provides a buffer area and site for defensive missile systems that will ward off an attack. The key to helping President Netanyahu and the Israeli people find both peace and security, some argue, may lie with Jordan. Jordan is perhaps the most stable political regime in the Arab world. King Abdullah leads a nation that is making significant progress in both democratization and improvement in the lives of the ordinary Jordanian, while providing bedrock security against outside extremist influences. Israel has to both respect and trust Jordan, and Jordan's security against outside threats has to be underpinned by equal aid from the United States, just as the United States provides aid to Israel. The likelihood of a destabilizing and anti-Israel regime emerging in Jordan is at present very remote. UK-US Intelligence in the 2020s will have to monitor carefully Jordanian stability. The threats to Israel lie much further to the east in Iran, and that country's extremist associations with other state and non-state actors. By the same token, Jordan is equally threatened by extremist groups from outside that will try to destabilize an otherwise progressive regime, with the vast majority of Jordanians loyal both to their political processes and their head of state.

Modern cruise and ballistic missile technology are such that the West Bank buffer zone is not relevant for Israel in terms of a ground-attack invasion from the east, particularly given relationships with both Jordan and the underpinnings provided by the United States. The major threats to both countries, other than extremist attacks from terrorist groups, are most likely to come from missile attacks. The very worst scenario for Israel would be a preemptive ballistic missile attack from Iran. In this and other missile scenarios, the West Bank does not play as a key geographic entity because of speed, times, and distance issues associated with the location of key targets in both Jordan and Israel if attacked by cruise and ballistic missiles. Some strategists argue that the West Bank can play a role insofar as it could be the site for a layered defensive missile network.

What the above illustrates is the critical intelligence underpinnings for both warnings and indicators and also for supporting policy decisions and military planning. Some argue that a settlement with Jordan over the West Bank can include the following: Jordan regains control of the West Bank and with United States oversight begins the management of both Palestinian and Israeli settlements in the area. In return, Jordan should grant to Israel several key sovereign air base sites in the West Bank where Israel may have full rights, permanent access for its military to man 24/7 defensive missile batteries and provide early warning radar systems. Such sites and systems will be of equal value to Jordan. In addition, it is argued that the United States could provide other key layers of defensive systems for both Jordan and Israel, in addition to the military systems that it provides under the various aid agreements. If these sorts of solution options are both realistic, achievable, and some form of progress is made in the 2020s, then UK-US Intelligence will be critical for establishing highly reliable intelligence systems to ensure that risks are mitigated.

From President Netanyahu's perspective, the issue of the strategic role of the West Bank has now taken on a whole new complexion, and one that guarantees Israeli access and presence for the above defensive systems. This is all hypothesis, but whatever does occur in the Middle East in the next ten-plus years will require a significant intelligence input that is not driven solely by US interests. The United States will also want to minimize deployment costs, except at times of rising tension in the region. The independence and capabilities of the other four nations of the Five Eyes intelligence community will be hugely significant in terms of independent and unvarnished assessments. Intelligence sharing is critical in any negotiation and agreement, and both Jordan and Israel will need to build confidence with themselves and mutually with the United States to share time-sensitive intelligence, complicated by the roles of Russia and China intervening at all levels of political-diplomatic-military-economic-arms sales activities. Put simply, good intelligence is about providing information to the user that enables them to make well-informed decisions well ahead of a decision point, never to be surprised, and always to have the upper-hand knowledge base over one's actual or potential adversary.

The Global Challenge from China

The emerging global power of China and its challenge to US military strength in East Asia poses fundamental questions about the nature and goals of Chinese policy for the long term, and how US-UK Intelligence can provide intelligence to help craft a strategy both in their best interests and in those of its friends and allies, not just in the region but also worldwide. In July 2019, the Chinese government published "China's National Defense in the New Era." This articulates China's public version of its defense policy. It is explicit about Taiwan and its "One China principle" and that, if necessary, it will fight for Taiwan. These are words to heed. China's stated GDP expenditures on defense and as a percentage of Chinese government spending are revealing, if accurate, and when compared with the GDP defense expenditures that the Chinese quote between 2012 and 2017 of the US (3.5%), Russia (4.4%), India (2.5%), the UK (2%), France (2.3%), Japan (1%), and Germany (1.2%). China states it spends 1.3 percent of GDP on defense. There is one statement that also resonates:

"China firmly believes that hegemony and expansion are doomed to failure." We assume that China means territorial expansion by aggressive means. This is at odds with China's militarization of the Spratly Islands. So, the question is, "Quo Vadis, China?"

The rise of China is self-evident, but the huge question exists as to what are China's long-and short-term goals, whose economic drivers, let alone military expansion, are reshaping the international security land and seascapes? At the same time, the United States rejected under President Trump the multilateral economic and political framework, witnessed by withdrawal from the Trans-Pacific Partnership, renegotiation of NAFTA, and threats to leave the World Trade Organization, compounded by punitive tariffs on China and

US allies, and rejection of the Iran Nuclear Agreement signed by key European allies, Russia, and China. The effect of all this has been to draw nations into the Chinese orbit, create disharmony with US NATO allies, and draw Russia and China closer. Punitive US sanctions have led to hugely negative consequences. The Biden administration has, at the time of writing in 2023, sought to reverse all the negative effects of the Trump administration. These have been largely successful, particularly in reenergizing NATO-US relations. This success was emblematic when Russia invaded Ukraine in February 2022. Most of all is the extraordinary successful growth of China's "Belt and Road Initiative" (BRI), a twenty-first-century "Silk Road" started in 2013, a trillion-dollar investment that embraces about eighty countries, strategically designed to guarantee that China will not only secure its own energy, trade routes, and key natural resources but also expand its investment in global port infrastructure and sea routes across all the world's oceans, stimulating demand for Chinese products and acquiring economic control through massive investments and loans that will not be repaid in some cases this century.

China has also articulated a "Polar Silk Road," stating that it is a "Near Arctic State." The means to achieve what are clearly stated Chinese goals is a "Maritime Grand Strategy," with the Chinese navy the key centerpiece. China seeks to gain access to and control of precious metal extraction and production in Russia, Central Asia, Latin America, and Africa. China's "Debt Diplomacy" is reaping benefits at the expense of the United States and its key allies. It enables China to soften hitherto strained relations with Japan, the Philippines, and Vietnam, lessening the friction resulting from Chinese occupation and militarization of the Spratly and Paracel islands in the South China Sea. The latter is overtly geared to creating a presence to counter the US Seventh Fleet, while enabling China two-hundred-nautical-mile territorial claims to fishing and undersea resource rights around every atoll and island, in spite of the International Court of Arbitration's declaration that China has no such legal or historic claims. The US has not attempted to enforce the ruling of the court in The Hague. Meanwhile, China has built naval facilities across the Indian Ocean in Gwadar, Pakistan, in Hambantota in Sri Lanka, and in Djibouti, with long-term port agreements with Cambodia, Indonesia, Malaysia, Brunei, Myanmar, Bangladesh, Tanzania, Namibia, Greece, and Italy.

Two successive US National Security advisors, Tom Donilon, a Washington lawyer (2010–2013), and Susan Rice, a policy aficionado (2013–2017), let all this happen with zero US counteractions with the hawkish John Bolton, more preoccupied with provoking conflict with Iran rather than paying attention to the detail that James Fanell provided in his briefing of the House Permanent Select Committee on Intelligence in May 2018. A trade and resource conflict is inevitable unless the United States shifts gears to a political-diplomatic-economic turnaround strategy, underwritten by the power of the United States Navy and Marine Corps, the forward-deployed round-the-clock presence that guarantees freedom of the seas, a rule-based international order, and the prevention of conflict over trade, resources, and those critical minerals deemed vital for not just national security but also the very heart and soul of the continuing digital revolution and its massive product line.

China is following the British maritime strategy and economic model that it pursued for centuries—the defense of seaborne trade and its support of overseas acquisitions and influence. China is investing "without risk," with zero shareholders to please. Investment in African mines brings nothing like the risk to US and European investors. China is stealing technology not just through well-known cyberpenetration and espionage but also through a simple and successful economic strategy—US and other foreign investors have and are going to China, investing, and then finding that China replicates their technology, production, and engineering plans, and then creates homegrown industries and companies. Foreign investment has and will die on the vine in due course. The response from the United

States and its key NATO allies has been appallingly paltry. Former secretary of defense, Jim Mattis, a wise and wonderfully astute US Marine general, has rightly observed that one key counterbalance is the "strategic convergence" of India and the United States, together with other key US allies, because, otherwise, Chinese hegemony in the Indo-Pacific region at the economic, political, and strategic levels will predominate. The huge danger of this is a twenty-first-century version and tragic specter of the 1930s economic implosion in East Asia that set Japan on not just a conflict course at sea but also a territorial aggrandizement that led to catastrophe for the world and dénouement on December 7, 1941. The global economy, the world, simply cannot afford to witness another conflict on this scale. There will be no winners, only losers all round. The United States and its allies, including convergence with India, must face this challenge with unprecedented diplomatic, economic, and political-military skill and fortitude.

Some of James Fanell's testimony was challenged by other experts, particularly his prognosis that China may invade Taiwan at some point in the 2020s.

Notwithstanding this aspect, his detailed description of China's expansionist policies and actions were thoroughly grounded in accurate intelligence. Moreover, he made the salient point that much of what China has done in the past ten years was clearly stated in their open literature. In other words, the Chinese have not attempted to hide their plans and programs. They have told us in no uncertain terms what they plan to do. It is possible for the United States in particular to slip into a position of action and reaction vis-à-vis increased Chinese military capabilities and operations seemingly intent on challenging the United States. China is overtly demonstrating what Chinese official writings convey—namely, that the American East Asian presence will be challenged and that China sees itself as the preeminent Asian power, with an intent to create a hegemony that will in due course extend to the outer island chains of the Western Pacific.

Action and reaction were very much phenomena of the Cold War: the Soviet Union would develop a capability, or extend its influence in various areas, or establish a new base, and the United States and NATO would counter such activities. The great game played itself out until the demise of the Soviet Union. What the United States and its allies must seriously consider now are the potentially negative impacts of following a similar pattern of behavior with China, of being led astray into costly and complex situations at all levels of political-military strategy. There are alternative ways to address the issues, problems, and challenges that lie ahead for the new generation of American leaders, who cannot afford the luxury of a Cold War standoff with massive economic implications. However, what the above does show quite clearly is that UK-US Intelligence and their Five Eyes partners, together with Japan, India, and other East Asia allies, will need to be extremely vigilant in the warnings and indicators domain, such that their political leaderships cannot be caught unawares by sudden and perhaps unprecedented drastic actions by China.

It is wise initially to revert to first principles when beginning the analysis that will lead to creating an enduring strategy for the US and its allies in East Asia. Does China resemble, or has it begun to replicate, the patterns of activities that have characterized the growth, and decline, of imperial powers and those nations that sought regional hegemony? Do the imperial models of ancient Greece and Rome, the Spanish, British, Hapsburg, Turkish, and Russian empires resemble and apply to what we see evolving in China? Do the militarist, expansionist territorial goals of Napoleon, the Nazis, Fascist Italy, and Imperial Japan connect with what we observe happening with a growing Chinese military capability, an economic juggernaut that is by no means yet in top gear, and with massive resource needs, particularly oil, that require overseas Chinese investment, foreign port facilities, and overseas political-military infrastructure?

The answer to much of the above is that China has led an extremely noninvasive approach to international relations in modern times, with certain exceptions.

The past five hundred years, since the European powers began their outward growth, exploration, colonization, and empire building, have witnessed China on a very different track. In that time, China has never invaded and permanently occupied a sovereign state or shown imperial intent. Since the Chinese revolution and the conclusion of World War II, China has for the most part lived inwardly. But there have been exceptions.

Gen. Douglas MacArthur's 1950 foray northward into North Korea and to the Yalu River provoked a response from China that was not surprising: its forces invaded south across the Yalu River and drove the United States back to the 39th parallel. From the Chinese perspective, the United States posed a threat to Chinese sovereignty and to a communist client state. In 1962, during the short Sino-Indian War, China invaded India briefly as a means of letting Jawaharlal Nehru's government know that China disapproved of India's support for the Dalai Lama and the Tibetan independence movement. After India suffered a defeat, China quickly withdrew, having made its point.

However, the Chinese invasion of Vietnam in February 1979, to signal Chinese disapproval of Vietnam's invasion of Cambodia to suppress China's client regime, the Khmer Rouge, led to an ignominious defeat. The war lasted just one month. China lost about twenty thousand troops, more in a matter of weeks than the United States lost in a single year of fighting in Vietnam. Moreover, a Vietnamese force of 100,000 border troops bloodied a Chinese army of 250,000, a humiliating defeat. The impact on China's leader, Deng Xiaoping, was dramatic.

China has supplied weapons and technology to nation states that run counter to US and its allies' interests. China has distinctive and clear-cut policies regarding all major international issues, whether it is UN policy in the Middle East or policy toward rogue nations (of which North Korea is a leading example). China, like any other country, pursues what it believes to be its national self-interest. US-UK Intelligence will have to monitor carefully Chinese pronouncements and actions so that changes do not come as surprises.

What China has *not* done is provide indications that it sees territorial expansion by invasion of other nations' territories as a way to extend Chinese power and influence.

It has mostly followed international law and agreements. There is no question that China could have marched into Hong Kong or Macau at any time without resistance. Instead, China waited until the legal expiration of treaty agreements that, in twenty-first-century hindsight, amounted to the blunt use of nineteenth-century imperial power by Portugal and Britain. Both territories were transitioned peacefully to Chinese rule. By contrast, an Argentinean dictatorship decided in 1982 to challenge Britain's long-standing rights and ownership of the Falkland Islands, and suffered the consequences. China has never made such moves. If there is a deviation from this trend, it may be economic and not militarist, and could in due course prove to be the seed of serious discord, the resource-hungry dragon. However, there are intelligence signs that the above may be too rosy a prognosis, that the Grand Maritime Strategy, which China is clearly pursuing, is a potential precursor to denouement. US-UK Intelligence will be pivotal in this regard.

China has repeatedly indicated that its inherent needs and destiny are bound to economic hegemony in East Asia. To that end, the People's Republic has begun a systematic set of claims, based on perceived historic rights, to key uninhabited reefs, atolls, and small islands in the South China Sea. China is now a self-evident economic Goliath.

At some point, its gross national product will equal and likely surpass those of the United States, Japan, and Germany. The danger is not economic competition, which is healthy and beneficial in the context of a well-managed, globally interconnected marketplace, but resource needs. China's massive population requires to be fed and sustained in keeping with its world economic position. China has a serious hold on key precious metals, particularly in the semiconductor and space industries, but in other areas, it is woefully dependent. Oil is the largest problem.

The exponential growth of Chinese oil demand could reach a possible supply and demand crisis situation in the mid to late 2020s. The country's planners are constantly looking for alternative suppliers and areas for investment and exploration. China is still using coal as a major energy source. The Western powers with green energy and conservation issues high on their national agendas see the Paris Accord as critical for all nations, and especially the two huge-population states of China and India, requiring increasing large investments in green solar, wind, and hydro energy sources.

There is no question that potentially both these nations can convert with the right leadership and investment to alternative energy sources. UK-US Intelligence will have to increasingly invest in economic intelligence, coupling their sources and methods with highly capable analyses from industry and especially the more prestigious academic institutions tracking global energy sources and distribution. The specter of a resource-hungry China replicating the Japanese resource-driven expansion policies of the 1930s, which culminated in the attack on Pearl Harbor, is not in sight in any shape or form at present or the foreseeable future. The US and the UK will have to increasingly devote more resources to economic intelligence in the strategic sense.

Chinese seizure of small islands and atolls in the South China Sea, and the militarization of these with runways, missile sites, radar and communications, exacerbated by aggressive naval posturing underpinning what the international legal community has declared as illegal claims to the Spratly and Paracel islands, are clearly matters of very serious concern. The Five Eyes have collected extensive intelligence on all these developments, and the public domain commercial satellite imagery of the Chinese South China Sea sites has made it evident to the world community what the Chinese have done in construction terms, showing in global media sources their clear intent. This is in flagrant violation of the International Court of Arbitration in The Hague, finding against Chinese claims in the South China Sea as not based on any legitimate historic rights or antecedents. To US-UK Intelligence and the Five Eyes community, these actions reflect a likely Chinese policy to continue militarization and claims not founded in the United Nations Convention on the Law of the Sea.

All this indicates willful intent to ignore international law, a most worrisome posture.

The US Navy and its allies are currently challenging all Chinese claims in the South China Sea by exercising regularly the rights of innocent passage within the historic international limits in all the areas claimed to be Chinese territory, by sailing aircraft carriers, cruisers, and destroyers into those waters that the Chinese claim as sovereign. This has led to near collisions at sea of Chinese and US warships and other hostile Chinese acts, such as intercepting US aircraft in international airspace that the Chinese claim as their national airspace. None of this bodes well for the future as the Chinese expand their navy in both numbers and capabilities, far exceeding what may be regarded as the classic naval mission of the protection of seaborne trade.

The legal concept of a two-hundred-mile economic zone has been generally accepted into the body of international law, but that zone and the law of the sea are the least developed and codified legalisms within the international community. Drawing two-hundred-mile economic zones around the disputed island chains of the South China Sea creates major challenges for dispute resolution. Vietnam has been at odds with China over island sovereignty issues for some time, and the geopolitics of the region place Japan, the Philippines, South Korea, Malaysia, Thailand, Singapore, and Indonesia in potential conflict with China over such claims as well. The wider issue of Chinese resource needs will not fade away. There are no signs of major green energy programs that will solve China's problems anytime soon. Coupled to China's increasing thirst for oil is its parallel policy of hard-currency accumulation and owning foreign indebtedness.

What then may China really want to achieve, given its military buildup, its naval exercises, and its posturing regarding Taiwan? What does China hope to gain by its ability to field new weapons systems that US-UK Intelligence and the Five Eyes have assiduously monitored and analyzed? The latter include anti-carrier, anti-access ballistic missiles, and anti-satellite systems, together with a considerable investment in electronic and cyber warfare skills and technology, and a growing fleet of submarines, both nuclear and non-nuclear, along with increasing moves into space and other intelligence/surveillance/reconnaissance domains. China has hypersonic missile systems, and the latest intelligence has revealed capable long-range high-speed drones. The Five Eyes community is concerned that China may, very simply, be planning on winning a war that it never fights. What is the essence of this analysis?

Such a war is about countervailing power, raising the order of battle of key assets to high levels, and creating constant challenges that require persistent US and allied presence, deployments, and basing at very high cost. At one level, it may be regarded as a war of attrition by other means, underpinned by sustainable economic growth and a Chinese military-industrial complex based on the new Chinese state capitalist model, which even some distinguished American economists have cited as being more efficient than the free-market capitalist model. US-UK Intelligence analysts then have to ask, Is this is a new form of hegemony or a unique Chinese version? The threat is not just the military buildup per se but the underlying single weakness in the otherwise rosy Chinese future: resource limitations and the increasing demand for oil and what is already being witnessed in Africa, with massive Chinese investment that is clearly resource oriented, particularly minerals. By beefing up its military strength, China wins the war it never fights by checkmating the United States, specifically the US Seventh Fleet, the key forward-deployed Asian representative of American presence, intent, technology, and firepower.

The intelligence to date does not bode well. China is pursuing quite simply a massive military modernization, with naval operations across the whole Indo-Pacific region and, put very directly, predatory economics. China is constantly strengthening the "Maritime Silk Road" in the Indian Ocean and demonstrating preparations for both combat and noncombat operations in the Indian Ocean, a huge change from pre-2010. In January 2016, China signed a ten-year agreement with Djibouti for port access and basing rights, ostensibly to protect Chinese commercial interests and citizens in Africa, and support counterterrorist operations. At the same time, this base provides China with a strategic posture adjacent to the critical Bab-el-Mandab Strait.

Similarly, with Chinese basing rights at the deep-water port of Gwadar, Pakistan, at Salalah in Oman, and in the Seychelles. In May 2019, China indicated that it would invest $10.7 billion in Oman. China will undoubtedly create "listening stations" in all these locations, as well as become a major arms supplier to the former US ally, Pakistan. All the ports in which China is investing are or will become "dual use" ports for commercial shipping and Chinese Navy port visits, repair and maintenance, and as key logistics hubs distant from mainland China. By the early 2020s, China will have the world's largest navy, signaling that China is no longer a land power but a maritime power whose trade is currently about 41 percent of GDP, and of that trade about 95 percent is seaborne. In 2020, China had about five thousand known registered ships.

So, what is the best strategy for the United States and its allies, and what requirements will be placed on US-UK Intelligence? First, none of the Five Eyes nations can contemplate a war with China. However, no responsible US leader can abide China creating an East Asian economic-political-military hegemony that may witness the demise of US influence and, with it, critical American economic interests. The Five Eyes navies led by the United States Navy plus other key regional allies such as Japan, India, and South Korea will have to return to a more regular and expansive presence in Far Eastern waters. This is critical to keeping the economic arteries healthy by the wise use of naval power. US-UK Intelligence and the Five Eyes become the centerpiece of the intelligence gathering and analysis to support these operations.

The solution may perhaps lie within the problem itself. While the United States reacts to Chinese moves—planning, for example, ways to implement new air-sea anti-access tactics and capabilities—essential points are possibly being missed. China's quest for economic hegemony by political-military means, in essence its Grand Maritime Strategy, can be addressed at the strategic level, because the United States and its allies have several critical factors in their favor. In the strategy that evolves from these factors, the US Navy, the other Five Eyes navies, and major Asian allies are important players. All will require coherent, accurate, and timely intelligence.

East and Southeast Asia and the wider Indo-Pacific region, stretching from the Malacca Straits across the Indian Ocean to East Africa and the key entry points to the Persian Gulf and the Red Sea, are joined economically, and therefore politically, by one medium—the sea. It is the means by which most of the trade of Asia, and thus the world, takes place.

Seaborne commerce is the enduring thread that runs through the history of the world since the age of discovery and expansion. Without oceanic trade, the global economy would collapse. The sea routes connecting all the Asian countries with the rest of the world are vital arteries. If, for whatever reason, they cease to function, the world will hemorrhage economically. The disparate Asian nations are interconnected and interdependent in this regard. The vital passages of the Malacca Straits and the Indonesian Archipelago run the routes that take trade onward through the South China Sea, the East China Sea, the Yellow Sea, the Sea of Japan, the Pacific Islands, and the trans-Pacific routes; those aquatic pathways are the lifelines of the world's trading nations. The protection of that trade, the maintenance of the freedom of the seas, and the enforcement of the laws of the sea present a huge strategic opportunity to bring together the Five Eyes nations and their allies in the region. Such a common effort can foster long-term peace and prosperity for all and ensure that East Asia is not destabilized by misplaced Chinese hegemonic intentions, underwritten by a clearly articulated Grand Maritime Strategy. China does not win a war that it never fights, and Asia can grow in wealth and prosperity with its Five Eyes and other key trading partners. This can be the genesis of a new strategy in Asia, one based on trade-route protection, maritime power, shared efforts based on shared interests, and supported in all regards by high-quality Five Eyes intelligence sources, methods, and analysis. This strategy's key ingredients include freedom of navigation, freedom of the seas, protection of seaborne trade, and rights of passage. What is required is a new "Asian Law of the Sea," either written or declaratory. Such a law would

- guarantee various maritime rights, including defining territorial rights, rights of access and passage, fishing and resource rights, and codify maritime conduct;
- provide unified policing and enforcement;

- provide agreement-based (and, in due course, treaty-based) means for regular international gatherings of the member states;
- take the Association of Southeast Asian Nations and other multi- and bilateral agreements to a new organization and forum for organizing and implementing a maritime code of conduct.

This new organization would be the vehicle for resolving issues associated with two-hundred-mile economic zones and disputes over island chains; for enforcing international law and human rights; and for combating piracy, smuggling, and terrorism. That is a formidable array of international activities that the Five Eyes nations can carry out with their regional partners. Such a cooperative undertaking can be the means to bring China into the family of Asian nations in ways that are neither belligerent nor challenging to the status quo. The strategy clearly places markers in the sand.

To be a nonparticipant is to take one's country out of the community of nations.

If China chooses a less cooperative, continual hegemonic course, then its Asian neighbors will have built themselves a fortified maritime community, linked by various agreements and obligations that will be formidable. In this environment, intelligence becomes absolutely vital. The most recent development of China creating bases and airfields from uninhabited reefs in disputed island areas in the South China Sea is a case in point. Open-source satellite imagery shows a clear Chinese intent to militarize these areas.

The alliance aspects are crucial. The good news is that the region's nations are on board. The Australians, the Malaysians, the Indonesians, the Thais, the South Koreans, the Japanese, the Philippines, and now the Vietnamese, signaled originally by US Secretary of Defense Robert Gates's successful groundbreaking visit back in late 2010, are increasingly joined in a common bond. At the center, in discreet fashion, has to be US-UK Intelligence and the Five Eyes as a whole, plus Japan and India, as the guardians against change and, worst case, surprise.

The Five Eyes navies and their close Asian allies are unique for multiple reasons, and one of them is the unifying force of the brotherhood of the sea that navies show toward one another. Sailors are gregarious people who are diplomats in myriad ways, and nothing is more unifying than port visits after joint exercises, rescue missions, disaster relief, and successful operations against drug runners and terrorists. Navies by themselves can implement policies that no amount of conventional diplomacy can hope to achieve. The United States in particular has existing resources that require little additional investment to make security-force assistance with all the participating nations a permanent and persistent feature of US naval diplomacy. Those should be the watchwords of this strategy: "US naval diplomacy," supported by Five Eyes intelligence and complemented by the intelligence services of key regional allies, particularly Japan, India, and South Korea. Vietnam may increasingly become an intelligence player in the above mix. Joint international protection of maritime trade, economic rights, and the enforcement of a new emerging law of the sea for Asia can be the means to peaceful ends. If China balks and insists on an open standoff characterized by "benign aggression," then there is little that the United States and its friends and allies can do, other than to make it very clear that they will never tolerate any form of overt aggression. The olive branch can be continuously offered, and hopefully at some stage will be accepted with magnanimity.

No one can successfully predict regime change in China. At present, this seems highly unlikely. What one can perhaps hypothesize is that the confluence of generational change, the very international trade that is making China great, cultural and travel exchanges, the internet, and technological sharing will overcome the inwardness and control mechanisms of the Chinese leadership. The specter of Tiananmen Square still looms large. China demonstrates a ruthless streak from time to time, and the concern for human rights are not part of China's political makeup. Only time will tell if this will evolve. The virtues of youth and the global economy combined eventually may make certain political transformations inevitable in China. However, this may be a rose-tinted view given that China today monitors every citizen's personal telephones, the internet, and restricts communications in keeping with a 1930s-style dictatorship, while suppressing any form of dissent or opposition to policies such as the treatment of ethnic and religious minorities.

One scenario can illustrate implementation of the new regional collective effort.

Regular joint exercises, guided by excellent current intelligence and projections, can be executed to protect shipping following the routes from the Southeast Asian straits to the Japanese Islands and South Korea. Such exercises can develop and train the region's nations in all domains of maritime warfare and seaborne trade protection.

For instance, in the anti-submarine warfare and anti-surface modes, those nations can show both capability and will, and if China elects to be a thorn in the side of its neighbors by offering up a belligerent passive-aggressiveness, then it will merely be providing training targets for the combined nations honing their skills. Hopefully, this will not occur, and China will show respect for and observance of the rights of free passage and the various economic zones. Indeed, China has as much at stake as any nation, increasingly dependent itself on the freedom of the seas for imported resources.

Change for the better in East Asia has been illustrated by the transformation of Vietnam, a nation that at the conclusion of the Vietnam War could barely sustain its population at the poverty level. Today, it has rejected the Marxist-Leninist model and pursues a state capitalist economy. Nothing is more symbolic of change than the $1.3 billion investment made by Intel outside Ho Chi Minh City. Vietnam's 95.54 million people are now at a new level of prosperity and growth, perhaps unthinkable at the time of another symbolic memory, the last US helicopter departing the empty Saigon embassy in 1975. Vietnam can become a close ally and major trading partner with the United States and its Five Eyes allies, and be integrated with the other Asian nations in a new Asian maritime strategy.

The United States and the United Kingdom with their Five Eyes intelligence allies should be strident in implementing the new strategy. It combines the maintaining of vital US and allied national interests, even to the extent of keeping the peace by preparing for war, with an internationalist maritime strategy that focuses on the enduring significance of the sea. The sea is both the means and the end in a modern US-UK and Five Eyes Asian strategy.

Peace in the Indo-Pacific Region and the Relationship with India

Back in the 1960s, US Secretary of State Dean Rusk advised President Kennedy that "India is key to countering China." The US went in an opposite direction, investing huge support across a broad spectrum of civil-military aid to Pakistan, driving India toward Russia for most of the Cold War, with the Soviet Union becoming India's chief arms supplier. Experience has shown that Pakistan cannot be trusted, in fact is duplicitous in many regards, as shown by the key Pakistani facility at Gwadar for China to have a naval base for the foreseeable future, with China now providing major arms supplies to Pakistan. US diplomacy with India has fortunately shown most positive signs. In 2015, President Obama issued a "US-India Joint Strategic Vision for the Asia-Pacific and the Indian Ocean Region." On April 11, 2016, in the *Times* of India, US Secretary Ashton Carter wrote a key lead article entitled "A Firm Strategic Handshake: The India-US Partnership Is Moving to Embrace Defense Tech Transfers and

Maritime Cooperation." On June 7, 2016, the White House issued a joint statement: "The United States and India: Enduring Global Partners in the 21st century." All this was converted to hard legislative fact in the US Congress.

In 2016, India was formally declared a "Major Defense Partner" (MDP), and this was underwritten in the US Defense Authorization Act 2017, cementing the MDP into US law.15 The Asia Reassurance Act of 2018 further solidified this. On June 8, 2016, Prime Minister Narendra Modi of India gave a groundbreaking "Address to a Joint Meeting of Congress." The so-called trust deficit between India and the US that had persisted since the US-Pakistan alliance was slowly and effectively being eroded, though it is still not quite there. With a population in 2018 of 1,349,217,956 (versus in China in 2019 1,409,517,397), India not just is the largest democracy in the world but also faces off against a single-party communist state that is now supporting India's chief political-military problem, Pakistan, exacerbated by China's presence next door in Gwadar, Pakistan.

To overcome decades of US-India mistrust characterized by India's desire to both appear and actually to be nonaligned, India's sense of US diplomatic ambiguities, its own internal bureaucratic inertia and sense of not wanting to move into another quasi "colonial orbit," albeit it the United States, there has to be several years of confidence building. Intelligence can be key to this because India needs all the help it can get given the Kashmir scenario, and China's support for and alignment with Pakistan. A combination of intelligence cooperation and sharing, plus a steady increase in naval cooperation can go hand in hand. The two are complementary.

In addition, the Five Eyes can extend intelligence relations beyond the maritime to assist India over its border disputes with Pakistan and likely Chinese operations with Pakistan against Indian key national security interests. The US Army and those of its Five Eyes allies may provide specialist technical support, complemented by ground, space, and other sources and methods that the Five Eyes have in spades.

On the critical maritime scene, Five Eyes navies can provide, over time, confidence-building intelligence support and across-the-board cooperation for both collection and analyses against China and its surrogates. The Indian Ocean is a maritime highway, and the type of intelligence that the UK and US can provide with the other three nations will help India better define its future naval force structure and investment. This has to be an incremental confidence-building process because all those nations not aligned with either China or Russia will need a strong Indian navy. It is likely that by the mid-2020s, India will have a 160-ship navy that will include 3 aircraft carriers, 60 major surface combatants, and 400 aircraft. As a value of the Indian defense budget, the navy will have increased from a mere 4 percent in 1960 to 8 percent in 1970, to 11 percent in 1992, and to 18 percent in 2009,16 and although this increase is laudable, an even higher percentage will be required to take the Indian navy from its sobriquet of the "Cinderella" service to the next level of operational performance, so that it can operate unilaterally with the US Navy and multilaterally with the Five Eyes navies. This interoperability between navies will require establishing secure intelligence links, discreet encrypted communications, and critical data links such as Link 16, a tactical data link network used by NATO, and all the attendant satellite communication connections. Common seamanship standards and protocols such as replenishment at sea, vertical replenishment, ammunition replenishments, and a host of key seamanship drills and maneuvers will have to become ingrained as second nature in a new generation of Indian naval personnel. To underpin these developments, India will need a "Grand Strategic" direction to enable the Indian navy's future leadership and its political oversight to move in unison to reduce US-Indian political ambiguities, achieve expectation goals, and slowly move India into the realm as the major maritime power in the Indian Ocean. Assisting India with the India-Pakistan scenario will help considerably through

US mechanisms such as the Defense Technology and Trade Initiative (DTTI) to leverage, for example, US Special Forces and rapid reaction cell capabilities in India's border disputes.

The sales of P-8 Poseidon maritime reconnaissance and ASW aircraft, SH-3 ASW helicopters, and aircraft carrier and jet engine technologies has helped reaffirm US commitment to India's growing navy. All this is good, and at the heart of change will be Five Eyes intelligence cooperation and collaboration.

The Russia of Vladimir Putin

Russia has clearly violated the norms of international behavior by its annexation of the Crimea and its invasion of Ukraine in February 2022. Russia's avowed objectives are not difficult to ascertain, whatever the pleadings of its leader.

Without its oil and gas productions and the exports that flow from these, the Russian economy would be in seriously worse shape than at present. The oligarchic nature of the Russian communist party, the roles of small controlling economic elites, and the Russian Mafia, plus the very nature of Vladimir Putin's background as a former KGB operative that makes him secretive and authoritarian, could add up to a recipe for long-term failure, particularly if at some point both the opposition groups and Russian masses coalesce into an effective alternative. The huge personal wealth accumulated by a tiny Russian minority must at some point come back to haunt them, but the exact nature and timing of such denouement is difficult to predict.

Vladimir Putin's personal treasure trove cannot be ignored by the Russian people and web users indefinitely. However, the converse of this is a perpetual Putin-led dictatorship with opposition groups stifled or, worst case, removed.

How the Ukraine war impacts Putin's political survival remains to be seen. At the time of writing in May 2023, Putin faces multiple challenges. However, he oversees a dictatorial state with vast means of controls and security. Opponents are imprisoned.

Two fundamental facts need to be stated. First, Russia's GDP, US$1,578 trillion in 2017–2018, is significantly less than that of the state of California, US$2.448 in 2015–2016. California had a population of 39.54 million in 2017, Russia 144.5 million in 2017.17 These core facts say an enormous amount. Second, Russia has nuclear weapons. Without these weapons, readers are encouraged to assess for themselves where they think that Russia would be in the international order, notwithstanding that Russia is a member of the United Nations Security Council and has veto power. Without nuclear weapons, and its oil and gas, it is likely that Russia would not have a lead place in the international order for the foreseeable future, unless an alliance with China matures beyond oil deals between the two leaders of Russia and China. Combined Russian-Chinese operations in East Asia focusing on Japan and other nations may become a serious matter for concern.

During the Cold War, the Soviet navy was a serious challenge. The whole NATO edifice kept the Soviet navy in check by and large. However, we should also note that the Berlin Wall could not have come down soon enough, given the technical strides that the Soviets appeared to have been making, with their ship and submarine build rates most worrisome. Glasnost and Perestroika changed all that, with Mikhail Gorbachev becoming general secretary of the Central Committee of the Communist Party of the Soviet Union in March 1985. How far Vladimir Putin wishes to put the clock back remains to be seen—indeed whether this is at all credible is an open question, given Russia's financial situation.

On the strategic missile submarine side of the equation, the Russians have, after a moribund period following the collapse of the Soviet Union, begun a program to rebuild its SSBN Fleet, with four

Borei-class SSBNs in the fleet and, according to the Russian News Agency Tass, another eleven expected to be built by 2020. The three remaining Delta III-class SSBNs and six Delta VI-class SSBNs will be gone from the inventory by the 2020s. The Russians are building the Yasen-class SSGN, with eight ordered so far, and an SSN class that is purported to begin building in 2016, with perhaps fifteen completed by 2035. News reports state that after the improved Kilo-class of six for the Black Sea Fleet is completed, the Russians will build a new air-independent improved Lada-class—perhaps 14–18 of these over a fifteen-year period, with most of the class commissioned in the 2020s.

Safety is a huge issue. Since 2000, the Russians had seven major nuclear submarine accidents. The worst of these was the *Kursk*, which exploded and sank with the loss of all hands. The nuclear incident in 2019 that killed a group of senior Russian scientists is still being analyzed at the time of writing, though it is suspected that a test nuclear propulsion unit became out of control. Russia's submarine force, until the recent resurgence, was older than thirty years. However, by positioning its remaining more capable submarines and new SSNs and SSBNs, together with its nuclear-capable bombers and land-based missiles, Putin's Russia can send unfavorable messages to the West, for example, moving nuclear weapons near to the Polish border, and certainly moving nuclear weapons into the Crimea during the current conflict will be seen by NATO as an aggressive act. The sustainment of US-UK Intelligence with full Five Eyes intelligence support is crucial in this environment to support NATO.

The Russian surface navy is not in good shape, much worse than perhaps media sources relate, with perhaps too grandiose plans for possible aircraft carriers, frigates, corvettes, and large destroyers on the order of fifteen thousand tons, together with a cruiser modernization program for the Kirov and Slava classes, and the Udaloy destroyers, though the Sovremennyy-class destroyers will be retired. In spite of the French Mistral-class amphibious ship debacle, it looks like the Russians may build two to three 14,000–16,000-ton amphibious ships, and four Ivan Gren-class amphibious ships in each of the Black Sea and Baltic Fleets. All of the above is very much dependent on both Russian yard capacity and finances. If all the above happened by about 2030, the Russian navy could in effect be back in serious business. The question for US-UK Intelligence is, Is this at all achievable? To date, unclassified Five Eyes data shows that the Russians have fallen behind almost every program with delays and major difficulties. The overall picture is reasonably clear: the Russian Navy will concentrate on strategic deterrence, the SSBN force, and coastal defense, with the blue water navy of the Cold War era still to be determined. Russian incursions, for example, near to UK airspace are by relatively aging moribund aircraft and have the aura of defunct Cold War saber rattling to very little effect.

The question for the West and specifically US-UK Intelligence is how to counter and modify Russian aggressive moves, short of direct confrontation. Where, for example, does the maritime mix play in this? Sanctions and diplomacy have impacted Russia, though the former have negative economic connotations for the West, particularly the European nations dependent on Russian energy sources.

Germany has made it very clear to both its EU partners and the United States that it needs Russian gas, and the undersea gas pipeline from Russia to Germany is the critical infrastructure. The Ukraine war has brought this sharply into focus. The US argument that Germany could be held hostage to Russian supply is countered by those analysts that argue that Putin's Russia desperately needs the income from German gas sales, and that the relationship is complementary, not potentially an economic hostage situation. The Ukraine war has changed the dynamics of this. Russia is now in 2023 busily finding other buyers of Russian energy, and China is clearly a major customer. Russia has found surrogates to circumvent sanctions imposed as a consequence of its invasion of Ukraine. Naval power in both the Baltic and Black Seas, judiciously applied with the forward-deployed allied presence of multinational naval forces, together with classical diplomacy, can send a clear message that aggression will not be rewarded. A US Navy and US Marine Corps MEF (Marine Expeditionary Force)–level surge into either or both seas, supported by the NATO navies, and supported by all elements of the Five Eyes intelligence community, sends not just a clear message of intent and deterrence. It shows solidarity of purpose and the clear military ability to stop aggression in its tracks. The Russian invasion of Ukraine, and a worst-case threat to NATO allies in the Baltic states, can be met with an unequivocal display of overwhelming naval and marine/amphibious power. US and other key NATO forces can display, by forward-deployed and persistent presence, a similar capability that was shown, for instance, at Inchon in the Korean War. A large and flexible amphibious force that is deployed from the sea, at short notice, with no requirements for shore support, can send a key message, along with diplomacy, in support of the allied cause. This involves therefore the classic display of naval expeditionary warfare based on three main tenets: forward-persistent presence, flexibility to use those forces in terms of the mix and combination of naval forces, and maneuver from the sea at a time and places of one's choosing. These abiding principles will be underpinned by US-UK and Five Eyes intelligence sources and methods, indicators and warning, and collective sustained analysis.

The psychological make up of our adversaries and those who wish the United Kingdom and the United States and their allies ill intent is a critical component of any analysis of their plans and operations. Intelligence that ignores or does not include such analysis is likely built on shifting sand. In the contemporary context, take the classic example of Vladimir Putin. Vladimir Putin is a Yuri Andropov lookalike, with Andropov later attaining the general secretaryship of the Soviet Communist Party, not unlike how Putin acceded to power. Everything Putin thinks and does is characterized by his KGB beginnings, his training, his actions, and therefore how he can be predicted to behave. This is vital in any US-UK Intelligence assessment of Russian intentions, plans, and operations. Personality is critical. We should look at Russia through the Putin lens and that of his key oligarchs. The Five Eyes and allies have to understand and analyze the inner mindset of Putin and his FSB operatives, his oligarchic friends, his security system, his deception techniques, and his electronic eavesdropping capabilities and procedures, of which cyberpenetration, for example, of the US 2016 election, is merely one among many. He and his closest staff, plus the trusted foot soldiers that make up Putin's coterie and do the real work on the ground, always have a strategy and plan. Unraveling that strategy and plan is step one. It is clear to the layperson that Putin very much wants sanctions lifted with the West and, at a more grandiose level, he has a desire to restore mother Russia to another level of recognition and self-aggrandizement for himself, at the expense whenever and wherever possible of what he sees as the old adversaries in NATO and their associated allies. Vladimir Putin sees the Five Eyes as adversaries.

The secret of Putin's success, as most likely measured by his criteria and KGB/FSB standards, is to be not directly exposed to direct evidence of his personal involvement in Russian intelligence operations. Putin's operatives' tradecraft is not to communicate while others listen, to launder money through multiple channels with no traceable fingerprints, to hold several passports and identities, to always guard their back and personal weaknesses whenever possible, and to disarm and dissemble with consummate urbanity. This is what the FSB and its surrogates in both the Russian Mafia and the wealthy oligarchs are very simply all about. The cultural and historical underpinnings are all there to be analyzed. The psychological makeup of the Russian leader and his immediate entourage holds the key to predicting Russian policies and their likely outcomes. There is clear and perceptible lineal descent at one level from the post–World War II Soviet leadership to Vladimir Putin. The lives and careers of Georgy Malenkov, Nikita Khrushchev, Leonid Brezhnev, Yuri Andropov, Konstantin Chernenko, to the great changes brought about by Mikhail Gorbachev, reveal aspects of their mindsets, behavior, and policies that enabled us to predict with reasonable accuracy their likely reaction to changing global geostrategic realities in the context of domestic Soviet politics and economics. The same applies to Vladimir Putin and his regime. US-UK Intelligence will be able to unravel many of Putin-authorized asymmetric and apparently non-state-sponsored covert operations and cyberspace initiatives by examining both his past and current dependence on means that run contrary to the maintenance of international order. Putin is not difficult to predict. The secret for US-UK Intelligence is to penetrate and contain the operations generated by this old-style KGB operative who has grasped the significance of the digital era. Hopefully, the Ukraine invasion will be Putin's fatal mistake. Time will tell. In May 2023, the war is still in progress.

Collection and Analysis

In some instances, the past may remain prologue in terms of the collection technologies and assessments that were employed successfully during the Cold War being applied to emerging post-2020 military threat systems of potential aggressor states.

This is particularly true of ELINT and MASINT collection against new systems and technologies, and to assess when they will gain initial operational capability (IOC) as they appear from the production lines of China, Russia, North Korea, Iran, and, to some extent, Israel. It is salutatory to recall that Israel supplied Argentina with various key military assets both during and after the Falklands conflict. For example, after the conflict, Israel refitted three Boeing 707 aircraft with advanced SIGINT equipment that was clearly not in the best interests of the Five Eyes community. The counterintelligence services of all the Five Eyes monitor commercial and military technology gathering by Israel and its surrogates and technical representatives, knowing that Israel has commercial and financial interests in understanding and garnering the latest Western technologies that it can use in its own industrial base.

The motive is very simply economic well-being, which is not unreasonable, except that it involves in essence taking Five Eyes technology, reproducing it, and then selling on the international markets.

Of course, China and Russia are much bigger and more serious targets for counterintelligence against classical technical espionage as well as perfectly legal acquisition of Western technology by surrogate means. The open societies of the Five Eyes are much more vulnerable than the closed and heavily secret and pervasive societies of China, Russia, North Korea, and Iran, where human rights have no legal standing. Penetration of programs in the very early stages of R & D through initial design and production of emerging advanced technologies in threat countries will require new and innovative collection methodologies. Take for example the development of hypervelocity weapons with speeds and ranges not contemplated during the Cold War. Similarly, with situational awareness, targeting, and space systems technologies, where there is in the case of the latter a growing need to deploy defensive counterspace systems because of adversary offensive counterspace systems. The Five Eyes require more resilient and defendable space assets. Similarly with networked, AI-intensive, and fully integrated advanced UUV (unmanned underwater vehicle) and UAV/UCAS systems, there will be major requirements to use the latest AI tools to enhance real-time intelligence collection and secure distribution without any possibility of interception and/or jamming.

All major threats see Five Eyes space assets as huge threats to their ability to cover up technical developments, initial testing, and then deployment. For instance, Five Eyes advanced space-based infrared systems have the capability to unmask myriad different threat developments. As AI becomes more and more commonplace within the interlaced Five Eyes collection networks, the overall ability of the major threats will be increasingly fraught to deceive and surprise. GPS vulnerability has been an issue for many years. Between October 16 and November 7, 2018, it was alleged by the Norwegian Ministry of Defense that the Russian military jammed NATO GPS signals during the largest NATO military exercise since the Cold War, Trident Juncture, in Norway, that involved fifty thousand US and NATO forces. Jamming evidently occurred in the Kola Peninsula. None of this is surprising, and, of course, it does tip NATO's hand to what the threat constitutes. I was shown in 2018 and held a GPS jamming device manufactured in China that could jam local commercial GPS signals within about a ten-mile radius. This is daunting if such devices are in the wrong hands, whether criminals, terrorists, malcontents, mentally unstable persons, or, worst-case, intelligence agents and deep-rooted undercover plants awaiting instructions in the event of hostilities. In 2013, a New Jersey man bought an illegal GPS jammer to thwart the tracking device in his company vehicle. His GPS jammer, bought online for less than $100, interfered with a new GPS guidance system called Smartpath being tested at Newark Liberty airport. Federal agents tracked his jamming signal to his truck. He received a very heavy fine, as well as losing his job.19

In the past seven years since the incident above, jamming technology has improved considerably. Military- and intelligence-grade jammers are in a league of their own from commercially accessible devices. US-UK Intelligence has the capability to collectively design and employ the most advanced anti-jam GPS devices that will undoubtedly both confuse and deceive the threat, while indeed homing weapons onto the source. The essential parameters of electronic warfare persist. Those who seek to do bad things with what may appear to be state-of-the-art offensive tools often become their own worst enemy.

Modern HUMINT

Perhaps the single biggest challenge facing those who manage clandestine HUMINT operations in the digital era is how to securely and covertly maintain contact with HUMINT sources without counterintelligence services detecting an agent. This is an important task. In the digital era, counterintelligence agencies have become adept at intercepting the discreet communications of those who are betraying their nations' secrets, however disguised and buried such communications may be. Classical dead letter drops and meetings that involve an agent avoiding counterintelligence followers are most likely a thing of the past and spy novels. Sheer physical access in such countries as North Korea and Iran is hugely challenging. Contacts are most likely to be made at official functions. The problem even in these situations where US-UK Intelligence operatives have diplomatic status is that the counterintelligence services of host nations will be fully active. They will be watching, listening, and videoing the activities of their nationals as they have iterations with diplomats, trade negotiators, visiting senior business executives, academic researchers, and so on. A report that was issued in Yahoo News on November 2, 2018, by two capable investigative journalists, Zach Dorman and Jenna McLaughlin, illustrates the above. They discovered that the CIA's internet-based communications system for covert exchanges with overseas agents was compromised. This happened between 2009 and 2013, with the compromise initiated in Iran. They state, "More than two dozen sources died in China in 2011and 2012 as a result, according to 11 former intelligence and national security officials," evidently disclosed under the apparent protection of anonymity. They continued: "The issue was that it (the communications system) was working well for too long with too many people. But it was an elementary system." According to their sources, Iran succeeded in breaking up a CIA HUMINT network that hampered US Intelligence collection against Iran's nuclear program. Dorman and McLaughlin state, "Two former US intelligence officials said that the Iranians cultivated a double agent who led them to the secret CIA communications system." The system was an online system. We are led to believe that once the Iranian double agent revealed to Iran's counterintelligence people the website, the Iranians then scoured the web for other likely operatives, revealing "who in Iran was visiting these sites, and from where, and began to unravel the wider CIA network." In May 2017, the *New York Times* reported the loss of thirty CIA agents in China, and in May 2018, CIA officer Jerry Lee, based in Beijing, was charged with spying for the Chinese. *Foreign Policy* magazine reported that "Chinese intelligence broke through the firewall separating it (CIA communications system) from the main covert communications system, compromising the CIA's entire asset network in that country."

One may conclude that perhaps China and Iran cooperated in these events.

Whatever the accuracy of the above claims, one fact is significant and has been verified. Back in 2008, a defense contractor named John Reidy blew the whistle on various inadequacies and vulnerabilities after his management would not listen to his technical concerns. His complaints were not adequately addressed, and he was fired from his position in November 2011. He had assessed that about 70 percent of CIA covert operations were compromised. One may speculate that if Reidy's concerns had been addressed early enough, then lives could have been saved.

Running Covert Agents

What these unclassified public reports illustrate is simply that running covert agents has never been more difficult than today and in the future, even in the case of the classic "walk-ins" where prospective agents visit Five Eyes diplomatic facilities or make contact with an official to start a dialogues of betraying their nations' secrets. Such facilities and overt US-UK Intelligence personnel in sensitive overseas cities such as Moscow, Beijing, Tehran, and Pyongyang are so heavily monitored by multiple surveillance systems and human assets that any individual entering or meeting with a foreign official is likely to be immediately identified. Perhaps long gone are the days when a key MI6 agent from the Cold War, Oleg Gordievsky, a senior KGB official who became head of the KGB (Rezident or station chief) in the London Rezidentura (station) may be recruited by direct contact under the eyes of Soviet counterintelligence. Ben Macintyre's fine book, *The Spy and the Traitor*, spells out in detail how MI6 recruited and ran Gordievsky until he was betrayed by no other than CIA's traitor, Aldrich Ames, as a result of his boss's security complacency and indiscretions. All the above calls into question the future value of HUMINT. US-UK Intelligence, however, has enormous combined strategic leverage when it comes to HUMINT, assuming that one avoids the notion that all HUMINT is about covert and clandestine agent-running. The enormous bandwidth of the digital era combined with international travel across every part of human endeavor means that there are new and challenging ways to exploit old-fashioned classical HUMINT. HUMINT is by no means dead, and it will take on new forms based on advanced technology, ingenuity, and innovation for which Bletchley Park forebears would be justly proud.

A new generation of original thinkers within US-UK Intelligence can indeed revolutionize HUMINT in unprecedented ways.

Climate Change

Climate change has to be a concern for US-UK Intelligence. The US and the UK with their many allies and friendly nations are together spending billions on national defense while our planet is threatened by the undeniable scientific evidence of climate change. The question is, Will the international community, and their intelligence communities specifically, be able to mobilize resources to counter this threat? The cascading effects of climate change are predicted to destabilize highly vulnerable regions and tens, and likely hundreds, of millions of people, including, for example, large centers of urban population in the United States. The United States walked away from the 2015 Paris Climate Agreement. This has been rectified by the Biden administration. Without United States' leadership and investment in countering the effects of climate change, there is a huge international gap, a task that the Five Eyes community as a whole needs to address. What is the key scientific evidence? The glaciers in Antarctica and the Himalaya mountains are melting, and these effects alone will significantly impact our planet. The melting Thwaites Glacier in Antarctica is the size of Florida, and if it melts completely, scientists estimate that global ocean levels will rise by two feet. January 2019 was the hottest month ever recorded in Australia, with 2017 and 2018 the hottest years ever recorded. Rising temperatures are estimated to melt one-third of the glaciers in the Hindu Kush region of the Himalayas.20

National security and climate change are inextricably linked. The US Department of Defense includes climate change in its threat data and analytics, while, conversely, the Trump White House challenged the global scientific community. This has fortunately been rectified. The United States' director of national intelligence has stated, "Global environmental and ecological degradation, as well as climate change, are likely to fuel competition for resources, economic distress, and social discontent." What is clearly required is international commitment and agreement, and for the US-UK Intelligence community and Five Allies to make a stand through technical intelligence support and do what the late Carl Sagan advocated, to stand together and "preserve and cherish the pale blue dot, the only home we've ever known." Drastic change will be needed, and US-UK Intelligence will become critical by using the vast array of technical intelligence tools to collect and analyze data in the service of the planet. A Five Eyes summit led by the US and the UK will have to continuously monitor and address how each nation can contribute to economic intelligence collection and analysis, together with the impact of climate change.

Appendix B

Influential Individuals and Mentors

Royal Navy Admiral Sir Reginald "Blinker" Hall

The Zimmermann Telegram was one of the greatest intelligence triumphs of British history. Its centenary was commemorated in 2017—and it is most important to recognize the continuity of events since 1917. The Royal Navy Admiral Sir Reginald "Blinker" Hall was the architect of this most famous intelligence coup of all time.

He was called "Blinker" because of a permanent facial twitch that he exploited with characteristic aplomb. Hall's genius lay in his early and extraordinarily successful exploitation of radio telegraphy and its cryptologic underpinnings. Hall did not know this at the time, but his actions and those of his key subordinates set the stage for arguably saving the civilized world from tyranny in the Nazi era as a result of critical intelligence cooperation and sharing of the most sensitive secrets. The Five Eyes owe much to Admiral Sir Reginald Blinker Hall. Without the foundations built by him and the maintenance of interwar capabilities, in spite of the financial downturn caused by the Great Depression, it is difficult to see how the British would have established by 1939 at Bletchley Park what would become a highly secret war-winning organization, working in total cooperation with the US Office of Naval Intelligence.

Blinker Hall was the son of the first director of British naval intelligence, William Henry Hall, so intelligence was in his blood when he entered the Royal Navy in 1884.

As a captain, Blinker Hall was the DNI throughout World War I, and because of his huge successes, he was promoted to rear admiral in 1917, after the Zimmermann Telegram. Later, he became vice admiral, 1922, and admiral, 1926.

The British Naval Intelligence Department (NID) was created in 1887, with mainly the defense of British imperial trade interests as a primary driver. In 1887, there were a mere ten staff officers with a budget of about five thousand pounds a year.

Many in the Royal Navy leadership were against such a staff, with senior officers such as Admiral Fisher disclaiming in no uncertain terms that a staff would "convert splendid sea officers into very indifferent clerks."

When Hall became the DNI and war was declared in August 1914, he faced much intransigence characterized by a combination of prejudice and ignorance.

Operational intelligence as we understand it today was primitive to nonexistent.

Hall took one extraordinary step that was to revolutionize naval warfare and which, with the benefit of hindsight today, may seem obvious but in 1914 was clouded in fog. Hall realized that exploitation of wireless telegraphy and its cryptography could be war winners, what modern parlance would characterize as technical game changers. Hall built wisely on the work of Sir Alfred Ewing, a professor of mechanical engineering at Cambridge, who was brought into the Admiralty as the director of naval education and then created the first ever cipher team. Hall's "Room 40" became the heart and soul of naval intelligence in World War I, building on Ewing's foundations, to create a cadre of first-class cryptographers. Hall's single biggest problem was interfacing with the Operations Division of the Admiralty, where there was institutional bias against new and mainly civilian technical experts advising operators on key intelligence from wireless intercepts. The issue was clear to Hall: the operators did not wish to share their operational data with Room 40 civilian cryptographers, and the latter were deprived of the key opportunity to both analyze and interpret cryptographic intelligence in light of current and planned British naval operations and, most of all, their German adversaries. This failure to make the wise use of such intelligence reached its nadir at Jutland, a subject that has been much underrated in understanding why Jutland was not the success that the Royal Navy wanted and the country expected.

So, what did Hall get up to between January and March 1917 that will forever live in the annals of any intelligence organization worldwide and provided a blueprint for Five Eyes intelligence much later? First, the overall political-military context in which Hall and his Room 40 team were operating. The United States was not in the war in January 1917. The Germans were planning on restarting unrestricted U-boat warfare from February 1, 1917, in an attempt to bring the British economy to its knees by attacking its most vital national interest, seaborne trade. This one fact could be the tipping point for the American president to convince his people to join the war on the allied side, remembering that in the United States in 1917, anti-British sentiment ran high, with a volatile and outspoken Irish American and German American population. Second, on January 11, 1917, the German foreign minister, Arthur Zimmermann, presented an encoded telegram to the US ambassador in Berlin, James W. Gerard, who agreed to transmit the telegram in its coded form. The American embassy transmitted this telegram on January 16, 1917, five days later.

Why would the German Foreign Ministry be using the American embassy to send its messages, in this case (the Zimmermann Telegram) via Washington, DC, to the German ambassador in Mexico City, Heinrich von Eckhardt? Hall and his staff had realized very early on that undersea communications cables could provide the source of great intelligence and also that by denying their use by cable cutting, an enemy could be deprived of vital communications. The British had cut the German transatlantic cable at the beginning of the war in 1914. The US was neutral in 1914 and permitted Germany limited use of its Europe to US transatlantic cable mainly because President Woodrow Wilson was encouraging peace talks and wanted to ensure that Berlin could talk with the US diplomatically. Zimmermann's telegram was instructing the German ambassador in Mexico City to inform the Mexican president, Carranza, that if the US entered the war against Germany, then Germany would support Mexico financially in fighting a war against the US to regain territory lost to Mexico in the wars with the United States, a bombshell of enormous proportions if made aware to the US government and people.

Hall's Room 40 was reading all the American traffic (that ran via cable from the US embassy in Denmark), including all German traffic, encrypted or otherwise, that was forwarded from the US Embassy in Berlin. The US cable went via the UK, and the intercept point was at a relay station at Porthcurno, near Land's End.

Hall's civilian cryptographers Nigel de Grey and William Montgomery brilliantly decrypted the Zimmermann telegram the following day after interception by the British on January 17, 1917. Why was this so speedy and efficient? Hall and his team had also pulled off two critical earlier coups. Room 40 had captured secretly during the Mesopotamian campaign the German Diplomatic Cipher 13040, and, as a result of very good clandestine relations with the Russians, Hall obtained the critical German Naval Cipher 0075 (the 007 part will not be lost on readers). The Russians had obtained this from the German cruiser *Magdeburg* after it was wrecked.

Hall had secretly nursed Russian relations.

The genius of Hall was what he did and did not do next. The Americans may well think that this was all a devious British plot to bring the United States into the war. The telegram was brutally explicit in two regards: on February 1, 1917, the Germans would resume unrestricted U-boat warfare, and a German-Mexican military alliance was proposed, with Germany as the funding source. Hall needed a cover story for his knowledge of the German codes and to avoid the Americans knowing that Room 40 was reading their and others' mail, while at the same time convincing Woodrow Wilson and his government that the telegram was real, not a British forgery. Hall never once consulted anyone in the British Foreign Office or within the Admiralty staff. He acted with his staff alone. He then decided on his "deception plan." This was the real genius of this extraordinary brilliant work by Hall and his team. Hall knew one key fact: the German embassy in Washington, DC, once it received the telegram, would have to transmit it to the German embassy in Mexico City. Hall knew that they used a commercial telegraph company. NID agents bribed a Mexican telegraph employee to yield the cipher, thereby enabling Hall to inform the Americans that this had come directly from the Mexican telegraph company from Washington, DC. Simple but brilliant. Hall also, in parallel, took another quite remarkable action, by great timing, by doing nothing until the Germans announced unrestricted U-boat warfare on February 1, 1917, after which the US broke off diplomatic relations with Germany on February 3, 1917. Hall then did two key things. He only informed the British foreign secretary on February 5, 1917, with an emphatic request that the British Foreign Office delay all diplomatic moves with the US until Hall himself took various actions.

With foreign office knowledge, Hall then met with the secretary of the US Embassy in London, Edward Bell, on February 19, 1917, and, the following day, Hall met with the US ambassador to the Court of St. James, Walter Hines Page, and handed him the telegram.

Three days later, Ambassador Page met with the British foreign secretary, Arthur Balfour, and on Hall's quite emphatic advice, he gave the American ambassador a copy of the stolen Mexican cipher text and the English translation of the full Zimmermann telegram. After some analysis and discussion in Washington, President Wilson was convinced. He went ahead and released the telegram to the US press on February 28, 1917, and this immediately inflamed American public opinion against both Germany and Mexico. Wilson and his top aides realized also that they had to protect the British "Mexican cipher" and British code-breaking capabilities. Herein lay the foundations of what became years later the beginning of what Humphrey Bogart, playing Rick Blaine, said at the very end of the 1942 movie *Casablanca* to Claude Rains, playing the cynical French police chief Capt. Louis Renault: "Louis, I think this is the beginning of a beautiful friendship." The American protection of Britain's secrets was indeed the beginning of a very special relationship.

Further positive news for Hall and his Room 40 team was that the Mexican president had been advised that German funding was unreliable and that a successful war with the United States was unlikely. Pres. Venustiano Carranza was also advised that even if German funding did materialize, their sister South American nations, Argentina, Brazil, and Chile, from whom Mexico would purchase arms, would likely be unsupportive of a Mexican alliance with Germany and a war with the United States. Nonetheless, the Mexican government did not enforce an embargo against Germany, much to the chagrin of the United States, and Mexico continued to do business with Germany throughout World War I. However, Mexico did not repeat history in World War II, declaring war on the Axis Powers on May 22, 1942.

The final coup de grace was delivered by none other than Arthur Zimmermann himself, who rashly announced on March 3, 1917, in a press conference, that the telegram was in fact true. He then very naively followed this with a statement in the Reichstag on March 29,

1917, that his plan had been for Germany to fund Mexico only if the Americans declared war on Germany. The United States Congress declared war on Germany on April 6, 1917, President Wilson having asked for this declaration on April 2, 1917.

Hall and his Room 40 team had triumphed, and Hall was promoted to rear admiral shortly thereafter.

The significance of Hall's achievements and relationship with his American counterparts has to be put in context, 103 years later in 2020. The US ambassador in London, Walter Hines Page (August 15, 1855–December 21, 1918) described Blinker Hall as the single most influential person, indeed genius, of World War I.

There is a memorial plaque in honor of Walter Hines Page in Westminster Abbey, in Westminster, London. He and Hall had a special relationship that bound both the United Kingdom and the United States forever in sharing sensitive intelligence.

Sir Michael Howard

After school at Wellington College and Christ Church, Oxford, Michael Howard (1922–) served in the Coldstream Guards in the Italian campaign, winning the Military Cross for gallantry at the first battle of Monte Cassino in 1944. He founded the Department of War Studies at King's College London, as a lowly assistant lecturer, and by the sheer weight of outstanding research and teaching, plus energetic and persistent leadership, grew a formidable but in those days a small department.

He left, just as I joined King's, to become successively at Oxford the Chichele Professor of the History of War and, from 1980 to 1989, the ultimate accolade of Regius Professor of Modern History, succeeding Prof. Hugh Trevor-Roper (later Lord Dacre), the famous author of the best-selling *The Last Days of Hitler*. Michael Howard completed his active academic career in the United States, as the Robert A.

Lovett Professor of Military and Naval History at Yale from 1989 to 1993. As a schoolboy at Bablake, I had read his *The Franco-Prussian War of 1870–71*, and even then at a young age, I had appreciated not just his mastery of detail but also the exquisite nature of his analysis and language. As I started research at King's, the turnover was in progress with his successor, Prof. Sir Laurence Martin (born 1928), who had studied at Christ's College, Cambridge, and Yale University. He spent ten years at King's before becoming vice chancellor of Newcastle University in 1978 and then director of Chatham House, the Royal Institute of International Affairs, in 1991. I got on very well with Laurence Martin. I liked his "American approach" to defense and intelligence, and as my research took shape, he rapidly realized, as did I, that others needed to become closely involved.

Bryan Ranft

I first had contact with Prof. Bryan Ranft at the Royal Naval College, Greenwich, where he was head of Naval History and International Affairs. Bryan was a World War II veteran, like Michael Howard, a Manchester Grammar School and Balliol College, Oxford, graduate before World War II broke out. At Balliol, he was a contemporary of Denis Healey (1917–2015), who became secretary of state for defense, 1964–1970, chancellor of the Exchequer, 1974–1979, and, finally, deputy leader of the Labor Party from 1980 to 1983. Like Ranft, Healey served in the British army in World War II from 1940 to 1945, reaching the rank of major in the Royal Engineers in the North Africa Campaign, Italian Campaign, and at the battle of Anzio. Healey came from modest beginnings and won a scholarship to Balliol College from Bradford Grammar School. At Oxford, Healey was a member of the Communist Party from 1937 to 1940, leaving the party when France fell to the Nazis. Healey was an outstanding Oxford scholar, gaining a "Double First" degree in 1940. At Balliol, besides Bryan Ranft, he became a lifelong friend and political rival of the future Conservative prime minister, Edward Heath, whom he succeeded as president of the Balliol Junior Common Room. Bryan

Ranft's Oxford DPhil thesis had been on the protection of seaborne trade, a brilliant study that traced the early origins in fine detail of how Britain had successfully pursued a maritime strategy primarily focused on the defense of trade.

Ranft and Healey came to serious intellectual blows during Healey's tenure at the Ministry of Defense, with Healey laying the grounds for the serious reduction in the size, shape, capabilities, and deployment of the Royal Navy. He canceled the aircraft carrier replacement program, thus ending effectively Royal Navy fixed-wing aviation once the last of the fleet carriers was decommissioned. Overseas bases were to be closed and the Royal Navy was to be withdrawn from persistent forward presence in the Far East and Mediterranean to become a North-East Atlantic Navy. There were serious budgetary issues that Healey faced, but Ranft argued that strategically his policies were unbalanced, with overemphasis on the British army of the Rhine commitments to the Central Front in Europe that many naval experts argued was unnecessary given the massive commitment by the US Army and the US Air Force, and underpinned by NATO's ability (read the United States) to use tactical nuclear weapons if the Red Army and its Warsaw Pact allies attempted to cross the FEBA (Forward Edge of the Battle Area). Ranft stated in several eloquently argued papers that Soviet expansionism and aggressive posturing was happening at sea, with Soviet Admiral Sergey Gorshkov (1910–1988) supported by the Soviet leadership following a classical maritime strategy to pursue the vital national interests of the Soviet Union.

Time would prove Ranft completely correct, but it was too late to undo the severe damage that Healey did to the force structure and therefore deployability of the Royal Navy.

Bryan Ranft rapidly realized that my research interests had polarized on a major unexplored topic in the late 1960s, which may seem unusual today with the total benefit of hindsight. I had been inspired and energized by both my work on the Naziera and also my intense interest in naval warfare and how intelligence had played a crucial role in the allied victory at sea in Europe and the Pacific. Bryan Ranft was indeed a wonderfully kindly man and generous human being.

Sir Harry Hinsley

Hinsley was born in Walsall in the English Midlands November 26, 1918, and died in Cambridge on February 16, 1998, aged seventy-nine, from lung cancer. He came from modest beginnings and was clearly gifted intellectually. Contrary to popular misconceptions of lack of opportunity for working-class children in the 1930s in what is often characterized as a class-ridden society, the young Harry won a place at Queen Mary's Grammar School in Walsall. In 1937, Hinsley won a distinguished scholarship to read history at St. John's College, Cambridge. He was an outstanding scholar at Cambridge, rewarded years later in 1985 by his election to a Fellowship of the British Academy (FBA). When war was declared by Neville Chamberlain on September 3, 1939, after the September 1, 1939, invasion of Poland by Nazi Germany, the Government Code and Cipher School at Bletchley Park was seeking the best and brightest minds to meet the Nazi challenge. He was interviewed by the director of Bletchley Park, the legendary Comm. Alexander "Alastair" Deniston, Royal Navy (December 1, 1881–January 1, 1961) and was very soon thereafter working in "Hut 4," a location that decades later, not until the late 1970s/early 1980s in fact, would become synonymous with war-winning codebreaking. Hut 4 provided the keys to critical successful operations against the Nazis and their allies, particularly in the hugely successful fight against the U-boats and helping the winning of the battle of the Atlantic by the most secretive clandestine means. Winston Churchill knew that without the maintenance of seaborne trade between the United States and the United Kingdom, the British war effort could die a painful death. His wartime speeches reflect this harsh reality. At Bletchley, Hinsley became intimately involved in parallel efforts in the United States, and particularly with the US Office of Naval Intelligence (ONI). Deniston recognized Hinsley's intellectual talent, together with other Bletchley luminaries such as Alan Turing and Gordon Welchman. In late 1943, Hinsley was in Washington DC, still a relatively young man, negotiating a highly classified SIGINT agreement with the United States.

Toward the end of the war, he was working for Sir Edward Travis, KCMG, CBE, (September 24, 1888–April 23, 1956), who was the operational head of Bletchley Park during World War II and later the head of Bletchley's successor, GCHQ. Travis was a critical person at Bletchley. He had joined the Royal Navy in 1906 as a paymaster officer and served in HMS *Iron Duke*. Between 1916 and 1918, he worked in the famous Room 40 under Capt. Blinker Hall. In 1925, Travis became Denniston's deputy at the GC&CS. During World War II, Travis became a critical player at Bletchley Park, about which much has been written in multiple books. Travis was instrumental in the signing of the 1943 UK-US BRUSA Agreement and the subsequent 1946 highly classified secret intelligence agreement, cementing the special relationship in the postwar period and laying the way for the creation of the Five Eyes intelligence agreements and the longest-lasting intelligence cooperation in history. Travis was knighted in June 1944, though the reasons for his knighthood were cloaked in disarming secrecy. On paper, it looked as if he was rewarded for diplomatic services, which, at one level, he indeed had been.

By war's end, after distinguished work, for which he was made an officer of the Order of the British Empire (OBE) in 1946, and having married the lady whom he met at Bletchley Park, Hilary Brett-Smith, Harry Hinsley was back at Cambridge, elected as a fellow of St. John's College in 1945. In 1969, when I began work with him, he had recently been elected professor of international relations, having published earlier in 1962 his major work, *Power and the Pursuit of Peace*, which was acclaimed internationally and sealed his academic reputation.

His work on the official history of British intelligence in World War II changed dramatically the worldview of historians, analysts, the media, current intelligence agencies and their employees, and the retired and serving military. His 1985 knighthood was justly deserved. He enjoyed the fruits of his labors and retirement from 1989, when he retired as master of St. John's College, Cambridge, until his passing in February 1998, at age seventy-nine. The one accolade I sought came on December 6, 1972, when I was awarded the degree of doctor of philosophy by the University of London, King's College.

Harry Hinsley, Sir Edward Travis, and John Titman in Washington, DC, in November 1945 (US National Archives).

Vice Admiral Sir Norman "Ned" Denning

One of the finest people that I was privileged to meet on a regular basis was retired vice admiral Sir Norman "Ned" Denning (1904–1979). He had been a member of the famous "Room 39" during World War II, and later in his career director of naval intelligence (1960–1964), deputy chief of the Defense Staff for Intelligence (1964–1967), and earlier, 1956–1958, he held a senior position at Greenwich. I first met

Admiral Denning through Bryan Ranft after the admiral had retired and was head of the famous "Defense and Security Media Advisory Board," or better known as the "D Notices Committee." The latter was the key committee that ensured that the British media did not unwittingly betray the UK's secrets via inadvertent news media. It meant that Admiral Denning had daily direct working relations with all the Fleet Street newspaper editors, the heads of the independent TV networks, and the BBC, together with any other source that may give away information detrimental to national security. I met with Admiral Denning regularly. He gave me unfettered access to his incredible experience and memory bank that was truly prodigious.

His career had spanned the greatest war in the history of our planet through to the Cold War. I soaked up his stories, his insights, his anecdotes, and, most of all, his wisdom. We would meet for about two hours at a time, often followed by lunch.

It was a huge privilege.

Admiral Denning was also the brother of Lord Justice Alfred Thompson "Tom" Denning (1899–1999), the Master of the Rolls (1962–1982), whom Margaret Thatcher described as "probably the greatest English judge of modern times." Lord Denning joined Lincoln's Inn in 1921 and was called to the Bar in June 1923, a distinguished graduate of Magdalen College, Oxford. I have been a barrister of Lincoln's Inn, called in November 1980, almost forty years ago at the time of writing, so by a wonderful quirk or irony of fate, I was privileged to know both of these brothers, who came from modest beginnings and ascended to the highest offices in the UK, belying any notion that Britain was a class-ridden society in the early and mid-twentieth century.

James McConnell

During my second year at Greenwich, my colleagues and I, both uniformed teaching personnel and civilian academics, welcomed an American who came to us from the US National Security Agency and the US Navy's key think tank, the Center for Naval Analyses, or CNA for short. This gentleman was James "Jamie" McConnell, an extraordinarily capable and well-established Soviet Union intelligence analyst and a specialist on all things Soviet navy. Jamie was a Columbia University graduate in Russian. He was now the only person at Greenwich who not only spoke fluent Russian, and could read the subtle nuances of Soviet military and strategic thought but also was the ultimate expert on Russian open sources and knew in great detail what these were, how to obtain them, and, most of all, how to interpret these sources against the highly classified intelligence sources, particularly SIGINT and HUMINT. He was a most welcome addition to Bryan Ranft's staff. He and I became not only close-working colleagues but also friends for life. Jamie McConnell was very much in the forefront of why I would be appointed to Washington, DC, in 1976, a career-changing event for me. I learned an enormous amount from Jamie about Russian sources and methods, and understanding their strategic thinking and how this devolved to their construction programs, operational deployments, and the use of naval power in pursuit of Soviet goals. He was immersed in Soviet military literature and thought. All this brushed off on me. I soaked up all that I could learn from someone who was the finest independent thinker, who did not and would not accept conventional wisdom as gospel.

This great attribute was to pay dividends for the United States Navy, the UK, and their allies in the years from the early 1970s to the demise of the Soviet Union. In due course, he and others, and I became one of them, would challenge various US intelligence assessments for both their accuracy and the data on which they were based. He had chosen to base himself at Greenwich rather than become attached to, say, the CIA chief of station's staff in the US Embassy in London, or work as a defense intelligence or naval intelligence analyst in the UK Ministry of Defence.

He wanted intellectual independence and the freedom to move around those parts of the UK community that had a solid intellectual base to its work on the Soviet Union. This would include academia as well as the defense and intelligence community. He shared with me his seminal thinking on the direction in which the Soviet Union was moving in terms of the role and mission, and the detailed tactical deployment, of their key naval nuclear deterrent assets, their SSBNs, the equivalent in the early 1970s to the UK-US Polaris submarines. He began to postulate what was to become an incredibly accurate rendition of Soviet naval strategic thinking, embodied in what he termed a "Withholding Strategy," that Soviet SSBNs were the fallback second-strike nuclear assets after initial nuclear Armageddon commenced, and that the Soviet would seek to protect them and keep them sacrosanct in what he called "bastions." The latter were going to be under the Arctic ice cap, with the Soviets seeking locations near polynyas, or thin ice covers above the Arctic Ocean, from which submarine-launched nuclear ballistic missiles could be launched as a second strike against the United States and its allies. This would entail the Soviets ice hardening their submarines and using the Arctic as the key bastion, others being defined as those sea areas within a defendable perimeter in the northern Norwegian Sea and the Barents Sea. These bastions would be fully protected by multiple tactical assets. This not just represented new and innovative thinking and assessment but also challenged conventional reports, analyses, and, most of all, US National Intelligence Assessments (NIEs). The difference lay in the delta between strictly conventional intelligence sources and methods, the analytical product derived from these, and the McConnell approach that married these data sources with Soviet open sources. The latter was not easily available to Western sources and was, more often than not, obtained by surreptitious means. They were not often available for public use in the Soviet Union and, although not classified as such, was nonetheless restricted in distribution. Added to these more discreet Soviet open sources were the technical papers that Soviet scientists and engineers published within their specialist communities, again not classified but nonetheless with restrictive access.

McConnell used these sources in spades and to great analytical effect. They were highly reliable, and if read beside the highly classified UK-US Intelligence sources, a new view could emerge of Soviet intentions. I immersed myself in his output, while realizing that we were all poor relations insofar as we could at best speak a few paltry words of Russian. McConnell was in a league of his own, and the UK benefited not just from his time at Greenwich but also, as a result, key British personnel became familiar with his methodology and product, learning greatly from him over the ensuing decades.

The Honorable Professor Alastair Buchan

I recall well in the early 1970s being notified that I had been selected together with one Royal Marine officer, two Army officers, and two Royal Air Force officers to attend a specially tailored course at Oxford University that was designed and led by the Honorable Professor Alastair Buchan (September 1918–February 1976, son of the famous author John Buchan and a former governor general of Canada), the Montague Burton Professor of International Relations at Oxford. Prior to Oxford, he had been director of the International Institute of Strategic Studies and commandant of the Imperial Defense College. He had fought in World War II in the Canadian army. The course was demanding and an inspiration. I was the only one to have a full career in intelligence, but the relationships that I built were enduring, and what I learned from Alastair Buchan and my other mentors in the 1960s, I have, very subconsciously and subliminally, used in writing this book.

David Kahn

Through my intelligence and academic associations, I was very familiar with the American David Kahn (born 1930), author of *The Codebreakers: The Story of Secret Writing*, a very fine description and analysis of the history of cryptography from ancient Egypt through to the time of publication in 1967. I had studied David Kahn's work during my doctoral research, so when he came to St. Antony's College, Oxford, as a research scholar, I planned to meet with him. David Kahn was awarded an Oxford DPhil in 1974 under the supervision of the Regius Professor of Modern History, Hugh Trevor-Roper, on modern German history. I was naturally keen to make his personal acquaintance. I visited him at Oxford during my many visits to the other Oxford luminaries mentioned earlier. I was intrigued by some of the difficulties that he experienced in publishing his book, with the US NSA wanting his publisher to redact various parts, even though he had used open sources. I gained much insight into his cryptologic research and how he had managed to amass such a monumental and magnificent data set. I regard David Kahn highly, and his work has, in my opinion, been unsurpassed. He later in life donated all his key research papers and personal documents to the NSA archives. From the earlier differences with the US government, David Kahn became a benefactor and much-respected historian of the cryptologic arts and sciences that the NSA community embraced as one of their own.

Peter Jay

Peter Jay (1937–) had been commissioned in the Royal Navy, had also worked as a civil servant in the Treasury, and then moved to journalism, becoming for ten years the economics editor of the *Times*. Peter Jay was clearly intellectually gifted, having gained a "First" in PPE at Christ Church, Oxford, where he was also president of the Oxford Union. Peter Jay was the son of Douglas Jay (later Baron Jay), a Labor Party politician.

He was a most capable and popular lecturer. He knew his subject extremely well and expounded with great clarity and humor. He answered questions on the British and world economies with consummate skill. I thought no more of this until one day I was

189

summoned to the admiral president's office. Rear Admiral "Teddy" Ellis was a delightful man in his last post in the service before retirement.

I knew his son well, who was also a Royal Navy officer close in seniority to myself.

The admiral said he wanted me to do him a favor. I was intrigued naturally.

He said that he could not order me to do what he was going to request but clearly hoped that I would concur. He said that he was aware that I knew Peter Jay through his visits to lecture and, here was the rub, he was the son-in-law of James Callaghan. The admiral explained that Peter Jay planned to sail this boat across the Atlantic to the United States. This was a time when there was no global positioning technology (GPS) and sailboats did not have Decca navigators or LORAN, a system that permitted ships to electronically plot their positions using radio bearings if they were in range of the LORAN transmitters. Peter Jay had let the admiral president know that he very much wanted instruction on how to do astronavigation and could he help find the right person to teach him. As it turned out, I was the only navigation instructor then on the college staff. Would I instruct him? "Yes, sir, delighted to do so," rolled off my tongue. The admiral was delighted, and I left his office with a few extra points to my credit. I dutifully obeyed, and, to be very frank, I thoroughly enjoyed the interaction. Peter Jay was exceptionally bright, and I taught him the necessary skills to help him navigate safely across the Atlantic.

Little did I realize that I was training the future ambassador to the United States and that his father-in-law would become prime minister. In Washington, DC, a few years later, at the British embassy, this would cause me a modicum of difficulty and explanation to my superiors—that is, my relationship with the new ambassador, who succeeded a distinguished and much-loved career diplomat, Sir Peter Ramsbotham (ambassador, 1974–1977), who was also very highly respected by the Americans and was a favorite of all the embassy staff. On becoming prime minister in 1979, Margaret Thatcher was quick to ensure Peter Jay's departure from the British embassy in Washington, replacing him with another career diplomat, Sir Nicholas Henderson.

Admiral Sir Nicholas Hunt and Admiral Sir James Eberle

Two senior Royal Navy officers during these years at sea were to have an abiding impact on my career and thinking. I had considerable respect for their leadership skills and their fine intellects. Both would in due course become four-star admirals and knighted for their services. The first was my captain in HMS *Intrepid*, Capt. Nicholas Hunt (1930–2013; commander in chief Fleet, and Allied commander in chief Channel and Eastern Atlantic, 1985–1987), father of the young boy that I knew at this time who became the British minister of health and then foreign secretary until his resignation in 2019, Jeremy Hunt, MP (born 1966).

While I was serving with Captain Hunt in HMS *Intrepid*, Rear Admiral James Eberle, a World War II veteran, was the flag officer Carriers and Amphibious Ships(1927–2018; commander in chief Fleet, 1979–1981; commander in chief Naval Home Command, 1981– 1982; in retirement director of the Royal Institute for International Affairs, 1984–1990).

Both these officers influenced my thinking as well as my leadership skills, and I would remain in touch with both for the rest of my naval career and, in the case of Admiral Hunt, after I returned to the United States permanently in 1983. They were thinkers, and both nurtured my own naval and strategic thinking. I owe them both a debt of gratitude for taking an interest in my career development. They set a wonderful example.

Daniel Patrick O'Connell

The year 1973 was the one hundredth anniversary of the Royal Naval College, Greenwich (RNC Greenwich closed in 1998 when British higher military education was consolidated for all services in one location at a Joint Services Command and Staff College in Watchfield, Oxfordshire). Today, this historic site is managed by the Greenwich Foundation for the Old Royal Naval College. I was privileged to be on the staff during this celebratory year, culminating in visit and dinner with Queen Elizabeth and other senior signatories. One key symposium-cum-conference that we held was I believe the first ever major gathering relating to the "Law of the Sea." As the junior member of the staff, at least by age, I was directed by the admiral president to run all the logistics for the conference. The good news was that this allowed me interface with all the guest speakers and conferees, and of these one stood out above all others, and he became the single most important contributor, giving a series of outstanding addresses. This was Prof. Daniel Patrick O'Connell (1924–1979), a New Zealander, born in Auckland, who was the Chichele Professor of Public International Law at Oxford, from 1972 until he died in 1979 in Oxford, and the author of what I regard as still the major works on the law of the sea: *The Influence of Law on Sea Power* and *The International Law of the Sea* (published posthumously).3

The latter is a definitive work. Through O'Connell's seminal work and the publication of the Conference Records, there was much impetus given through British government and naval channels to what became the United Nations Convention on the Law of the Sea (UNCLOS for short), signed on December 10, 1982, by157 signatory nations, with an effective date of November 16, 1994. Because of my logistics tasking, I interacted with Professor O'Connell, and he became very interested in our joint ideas on the intersection of intelligence with the law of the sea as he envisaged it in preserving international order, not simply on the high seas per se but in the wider ramifications for international peace and order. I made several subsequent visits to Oxford to develop these ideas. My visits to Professor O'Connell also enabled me to renew the close associations developed with both Professor Buchan and Professor Trevor-Roper. It was an illuminating intellectual experience to see the coalescence of law, intelligence, and recent modern history coupled to their prognoses for the Cold War and dealing with the Soviet Union and its Warsaw pact allies.

My involvement in the law of the sea through Professor O'Connell encouraged me to take a much wider and more detailed look at legal issues that much later would stand me in good stead when addressing international terrorism and the role of the sea, gun running, human trafficking, the international trade in drugs via the oceans of the world, and illegal weapons shipment. Today, Chinese encroachments in the South China Sea and a ruling by the International Court of Arbitration in The Hague against China continue my focus on not just the intelligence implications but also the intertwined legal aspects. I became so involved intellectually in the law of the sea aspects that on July 29, 1975, while I was at sea in one of my next appointments after Greenwich, I was admitted to Lincoln's Inn, one of the four Inns of Court, to become in due course a British barrister.

Admiral Sir Herbert Richmond

The Greenwich academic staff had a private dining club that was only open to established academics in the key domains of naval strategy, plans, intelligence, and operations, and the whole panoply of current international relations and politics that underscored all the above. It was a select few, and I was privileged to join the "Herbert Richmond Dining Club," named after Admiral Sir Herbert Richmond (1871–1946) who led, with others, the founding of *The Naval Review* in October 1912 with the following goal: "To promote the advancement and spreading within the Service (the Royal Navy) of knowledge relevant to the higher aspects of the Naval Profession." *The Naval*

Review to this day is a vital source of high-quality thinking and discourse on all matters relevant to maritime strategy and operations and the myriad associated political-economic-social-diplomatic and historical factors. Richmond was not just a highly successful seagoing commander but also a distinguished intellectual, becoming after his retirement as a four-star admiral the Vere Harmsworth Professor of Imperial and Naval History from 1934 to 1936 and the Master of Downing College, Cambridge University from 1934 to 1946. He has been described as "perhaps the most brilliant naval officer of his generation," and as a first-class naval historian, he was called the "British Mahan." He was successively in charge of the Senior Officers Course and then the admiral president of the Royal Naval College, Greenwich 1920–1922. After retirement from the Royal Navy, he had the foresight very early on to see the impact of the emerging Japanese threat and what the British government should do to counteract what he saw would become Japanese expansionism.

Vice Admiral Sir Roy "Gus" Halliday

When I served in Washington, DC, in the mid-1970s, my reporting chain would be via Op-96 in the Office of the Chief of Naval Operations in the Pentagon to the British Naval Attaché, Rear Admiral Roy "Gus" Halliday (1923–2007). Admiral Halliday was a distinguished World War II veteran who won the Distinguished Service Cross (DSC) flying from HMS *Illustrious* and HMS *Victorious* against the Japanese from the British Pacific Fleet. He had been shot down and was rescued by HMS *Whelp*, whose first lieutenant was Lt. Prince Philip of Greece, who lent Halliday a spare uniform, and later the two of them celebrated on a "run ashore" in Fremantle. Halliday was back on board HMS *Victorious* in time to take part in the raids on the airfields on the Sakishima Islands in March to May 1945. He was awarded the DSC for his courageous efforts, and he also received a "Mention in Dispatches" for his flying during Operation Meridian. After the Japanese surrender, he learned that his cabinmate, Ken Burrenston, had been shot down over Palembang, captured by the

Japanese, and then beheaded at the notorious Changi prisoner-of-war camp two days after the Japanese surrender, a heinous war crime. After a distinguished postwar career, he was appointed head of naval intelligence in 1973 (the DNI position had been abolished as part of the 1967centralization initiated by Minister of Defence Denis Healey) as a commodore, from which post he was promoted to rear admiral in 1975 and appointed naval attaché and commander of the British Navy Staff in Washington, DC. In 1978, now vice admiral Halliday became the deputy chief of the Defense Staff (Intelligence), and on retirement from the Royal Navy in 1981, he was made the director-general Intelligence at the Ministry of Defence from 1981 to 1984. I was privileged to work for Admiral Halliday in his various roles and appointments, and he became a significant champion of my interests and career development during and after my tour in Washington, DC.

Admiral Carlisle "Carl" Trost

My American naval report in Washington, DC, in the mid-1970s was Rear Admiral Carlisle Trost, Op-96 (born April 24, 1930). He has always been known as Carl.

From Illinois, Admiral Trost graduated first in the US Naval Academy class of 1953.

He became a submariner and had an extraordinarily successful career; illustrious would be a much better description. In May 1986, he was nominated by Pres. Ronald Reagan to succeed Admiral James Watkins as chief of naval operations (CNO). Admiral Trost served as CNO from July 1986 to June 1990. I was therefore unbelievably fortunate to have as my US Naval direct report the officer would in due course become the CNO. Between Admiral Halliday and Admiral Trost, who could ever expect to have such fine leaders with such distinguished careers both behind and ahead of them?

Vice Admiral Samuel L. Gravely Jr.

My finale during my appointment in Washington, DC, in the mid-1970s was actual sea time, in the nuclear-powered cruiser USS *Bainbridge* (CGN 25) in Third Fleet, US Pacific Fleet. I deployed for Exercise Varsity Sprint in the Pacific, sailing from San Diego. This was an enormous eye-opener for me on just how prodigious the capabilities of the US Navy were. *Bainbridge* had recently fitted the Naval Tactical Data System (NTDS), by far the most advanced system of its kind in the world. I gained enormous hands-on experience on board *Bainbridge*.

The commander of the Third Fleet, Vice Admiral Samuel L. Gravely Jr. (1922–2004), was a remarkable and truly wonderful person and leader. I got to know him well during my time on *Bainbridge*. He was the first African American to serve aboard a fighting ship as an officer, the first to command a US Navy ship, the first to become a flag officer, and the first to command a numbered fleet, a hugely remarkable achievement for his generation. He and I interacted on many subjects, not least naturally the ongoing Sea War '85 project, Soviet intelligence matters, and comparisons and contrasts between the US Navy and the Royal Navy. He invited me to stand with him regularly on *Bainbridge*'s bridge wings as we conducted various evolutions. During Varsity Sprint, *Bainbridge* demonstrated just how powerful a tool the NTDS was when coupled to the Terrier missile system. I transferred by helicopter to several other ships for short visits, including the battle group's aircraft carriers. It was a happy time, a great learning experience, and I hope that in my own small ways, I contributed.

I stayed in touch with Admiral Gravely after I returned to the UK, corresponding by private letter. He retired in 1980, and I was most upset when my schedule back in London would not permit me to attend his retirement ceremony at the Defense Communications Agency, where he was director. I regard him to this day as one of the finest people that I have been privileged to know.

USS *Bainbridge* (CGN 25) (Wikimedia Commons, US Navy)

Vice Admiral Samuel Gravely, United States Navy (Arlington Cemetery)

GLOSSARY OF TERMS

ACINT: Acoustic Intelligence

AIS: Automatic Identification System

ASIO: Australia Security and Intelligence Organization

ASIS: Australia Secret Intelligence Service

C: the initial designating the director of the British Secret Intelligence Service (the first director of SIS was Capt. Sir Mansfield Cumming, Royal Navy, who signed his documents with just the letter *C*.)

CIA: Central Intelligence Agency

CinCPac: commander in chief US Pacific Command

CinCPacFleet: commander in chief US Pacific Fleet

CinCUSNavEur: commander in chief US Naval Forces Europe

CJCS: chairman of the Joint Chiefs of Staff

CNO: chief of naval operations

CNA: Center for Naval Analyses

COMINT: Communications Intelligence

COMSUBPAC: commander Submarine Forces US Pacific Fleet

CONOPS: Concepts of Operation

CSE: Communications Security Establishment

DARPA: Defense Advanced Research Projects Agency

DIA: Defense Intelligence Agency

DIS: Defence Intelligence Staff (later DI—Defence Intelligence)

DNA: deoxyribonucleic acid

DNI: director of naval intelligence (UK and US) and director of national intelligence (US)

DOE: Department of Energy (US)

ELECTRO-OPINT: Electro-Optical Intelligence

ELINT: Electronic Intelligence

FBE: Fleet Battle Experiment

FBI: Federal Bureau of Investigation

FEBA: Forward Edge of the Battle Area

FISC: Foreign Intelligence Surveillance Court

FSB: Federal Security Service (Russia)

GC&CS: Government Code and Cypher School

GCHQ: Government Communications Headquarters

GCSB: New Zealand Government Communications Security Bureau

GEOINT: Geospatial Intelligence

GRU: Intelligence Directorate of the General Staff of the Armed Forces of the former Soviet Union and currently of the Russian Federation

HASC: House Armed Services Committee

HPSCI: House Permanent Select Committee on Intelligence

IAEA: International Atomic Energy Authority

IMINT: Imagery Intelligence

IOC: Initial Operational Capability

ISIS: Islamic State in Iraq and Syria

I & W: indicators and warning

JIC: Joint Intelligence Committee

KGB: The Committee for State Security was the main security agency of the Soviet Union from March 1954 until December 1991.

LASINT: Laser Intelligence

LOE: Limited Objective Experiment

MAD: Mutual Assured Destruction

MAD: Magnetic Anomaly Detector

MASINT: Measurement and Signature Intelligence

MI5: British Security Service

MI6: British Secret Intelligence Service (SIS)

NAB: New Zealand National Assessment Bureau

NATO: North Atlantic Treaty Organization

NCSC: National Cyber Security Center

NCTC: National Counterterrorism Center

NGA: National Geospatial Agency

NID: Naval Intelligence Department

NRO: National Reconnaissance Office

NSA: National Security Agency

NSC: National Security Council (UK and US)

NUCINT: Nuclear Intelligence

NZSIS: New Zealand Secret Intelligence Service

ONI: Office of Naval Intelligence

PFIAB: President's Foreign Intelligence Advisory Board

RADINT: Radar Intelligence

RCMP: Royal Canadian Mounted Police

RDA: R & D associates

RF/EMPINT: Radio Frequency and Electromagnetic Pulse Intelligence

RINT: Radiation Intelligence

SEAL: US Navy Sea Air Land Special Force Operator

SIGINT: Signals Intelligence

SOSUS: Sound Surveillance System

SSBN: nuclear-powered ballistic missile submarine

SSGN: nuclear-powered guided missile submarine

SSK: non-nuclear-powered diesel or air-independent propulsion submarine

SSN: nuclear-powered attack submarine

TTPs: tactics, techniques, and procedures

UAV: unmanned aerial vehicle

UCAV: unmanned combat aerial vehicle

UNCLOS: United Nations Convention on the Law of the Sea

UNO: United Nations Organization

UUV: unmanned underwater vehicle

WMD: weapon(s) of mass destruction

BIBLIOGRAPHY

Abshagen, K. H. *Canaris*. Translated by A. H. Brodrick. London: Hutchinson, 1956.

Admiralty British. Fuhrer Conference on Naval Affairs. Admiralty 1947. London: Her Majesty's Stationery Office.

Aid, M. *Secret Sentry: The Untold History of the National Security Agency*. New York: Bloomsbury, 2009.

Aldrich, R. J. Editor. *British Intelligence, Strategy, and the Cold War. 1945–1951*. London: Routledge, 1992.

Aldrich, R. J. Editor. *Espionage, Security, and Intelligence in Britain, 1945–1970*. Manchester: Manchester University Press, 1998.

Aldrich R. J. *Intelligence and the war against Japan: Britain, America and the Politics of Secret Service*. Cambridge: Cambridge University Press, 1999.

Aldrich R. J. *The Hidden Hand: Britain, America, and Cold War Secret Intelligence*. London: John Murray, 2001.

Aldrich R. J., G. Rawnsley and M. Y. Rawnsley, eds. *The Clandestine Cold War in Asia 1945–1965*. London: Frank Cass, 1999.

Aldrich R. J. and M. F. Hopkins, eds. *Intelligence, Defense, and Diplomacy: British Policy in the Post War World.* London: Frank Cass, 1994.

Aldrich, Richard J. *GCHQ: The Uncensored Story of Britain's Most Secret Intelligence Agency.* London: Harper Press, 2010.

Alsop, Stewart and Braden, Thomas. *Sub Rosa. The OSS and American Espionage.* New York: Reynal and Hitchcock, 1946.

Andrew, C. M. *Secret Service: The Making of the British Intelligence Community.* London: Heinemann, 1985.

Andrew, C. M. *For the President's Eyes Only: Secret Intelligence and the American Presidency from Washington to Bush.* London: Harper Collins, 1995.

Andrew, C. M. *Defense of the Realm. The Official History of the Security Service.* London: Allen Lane, 2009.

Andrew, C. M. and D. Dilks, eds. *The Missing Dimension: Governments and Intelligence Communities in the Twentieth Century.* London: Macmillan, 1982.

Andrew, C. M. and O. Gordievsky. *KGB: The Inside Story.* London: Hodder and Stoughton, 1990.

Andrew, C. M. and V. Mitrokhin. *The Sword and the Shield: The Mitrokhin Archive and the Secret History of the KGB.* New York: Basic Books, 1999.

Arnold, H. *Global Mission. Chief of the Army Air Forces 1938–1946.* New York: Harper, 1949.

Assman, K. *Deutsche Seestrategie in Zwei Welkriegen.* Vowinckel. Heidelberg: Heidelberg Press, 1959.

Aston, Sir George. *Secret Service*. London: Faber and Faber, 1939.

Bamford, J. *The Puzzle Palace: America's National Security Agency and its Special Relationship with GCHQ.*

London: Sidgwick and Jackson, 1983.

Bamford, J. *Body of Secrets: How NSA and Britain's GCHQ Eavesdrop on the World*. New York: Doubleday, 2001.

Bamford, J. *The Shadow Factory: The Ultra-Secret NSA from 9/11 to Eavesdropping on America.*

New York: Doubleday, 2008.

Barrass, Gordon S. *The Great Cold War: A Journey through the Hall of Mirrors*. Stanford, California: Stanford University, 2009.

Barry and Creasy. *Attacks on the Tirpitz by Midget Submarines.* September 1943. *London Gazette*, July 3, 1947.

Beardon, Milton, and James Risen. *The Main Enemy: The Inside Story of the CIA's Final Showdown with the KGB*. London: Penguin Random House, 2003.

Bibliography • 229

Bedell Smith, W. *Eisenhower's Six Great Decisions*. London: Longmans, 1956.

Bennett, G. *Churchill's Man of Mystery: Desmond Morton and the World of Intelligence*. London: Routledge, 2007.

Bennett, R. *Ultra in the West: The Normandy Campaign of 1944–1945*. London: Hutchinson, 1979.

Blackburn, D. and W. Caddell. *Secret Service in South Africa*. London: Cassell and Company London, 1911.

Belot, R. *The Struggle for the Mediterranean 1939–1945*. Oxford: Oxford University Press, 1951.

Benjamin, R. *Five Lives in One. An Insider's View of the Defence and Intelligence World*. Tunbridge Wells: Parapress, 1996.

Benson, R. L. and R. Warner. *Venona: Soviet Espionage and the American Response, 1939–1957. Menlo Park*.

California: Aegean Park Press, 1997.

Bilton, M. and P. Kosminksy. *Speaking Out: Untold Stories from the Falklands War*. Grafton: Grafton, 1987.

Booth, K. *Navies and Foreign Policy*. New York: Croom Helm, 1977.

Borovik, Genrikh. *The Philby Files: The Secret Life of Master Spy Kim Philby—KGB Archives Revealed*. London: Little Brown, 1994.

Brodie, Bernard. *Strategy in the Missile Age*. Princeton: Princeton University Press, 1959.

Brodie, Bernard. *The Future of Deterrence in U.S. Strategy*. California: University of California Press, 1968.

Brodie, Bernard. *War and Politics*. London: Macmillan, 1973.

Buchan, Alastair. *War in Modern Society*. Oxford: Oxford University, 1966.

Buchan, Alastair. *The End of the Postwar Era: A New Balance of World Power*. Oxford: Oxford University, 1974.

Cable, James. *Britain's Naval Future*. Annapolis, Maryland: US Naval Institute Press, 1983.

Calvocoressi, P. *Top Secret Ultra*. London: Cassell and Company London, 1980.

Carrington, Lord. *Reflect on Things Past. The Memoirs of Lord Carrington*. London: Collins, 1988.

Carl, Leo D. *The International Dictionary of Intelligence*. Virginia: McLean, 1990.

Carter, Miranda. *Anthony Blunt: His Lives*. London: Farrar, Straus, & Giroux, 2001.

Cater, D. *The Fourth Branch of Government*. Boston: Houghton Mifflin, 1959.

Cavendish, A. *Inside Intelligence*. London: Harper Collins, 1990.

Cherkashin, A. *Spy Handler. Memoirs of a KGB Officer*. New York: Basic Books, 2005.

China. The State Council Information Office of the People's Republic of China: In the New Era. July 2019. This is an open-source Chinese government official publication and policy statement.

Clayton, A. *The Enemy Is Listening: The Story of the Y Service*. London: Hutchinson, 1980.

Cockburn, Andrew and Leslie: *Dangerous Liaison. The Inside Story of the US-Israeli Covert Relationship*. Place: Harper Collins, 1991.

Cocker, M. P. *Royal Navy Submarines 1901–1982*. London: Frederick Warre Publications, 1982.

Cole, D. J. *Geoffrey Prime: The Imperfect Spy*. London: Robert Hale, 1998.

Colvin, I. *Chief of Intelligence*. London: Gollanz, 1951.

Colomb J. C. R. "Naval Intelligence and the Protection of Shipping in War," *RUSI Journal*, vol. 25 (1882): 553–590.

Compton-Hall, Richard. *Subs versus Subs. The Tactical Technology of Underwater Warfare*. London: David and Charles Publishers, 1988.

Copeland, B. J. *Colossus: The Secrets of Bletchley Park's Code-Breaking Computers*. Oxford: Oxford University Press, 2006.

Corera, Gordon. *MI6: Life and Death in the British Secret Service*. London: Harper Collins, 2012.

Dalein, D. J. *Soviet Espionage*. Oxford: Oxford University Press, 1955.

Deacon, R. *A History of the British Secret Service*. London: Muller, 1969.

De Silva, P. *Sub Rosa: The CIA and the Use of Intelligence*. New York: Times Books, 1978.

Dismukes, B. and McConnell J. *Soviet Naval Diplomacy*. New York: Pergamon Press, 1979.

Driberg, T. *Guy Burgess*. London: Weidenfeld and Nicholson, 1956.

Dulles, Allen. *The Craft of Intelligence*. New York: Harper and Row, 1963.

Dumbrell, J. *Special Relationship: Anglo-American Relations from the Cold War to Iraq*. London: Palgrave, 2006.

Earley, Peter. *Confessions of a Spy: The Real Story of Aldrich Ames*. New York: Putnam & Son, 1997.

Elliott, G. and H. Shukman. *Secret Classrooms. An untold story of the Cold War*. London: St. Ermin's Press, 2002.

Everitt, Nicholas. *British Secret Service during the Great War*. London: Hutchinson, 1920.

Ewing, A. W. *The Man of Room 40. The Life of Sir Alfred Ewing*. London: Hutchinson, 1939.

Fahey, J. A. *Licensed to Spy*. Annapolis, Maryland: US Naval Institute Press, 2002.

Falconer, D. *First into Action: A Dramatic Personal Account of Life in the SBS*. London: Little Brown, 2001.

Fanell, James. "China's Worldwide Military Expansion." Testimony and Statement for the Record. US House of Representatives Permanent Select Committee on Intelligence. Hearing, May 15, 2018. Rayburn Building, Washington, DC.

Fishman, Charles. *One Giant Leap. The Impossible Mission That Flew Us to the Moon*. New York: Simon and Schuster, 2019.

Fitzgerald, P. and M. Leopold. *Strangers on the Line: A Secret History of Phone-Tapping*. London: Bodley Head, 1987.

Freedman, Sir Lawrence. *Strategy*. Oxford: Oxford University Press, 2013.

Freedman, Sir Lawrence. *Official History of the Falklands Campaign. Volumes 1 and 2*. London: Routledge, 2005.

Freedman, Sir Lawrence and Gamba-Stonehouse, V. *Signals of War: The Falklands Conflict of 1982*. Princeton: Princeton University Press, 1991.

Freedman, Sir Lawrence. *A Choice of Enemies: America Confronts the Middle East*. Oxford: Oxford University Press, 2008.

Friedman, Norman. *Submarine Design and Development. Conway Maritime Press*. London: Conway, 1984.

Friedman, Norman. *The Fifty-Year Conflict: Conflict and Strategy in the Cold War*. Annapolis. Maryland: Naval Institute Press, 2007.

Foote, A. *Handbook for Spies*. London: Museum Press, 1949.

Foot, M. R. D. *SOE in France*. London: Her Majesty's Stationery Office, 1964.

Friedman, W. F. and C. J. Mendelsohn. *The Zimmermann Telegram of January 16, 1917 and its Cryptographic Background*. US War department, Office of the Chief Signal Officer. Washington, DC: US Government Printing Office, 1938.

Frost, M. *Spyworld: Inside the Canadian and American Intelligence Establishments*. Toronto: Doubleday, 1994.

Fuchida, Mitsuo and Okumiya Masutake. Edited by Roger Pineau and Clarke Kawakami. *Midway: The Battle that Doomed*

Japan, the Japanese Navy's Story. Annapolis, Maryland: Blue Jacket, 1955.

Gaddis, John Lewis. *The Cold War.* London: 2007.

Ganguly, Sumit and Chris Mason. "An Unnatural Partnership? The Future of US-India Strategic Cooperation. Strategic Studies Institute." US Army War College. May 2019.

Gates, Robert. *From the Shadows: The Ultimate Insider's Story of Five Presidents and How They Won the Cold War.* New York: Simon & Schuster, 2006.

George, James, ed. *The Soviet and Other Communist Navies.* Annapolis, Maryland: US Naval Institute Press, 1986.

Godfrey, Vice Admiral John. *Naval Memoirs.* London: National Maritime Museum Greenwich, 1965.

Goodman, M. S. *Spying on the Nuclear Bear: Anglo-American Intelligence and the Soviet Bomb.* Stanford, California: Stanford University Press, 2007.

Gordievsky, Oleg. *Next Stop Execution: The Autobiography of Oleg Gordievsky.* London: Whole Story, 1995.

Graham, G. S. *The Politics of Naval Supremacy.* Cambridge: Cambridge University Press, 1965.

Grant, R. M. *U-Boat Intelligence, 1914–1918.* Connecticut: Hamden, 1969.

Grayson, W. C. *Chicksands. A Millennium History.* London: Shefford Press, 1992.

Grimes, Sandra, and Jeanne Vertefeuille. *Circle of Treason: A CIA*

Account of Traitor Aldrich Ames and the Men He Betrayed. Annapolis, Maryland: Naval Institute Press, 2012.

Halevy, Efraim. *Man in the Shadows: Inside the Middle East Crisis with a Man Who Led the Mossad.* London: Weidenfeld and Nicholson, 2006.

Harper, Stephen. *Capturing Enigma: How HMS Petard Seized the German Naval Codes.* London: The History Press, 2008.

Hastings, Max with Simon Jenkins. *The Battle for the Falklands.* New York: W.W. Norton and Company, 1983.

Healey, D. *The Time of My Life.* London: Michael Joseph, 1989.

Helms, Richard. *A Look over My Shoulder: A Life in the Central Intelligence Agency.* New York: Random House, 2003.

Hendrick, B. J. *The Life and Letters of Walter H. Page.* Garden City, New York: Yale University Press, 1922.

Herman, M. *Intelligence Power in Peace and War.* Cambridge: Cambridge University Press, 1992.

Herman, M. *Intelligence Services in the Information Age.* London: Cassell and Company London, 2001.

Higham, R. *Armed Forces in Peacetime. Britain 1918–1940. A Case Study.* London: Foulis Press, 1963.

Hill, Rear Admiral J. R. *Anti-Submarine Warfare.* United States Naval Institute Press. Annapolis, Maryland, 1985.

Hill, Rear Admiral J. R., ed. *Oxford Illustrated History of the Royal Navy*. Oxford: Oxford University Press, 1995.

Hill, Rear Admiral J. R. *Lewin of Greenwich. The Authorized Biography of Admiral of the Fleet Lord Lewin*. London: Cassell and Company London, 2000.

Hillsman, Roger. *Strategic Intelligence and National Decisions*. Cambridge: Cambridge University Press, 1956.

Hinsley, F. H. *British Intelligence in the Second World War*. London: Her Majesty's Stationery Office, 1979–1990.

Hinsley, F. H. *Hitler's Strategy*. Cambridge: Cambridge University Press, 1951.

Hinsley, F. H. and A. Stripp, eds. *Code-Breakers: The Inside Story of Bletchley Park*. Oxford: Oxford University Press, 1993.

Hoffman, David E. *The Billion Dollar Spy: A True Story of Cold War Espionage and Betrayal*. New York: Penguin Random House, 2015.

Hollander, Paul. *Political Will and Personal Belief: The Decline and Fall of Soviet Communism*. New Haven, Connecticut: Yale University, 1999.

Howard, Sir Michael. *Captain Professor: A Life in War and Peace*. New York: Continuum Press, 2006.

Howard, Sir Michael. *Liberation or Catastrophe: Reflections on the History of the 20th Century*. London: A and C Black, 2007.

Howe, Geoffrey. *Conflict of Loyalty*. London: Macmillan, 1994.

Hunt, Sir David. *A Don at War*. London: Harper Collins, 1966.

International Institute for Strategic Studies (IISS). *The Military Balance Collection*. London: IISS, 2020.

Ireland, Bernard. With Eric Grove. *War at Sea 1897–1997*. London: Harper Collins and Janes, 1997.

James, Admiral Sir William. "The Eyes of the Navy. Room 40." *Edinburgh University Journal*, no. 22 (Spring 1965): 50–54.

Janes Fighting Ships. London: Janes Publishing, 1960–2015.

Jeffery, Keith. *MI6: The History of the Secret Intelligence Service, 1909–1949*. London: Penguin Random House, 2010.

Jenkins, R. *Life at the Centre*. London: Macmillan, 1991.

Johnson, Adrian L., ed. *Wars in Peace*. London: Royal United Service Institution, 2014.

Johnson, T. R. *American Cryptology during the Cold War, 1945–1989*. Volumes 1–4. United States National Security Agency. Declassified in 2009.

Jones, Nate, ed. *Able Archer '83: The Secret History of the NATO Exercise That Almost Triggered Nuclear War*. New York: The New Press, 2016.

Jones, R. V. *Most Secret War*. London: Hamish Hamilton Limited, 1978.

Kagan, Neil and Stephen G. Hyslop. *The Secret History of World War 2*. Washington, DC: National Geographic.

Kahn, David. *The Codebreakers*. London: Weidenfeld & Nicholson, 1966.

Kalugin, O. and F. Montaigne. *The First Directorate: My First 32 Years in Intelligence and Espionage against the West—the Ultimate Memoirs of a Master Spy.* New York: St. Martin's Press, 1994.

Kendall, W. "The Functions of Intelligence." *World Politics*, no. 4, vol. 1 (July 1949): 542–552.

Kegan, John. *Intelligence in War.* New York: Vintage Books & Random House, 2002

Kendall, Bridget. *The Cold War: A New Oral History of Life between East and West.* London: Penguin Books, 2018.

Kent, S. *Strategic Intelligence for American World Policy.* Oxford: Oxford University Press, 1949.

Korbel, J. *The Communist Subversion of Czechoslovakia, 1938–1948.* Oxford: Oxford University Press, 1959.

Kot, S. *Conversations with the Kremlin and Dispatches from Russia.* Oxford: Oxford University Press, 1963.

Krupakar, Jayanna. "Chinese Naval Base in the Indian Ocean. Signs of a Maritime Grand Strategy." *Strategic Analysis*, no. 3, vol. 41 (2017): 207–222

Lamphere, R. J. and T. Shachtman. *The FBI-KGB War: A Special Agent's Story.* London: W. H. Allen, 1986.

Lewis, Norman. *The Honoured Society.* London: Collins, 1964

Liddell-Hart, Sir B. H. *Strategy—the Indirect Approach.* London: Faber & Faber, 1954.

Liddell-Hart, Sir B. H. *The Other Side of the Hill.* London: Cassell, 1951.

Liddell-Hart, Sir B. H. *Memoirs in Two Volumes*. London: Cassell, 1965.

Liddell-Hart, Sir B. H. *The Real War, 1914–1918*. Boston: Little Brown & Company, 1930.

Lockhart, Sir Robert Bruce. *Memories of a British Agent*. London: Putnam, 1932.

Lockhart, Robin. *The Ace of Spies*. London: Hodder & Stoughton, 1967.

Lyubimov, Mikhail. *Notes of a Ne'er-Do-Well Rezident or Will-o'-the-Wisp*. Moscow: 1995.

Lyubimov, Mikhail. *Spies I Love and Hate*. Moscow: AST Olimp, 1997.

Macintyre, Ben. *The Spy and the Traitor*. London: Crown Publishing Group, 2018.

Marder, A. J. *From the Dreadnought to Scapa Flow*. 5 Volumes. Oxford: Oxford University Press, 1940.

Marder, A. J. *The Anatomy of British Sea Power*. New York: Alfred Knopf, 1940.

Martin, Sir Laurence. *Arms and Strategy*. London: Weidenfeld & Nicholson, 1973.

Mathams, R. H. *Sub-Rosa: Memoirs of an Australian Intelligence Analyst*. Sydney: Allen & Unwin, 1982.

McGehee, R. W. *Deadly Deceit: My 25 Years in the CIA*. New York: Sheridan Square, 1983.

McKay, Sinclair. *The Secret Life of Bletchley Park.* London: Aurum Press Limited, 2010.

McKay, Sinclair. *The Lost World of Bletchley Park.* London: Aurum Press Limited, 2013.

McKay, Sinclair. *The Secret Listeners.* London: Aurum Press Limited, 2013.

McKnight, D. *Australia's Spies and Their Secrets.* London: University College London Press, 1994.

McLachlan, Donald. *Room 39. Naval Intelligence in Action, 1939–1945.* London: Weidenfeld & Nicholson, 1968.

Mikesh, R. C. B-57: *Canberra at War.* London: Ian Allan, 1980.

Mitchell, M. and T. Mitchell. *The Spy Who Tried to Stop a War: Katharine Gun and the Secret Plot to Sanction the Iraq Invasion.* London: Polipoint Press, 2008.

Monat, P. *Spy in the US.* New York: Harper & Row, 1961.

Montagu, E. E. S. *The Man Who Never Was.* London: Evans Brothers, 1953.

Montgomery Hyde, H. *George Blake: Superspy.* London: Futura, 1987.

Moore, Charles. *Margaret Thatcher: The Authorized Biography. Volume 2. Everything She Wants.* London: Allen Lane, 2015.

Moorehead, A. *The Traitors.* London: Hamish Hamilton, 1952.

Morley, Jefferson. *The Ghost: The Secret Life of CIA Spymaster James Jesus Angleton.* London: St. Martin's Press, 2017.

Murphy, D. E., S. A. Kondrashev, and G. Bailey. *Battleground Berlin:*

CIA vs. KGB in the Cold War. New Haven: Yale University Press, 1997.

Nicolai, Colonel W. *The German Secret Service.* Translated by G. Renwick. Frankfurt am Main: Fischer, 2007.

Nott, J. *Here Today Gone Tomorrow: Recollections of an Errant Politician.* London: Politico's, 2002.

Oberdorfer, Don. *From the Cold War to a New Era: The United States and the Soviet Union, 1983–1991.*

Baltimore, Maryland: John Hopkins University Press, 1998.

Orlov, Alexander. *Handbook of Intelligence and Guerrilla Warfare.* London: Cresset Press, 1963.

Packard, W. *A Century of Naval Intelligence.* Washington, DC: Office of Naval Intelligence, 1996.

Parrish, T. *The Ultra Americans: The US Role in Breaking Nazi Codes.* New York: Stein and Day, 1986.

Parker, Philip, Editor. *The Cold War Spy Pocket Manual.* Oxford: Pool of London Press, 2015.

Paterson, M. *Voices of the Codebreakers: Personal Accounts of the Secret Heroes of World War Two.* Newton Abbot: David and Charles, 2007.

Pavlov, V. *Memoirs of a Spymaster: My Fifty Years in the KGB.* New York: Carroll and Graf., 1994.

Pawle, G. *The Secret War.* London: Harrap, 1972

Pearson, John. *The Life of Ian Fleming.* London: Jonathan Cape, 1966.

Petter, G. S. *The Future of American Secret Intelligence*. Washington, DC: Hoover Press, 1946.

Petrov, Vladimir and Evdokia. *Empires of Fear*. London: Andre Deutsch, 1956.

Philby, Kim. *My Silent War*. New York: Grove Press, 1968.

Pincher, C. *Too Secret Too Long*. London: Sidgwick and Jackson, 1984.

Pincher, C. *Traitors: Labyrinths of Treason*. London: Sidgwick and Jackson, 1987.

Pincher, Chapman. *Treachery: Betrayals, Blunders, and Cover Ups: Six Decades of Espionage*. Edinburgh: Mainstream Publishing, 2012.

Polmar, Norman. *The Ships and Aircraft of the US Fleet*. Volumes. Annapolis, Maryland: United States Naval Institute Press, 1984.

Powers, T. *The Man Who Kept the Secrets: Richard Helms and the CIA*. London: Weidenfeld and Nicholson, 1979.

Pratt, F. *Secret and Urgent. The Story of Codes and Ciphers*. London: Robert Hale, 1939.

Primakov, Yevgeny. *Russian Crossroads: Toward the New Millennium*. New Haven, Connecticut: Yale, 2004.

Prime, R. *Time of Trial: The Personal Story behind the Cheltenham Spy Scandal*. London: Hodder & Stoughton, 1984.

Raeder, E. *Struggle for the Sea*. Translated by Edward Fitzgerald. London: Kimber, 1959.

Ramsay, Sir Bertram Home. "The Evacuation from Dunkirk, May–June 1940," the *London Gazette*, July 17, 1947.

Ramsay, Sir Bertram Home. "Assault Phases of the Normandy Landings, June 1944," the *London Gazette*, October 30, 1947.

Ranft, Bryan, ed. *Technical Change and British Naval Policy 1860–1939*. London: Hodder and Stoughton, 1977.

Ranelagh, J. *The Agency: The Rise and Decline of the CIA*. New York: Simon and Shuster, 1986.

Ranft, Bryan. "The Naval Defense of British Sea-Borne Trade, 1860–1905." DPhil thesis, Balliol College, Oxford University, 1967.

Ransom, H. H. *Central Intelligence and the National Security*. Oxford: Oxford University Press, 1958.

Ratcliffe, P. *Eye of the Storm: Twenty-Five Years in Action with the SAS*. London: Michael O'Mara, 2000.

Rej, Abhijnan. "How India's Defense Policy Complicates US-India Military Cooperation." US Army War College. February 26, 2019. https://warroom.armywarcollege.edu/articles/indias-defense-policy-and-us/.

Richelson, J. *A Century of Spies: Intelligence in the Twentieth Century*. Oxford: Oxford University Press, 1995.

Richelson, J. *The US Intelligence Community*. New York: Ballinger, 1989.

Richelson, J. *The Wizards of Langley: Inside the CIA's Directorate of Science and Technology*. Boulder, Colorado: Westview Press, 2001.

Richelson, J. and D. Ball. *Ties that Bind: Intelligence Cooperation between the UKUSA Countries.* Boston: Allen and Unwin, 1985.

Report of the Security Commission, May 1983. Cmnd 8876. Her Majesty's Stationery Office, 1983.

Report of the Security Commission, October 1986. Cmnd 9923. Her Majesty's Stationery Office, 1986.

Rintelen, Captain Franz Von. *The Dark Invader.* London: Peter Davis, 1933.

Roberts, Captain Jerry. *Lorenz. Breaking Hitler's Top Secret Code at Bletchley Park.* Cheltenham: The History Press, 2017.

Roskill, S. W. *The War at Sea. 1939–1945.* Three Volumes. London: Her Majesty's Stationery Office, 1954–1961.

Roskill, S. W. *Hankey, Man of Secrets.* London: Collins, 1969.

Rowan, R. W. *The Story of Secret Service.* London: Miles, 1938.

Ruge, F. *Sea Warfare 1939–1945. A German Viewpoint.* Translated by M. G. Saunders. London: Cassell, 1957.

Ryan, C. *The Longest Day, June 6, 1944.* New York: Simon & Schuster, 1960.

Sainsbury, A. B. *The Royal Navy Day by Day.* London: Ian Allen Publications, 1993.

Saran, Samir and Verma Richard Rahul. "Strategic Convergence: The United States and India as Major Defense Partners." Observer Research Foundation (ORF), June 25, 2019.

Scott, James. *The Attack on the Liberty. The Untold Story of Israel's Deadly 1967 Assault on a US Spy Ship*. New York: Simon & Schuster, 2009.

Schelling, W. R. *Strategy, Politics, and Defense Budgets*. New York: Columbia University Press, 1962.

Schull, J. *The Far Distant Ships. An Official Account of Canadian Naval Operations in the Second World War*. Ottawa: Ministry of National Defence, 1962.

Schurman, D. M. *The Education of a Navy: The Development of British Naval Strategic Thought, 1867–1914*. Oxford: Oxford University Press, 1966.

Sebag Montefiore, Simon. *Stalin: The Court of the Red Tsar*. London: Vintage, 2003.

Showell, Jak P. Mallmann. *German Naval Code Breakers*. London: Ian Allan Publishing, 2003.

Sides, Hampton. *On Desperate Ground. The Marines at the Reservoir. The Korean War's Greatest Battle*. New York: Doubleday, 2018.

Sillitoe, Sir Percy. "My Answer to Critics of MI5." The *Sunday Times*, November 22, 1953.

Singh, Zorawar Daulet. "Foreign Policy and Sea Power. India's Maritime Role." Center for Policy Research, Delhi. *Journal of Defense Studies*, no. 4, (2017).

Smith, B. F. *The Ultra-Magic Deals and the Most Secret Special Relationship 1940–1946*. Shrewsbury: Airlife Publishing, 1993.

Smith, B. F. *Sharing Secrets with Stalin: How the Allies Traded*

Intelligence, 1941–1945. Kansas: University of Kansas Press, 1996.

Smith, M. *New Cloak. Old Dagger: How Britain's Spies Came in from the Cold*. London: Victor Gollanz, 1996.

Smith, M. *Station X: The Code-Breakers of Bletchley Park*. London: Channel Four Books, 1998.

Smith, M. *The Emperor's Codes: Bletchley Park and the Breaking of Japan's Secret Ciphers*. London: Bantam, 2000.

Smith, M. *The Spying Game: A Secret History of British Espionage*. London: Politico's, 2003.

Smith, M. *Killer Elite: The Inside Story of America's Most Secret Operations Team*. New York: St. Martin's Press, 2007.

Smith, M. and R. Erskine, eds. *Action this Day: Bletchley Park from the Breaking of the Enigma Code to the Birth of the Modern Computer*. London: Bantam, 2001.

Sontag, S. and Drew, C. *Blind Man's Bluff: The Untold Story of American Submarine Espionage*. New York: Public Affairs, 1998.

Stafford, D. *Spies beneath Berlin*. Second Edition. London: John Murray, 2002.

Stein, H., ed. *American Civil-Military Decisions*. Birmingham, Alabama: University of Alabama Press, 1963.

Steinhauer, G. and Felsted, S. T. *The Kaiser's Master Spy*. London: John Lane, Bodley Head, 1930.

Strip, A. J. *Code Breakers in the Far East*. London: Frank Cass, 1989.

Strong, Major General Sir Kenneth. *Intelligence at the Top*. London: Cassell, 1968.

Sudoplatov, P. *Special Tasks: The Memoirs of an Unwanted Witness—a Soviet Spymaster*. London: Little Brown, 1994.

Sunday Express Magazine, London. *War in the Falklands: The Campaign in Pictures*. London: Weidenfeld & Nicholson Ltd., 1982.

Svendsen, A. *Intelligence Cooperation and the War on Terror: Anglo-American Security Relations after 9/11*. London: Routledge, 2009.

Thakur, Arvind and Michael Padgett. "Time is Now to Advance US-India Defense Cooperation," *National Defense*, May 31, 2018.

Thatcher, M. *The Downing Street Years*. London: Harper Collins, 1993.

Thomas, R. *Espionage and Secrecy: The Official Secrets Act 1911–1989 of the United Kingdom*. London: Routledge, 1991.

Thompson, Julian. *No Picnic. 3 Commando Brigade in the South Atlantic 1982*. New York: Hippocrene Books, 1985.

Thompson, Tommy. "The Kremlinologist. Briefing Book Number 648." George Washington University, November 2018.

Thomson, Sir Basil. *The Story of Scotland Yard*. London: Grayson & Grayson, 1935.

Trento, Joseph J. *The Secret History of the CIA*. Roseville, California: Prima Publishing, 2001.

Tuchman, Barbara W. *The Zimmermann Telegram*. New York: Viking Press, 1958.

Toynbee, A., ed. *Survey of International Relations, 1939–1946*. Oxford: Oxford University Press, 1952.

United States Department of Defense. "Preparedness, Partnerships, and Promoting a Networked Region." Indo-Pacific Strategy Report. Washington, DC, June 1, 2019.

United States Department of Defense. Soviet Military Power. An annual publication from September 1981 to September 1990. This series may be obtained from the Superintendent of Documents, US Government Printing Office, Washington, DC, 20402. This outstanding series, contains extensive unclassified detail of Soviet: Policies and Global Ambitions; Forces for Nuclear Attack; Strategic Defense and Space Operations; Forces for Theater Operations; Readiness, Mobility, and Sustainability; Research, Development, and Production; Political-Military and Regional Policies; the US response.

United States Department of State. "Intelligence: A Bibliography of its Functions, Methods, and Techniques." Part 1. December 1948. Part 2. April 1949.

Urban, M. *UK Eyes Alpha: The Inside Story of British Intelligence*. London: Faber and Faber, 1996.

Vickers, Philip. *A Clear Case of Genius. Room 40's Code-Breaking Pioneer. Autobiography of Admiral Sir Reginald Hall*. Cheltenham: The History Press, 2017.

Vincent. J. *The Culture of Secrecy: Britain 1832–1988*. Oxford: Oxford University Press, 1998.

Waters, D. W. *A Study of the Philosophy and Conduct of Maritime War, 1815–1945*. Parts 1 and 2. Published privately. Copies are in the UK Ministry of Defence Library (Navy), and the National Maritime Museum, London.

Weiner, Tim, David Johnston and Neil A. Lewis. *Betrayal: The Story of Aldrich Ames, an American Spy*. London: Penguin Random House, 1996.

Wells, Anthony. "The 1967 June War: Soviet Naval Diplomacy and the Sixth Fleet—a Reappraisal." Center for Naval Analyses, Professional Paper 204, 1977, Department of the Navy.

Wells, Anthony. "NATO and US Carrier Deployment Policies." Center for Naval Analyses, February 1977, Department of the Navy.

Wells, Anthony. "Sea War '85 Scenario." With Captain John L. Underwood, United States Navy. *Center for Naval Analyses*, April 1977, Department of the Navy.

Wells, Anthony. "NATO and Carrier Deployment Policies: Formation of a New Standing Naval Strike Force in NATO." Center for Naval Analyses, April 1977, Department of the Navy.

Wells, Anthony. "The Application of Drag Reduction and Boundary Layer Control Technologies in an Experimental Program." Report for the Chief Naval Architect, Vickers Shipbuilding and Engineering Ltd., January 1986.

Wells, Anthony. "Preliminary Overview of Soviet Merchant Ships in SSBN Operations and Soviet Merchant Ships and Submarine Masking." SSBN Security Program, Department of the Navy, 1986, US Navy Contract N00016-85-C-0204.

Wells, Anthony. "SSBN Port Egress and the Non-Commercial Activities of the Soviet Merchant Fleet: Concepts of Operation and War Orders for Current and Future Anti-SSBN Operations." SSBN Security program, 1986, Department of the Navy, US Navy Contract N136400.

Wells, Anthony. "Overview Study of the Maritime Aspects of the Nuclear Balance in the European Theater." US Department of Energy Study for the European Conflict Analysis Project, October 1986, US Department of Energy.

Wells, Anthony. "The Soviet Navy in the Arctic and North Atlantic." *National Defense*, February 1986.

Wells, Anthony. "Soviet Submarine Prospects 1985–2000," The *Submarine Review*, January 1986.

Wells, Anthony. "A New Defense Strategy for Britain." *Proceedings of the United States Naval Institute*, March 1987.

Wells, Anthony. "Presence and Military Strategies of the USSR in the Arctic." Quebec Center for International Relations, Laval University Press, 1986.

Wells, Anthony. "Soviet Submarine Warfare Strategy Assessment and Future US Submarine and Anti-Submarine Warfare Technologies." Defense Advanced Research Projects Agency, March 1988, US Department of Defense.

Wells, Anthony. "Operational Factors Associated with the Software Nuclear Analysis for the UGM-109A Tomahawk Submarine-launched Land Attack Cruise Missile Combat Control System Mark 1." Department of the Navy, 1989.

Wells, Anthony. "Real Time Targeting: Myth or Reality." *Proceedings of the United States Naval Institute*, August 2001.

Wells, Anthony. "US Naval Power and the Pursuit of Peace in an Era of International Terrorism and Weapons of Mass Destruction." The *Submarine Review*, October 2002.

Wells, Anthony. "Limited Objective Experiment ZERO." The Naval Air Systems Command, July 2002, Department of the Navy.

Wells, Anthony. "Transformation—Some Insights and Observations for the Royal Navy from across the Atlantic." *The Naval Review*, August 2003.

Wells, Anthony. "Distributed Data Analysis with Bayesian Networks: A Preliminary Study for the Non-Proliferation of Radioactive Devices." With Dr. Farid Dowla and Dr. G. Larson, December 2003, The Lawrence Livermore National Laboratory.

Wells, Anthony. "Fiber Reinforced Pumice Protective Barriers: To Mitigate the Effects of Suicide and Truck Bombs." Final Report and recommendations. With Professor Vistasp Kharbari, Professor of Structural Engineering, University of California, San Diego, August 2006. For the Naval Air Systems Command, Department of the Navy. Washington, DC.

Wells, Anthony. "Weapon Target Centric Model. Preliminary Modules and Applications. Two Volumes." Principal Executive Officer Submarines, August 2007, Naval Sea Systems Command, Department of the Navy.

Wells, Anthony. "They Did Not Die in Vain. USS Liberty Incident— Some Additional Perspectives." *Proceedings of the United States Naval Institute*, March 2005.

Wells, Anthony. "Royal Navy at the Crossroads: Turn the Strategic

Tide. A Way to Implement a Lasting Vision." *The Naval Review*, November 2010.

Wells, Anthony. "The Royal Navy Is Key to Britain's Security Strategy." *Proceedings of the United States Naval Institute*, December 2010.

Wells, Anthony. "The Survivability of the Royal Navy and a New Enlightened British Defense Strategy." The *Submarine Review*, January 2011.

Wells, Anthony. "A Strategy in East Asia That Can Endure." *Proceedings of the United States Naval Institute*, May 2011. Reprinted in the *Naval Review*, August 2011, by kind permission of the United States Naval Institute.

Wells, Anthony. "Tactical Decision Aid: Multi Intelligence Capability for National, Theater, and Tactical Intelligence in Real Time across Geographic Pace and Time." May 2012, Department of the Navy and US National Intelligence community.

Wells, Anthony. "Submarine Industrial Base Model: Key Industrial Base Model for the US Virginia Class Nuclear Powered Attack Submarine." With Dr. Carol V. Evans. Principal Executive Officer Submarines, Naval Sea Systems Command, Department of the Navy.

Wells, Anthony. "The United States Navy, Jordan, and a Long-Term Israeli-Palestinian Security Agreement." The *Submarine Review*, Spring 2013.

Wells, Anthony. "Admiral Sir Herbert Richmond: What Would He Think, Write and Action Today?" The *Naval Review Centenary Edition*, February 2013.

Wells, Anthony. "Jordan, Israel, and US Need to Cooperate for

Missile Defense." *United States Naval Institute News*, March 2013.

Wells, Anthony. "A Tribute to Admiral Sir John 'Sandy' Woodward." *United States Naval Institute News*, August 2013.

Wells, Anthony. "USS Liberty Document Center." Edited with Thomas Schaaf. A document website produced by SiteWhirks, Warrenton, Virginia. September 2013. This site was transferred to the United States Library of Congress in April 2018, to be maintained in perpetuity for the benefit of scholars, analysts, and historians. USSLibertyDocumentCenter.org.

Wells, Anthony. "The Future of ISIS: A Joint US-Russian Assessment." With Dr. Andrey Chuprygin. The *Naval Review*, May 2015.

Wells, Anthony. *A Tale of Two Navies. Geopolitics, Technology, and Strategy in the United States Navy and the Royal Navy, 1960–2015.* Annapolis, Maryland: United States Naval Institute Press, 2017.

Wells, Anthony and Phillips, James W., Captain US Navy (retired). "Put the Guns in a Box." *Proceedings of the United States Naval Institute*, Annapolis, Maryland, June 2018.

Wemyss, D. E. G. *Walker's Group in the Western Approaches*. Liverpool: Liverpool Post and Echo, 1948.

Werner, H. A. *Iron Coffin. A Personal Account of German U-boat Battles of World War Two*. London: Arthur Barker, 1969.

West, N. *A Matter of Trust: MI5 1945–1972*. London: Weidenfeld and Nicholson, 1982.

West, N. *GCHQ: The Secret Wireless War, 1900–1986*. London: Weidenfeld and Nicholson, 1986.

West, N. *The Secret War for the Falklands*. London: Little Brown, 1997.

West, N. *Venona*. London: Harper Collins, 1999.

West, N. *At Her Majesty's Secret Service: The Chiefs of Britain's Intelligence Agency, MI6*. London: Greenhill Books, 2006.

Westad, Odd Arne. *The Cold War: A World History*. Oxford: Oxford University Press, 2017.

Wheatley, R. *Operation Sea Lion. German Plans for the Invasion of England, 1939–1942*. Oxford: Clarendon Press, 1958.

Wilkinson, N. *Secrecy and the Media: The Official History of the UK's D-Notice System*. London: Routledge, 2009.

Wilmot, C. *The Struggle for Europe*. London: Harper Collins, 1952.

Wilson, H. *The Labour Government 1964–1970: A Personal Record*. London: Michael Joseph, 1971.

Winterbotham, F. *The Ultra Secret*. London: Weidenfeld & Nicholson, 1974.

Wohlstetter, R. *Pearl Harbor, Warning and Decision*. London: Methuen, 1957.

Wolin, S. and R. M. Slusser. *The Soviet Secret Police*. London: Methuen, 1957.

Womack, Helen, ed. *Undercover Lives: Soviet Spies in the Cities of the World*. London: Orion Publishing Company, 1998.

Wood, D. and D. Dempster. *The Narrow Margin*. London: Hutchinson, 1961.

Woodward, Admiral Sir John "Sandy." *One Hundred Days. The Memoirs of the Falklands Battle Group Commander.* With Patrick Robinson. Annapolis, Maryland: United States Naval Institute Press, 1992.

Woodward, L. *My Life as a Spy*. London: Macmillan, 2005.

Wright, P, with Greengrass, Paul. *Spycatcher. The Candid Autobiography of a Senior Intelligence Officer.* New York: Viking, 1987.

Wylde, N., ed. *The Story of Brixmis, 1946–1990*. Arundel: Brixmis Association, 1993.

Young, J. and J. Kent. *International Relations since 1945*. Oxford: Oxford University Press, 2004.

Young, J. W. *The Labour Governments, 1964–1970: International Policy.* Manchester: Manchester University Press, 2003.

Zimmerman, B. *France, 1944. The Fatal Decisions*. London: Michael Joseph, 1956.

AUTHOR'S BIOGRAPHY AND PUBLICATIONS

Dr. Anthony R. Wells

Dr. Anthony R. Wells (taken in Prague, Czech Republic)

Anthony Wells is unique insofar as he is the only living person to have worked for British intelligence as a British citizen and US intelligence as a US citizen, and to have also served in uniform at sea and ashore with both the Royal Navy and the US Navy. He is a fifty-year veteran of the Five Eyes intelligence community. In 2017, he was the keynote speaker on board HMS *Victory* in Portsmouth, England, to commemorate the one hundredth anniversary of the famous Zimmermann Telegram intelligence coup by "Blinker Hall" and his Room 40 team in British Naval Intelligence. The guest of honor was Her Royal Highness Princess Anne, with the Five Eyes community, past and present, represented from the United States, the United Kingdom, Canada, Australia, and New Zealand. Dr. Wells, or Commander Wells, was trained and mentored in the late 1960s by the very best of the World War II intelligence community, including Sir Harry Hinsley, the famous Bletchley Park code breaker, official historian of British intelligence in the Second World War, master of St. John's College, Cambridge, and vice chancellor of Cambridge University. Sir Harry Hinsley introduced Dr. Wells to the Enigma data before it became public knowledge. Dr. Wells received his PhD in War Studies from King's College, University of London, in 1972. He holds bachelor's and master's degrees from the University of Durham, and a master's degree from the London School of Economics. He was trained at Britannia Royal Naval College, Dartmouth, and received his advanced training at the School of Maritime Operations. He was called to the Bar by Lincoln's Inn in November 1980. Anthony Wells has four children and eight grandchildren and lives on his farm in Virginia. He is a member of the Naval Order of the United States and was appointed an honorary crew member of USS *Liberty* by the USS Liberty Veterans Association. USS *Liberty* is the most highly decorated warship in the history of the US Navy for a single action, attacked by Israeli air and surface forces on August 8, 1967, in the eastern Mediterranean. Dr. Wells is the third chairman of the USS Liberty Alliance, succeeding the late admiral Thomas Moorer, former chairman of the US Joint Chiefs of Staff and Chief of Naval Operations, and the late rear admiral Clarence "Mark" Hill, former distinguished US naval aviator and battle group commander. He is a retired US national ski patroller and instructor, and a life member and former president of the Plains, Virginia, Volunteer Fire and Rescue Company. Wells is an FAA commercial pilot with single and multi-engine, land and sea, instrument, and flight instructor ratings.

Dr. Wells was the technical director of Fleet Battle Experiments ALPHA and BRAVO in the Third Fleet, United States Pacific Fleet. He was the chief executive officer of TKC International LLC, a specialist company supporting the US Intelligence Community and Department of Defense, for twenty-five years. He held top-secret SCI and special access clearances.

Anthony Wells's Publications

Literary Awards
In 2013 and 2017, the United States Submarine League presented Dr. Anthony R. Wells with Literary Awards for Articles in the *Submarine Review*.

Books
German Public Opinion and Hitler's Policies, 1933–39. 1968. Electronic version available at Durham University Library, UK—access www to Durham University Library and enter database with title and/or author name. Electronic and hard copy versions available.

Studies in British Naval Intelligence, 1880–1945. 1972. Electronic version available via the www British Library (ETHOS), and also King's College, London—www and then enter the database with title and/or author name. Electronic and hard copy versions available. Also simply enter title, and by Anthony Roland Wells and a www edition is available online.

Training and the Achievement of Management Objectives, the Solution of Management Problems, and as an Instrument of Organizational

Change. 1974. The London School of Economics and Political Science.

Technical Change and British Naval Policy. Edited by Bryan Ranft, Hodder and Stoughton, London, 1977, and Holmes and Meier, New York, NY.

War and Society. Edited by Brian Bond and Ian Roy, Croom Helm, London, 1977, and Holmes and Meier, New York, NY.

Soviet Naval Diplomacy. Edited by B. Dismukes and J. McConnell, Pergamon Press, 1979.

The Soviet and Other Communist Navies. Edited by James George, US Naval Institute Press, Annapolis, Maryland, 1986.

Black Gold Finale. A novel. Dorrance Publishing Company, 2009.

The Golden Few. A novel. Dorrance Publishing Company, 2012.

A Tale of Two Navies: Geopolitics, Technology, and Strategy in the United States and the Royal Navy, 1960–2015. US Naval Institute Press, Annapolis, Maryland, January, 2017.

Between Five Eyes. Casemate Publishers, Oxford, UK & Havertown, Pennsylvania, September, 2020.

Room 39 and the Lisbon Connection. A novel. Xlibris, Bloomington, Indiana, June 2021.

Crossroads in Time Philby & Angleton. A Story of Treachery. A novel. Palmetto Publishing, Charleston, South Carolina, 2022 and Austin Macauley Publishers, London, 2022.

Gone to Earth A Young American Woman Disappears in the South Pacific.

Based on a true story. A novel. Xlibris, Bloomington, Indiana, 2022.

How Strategic Airpower Has Tipped the Balance on the Global Stage from the 100th Bomb Group to the Falklands and Beyond. With Commander Nigel "Sharkey" Ward, DSC, AFC, Royal Navy (retired). To be published in 2023.

Guarding against Extremism in the 21st Century: A Lesson from the Past German Public Opinion and Hitler's Policies 1933–1939. XLibris, Blommington, Indiana, 2023.

Intrepid's Footsteps Sustaining US-UK Intelligence in an Era of Global Challenges. A personal memoire. To be published in 2023.

Articles
"Admirals Hall and Godfrey—Doyens of Naval Intelligence (Two Parts)." The *Naval Review*, 1973.

"Staff Training and the Royal Navy (Two Parts)." The *Naval Review* 1975, 1976.

"The 1967 June War: Soviet Naval Diplomacy and the Sixth Fleet—a Reappraisal." Center for Naval Analyses, Arlington, Virginia. Professional Paper 204, October 1977.

"The Center for Naval Analyses." Professional Paper Number 197, December 1977. Department of the Navy, Washington, DC, Center for Naval Analyses.

"The Soviet Navy in the Arctic and North Atlantic." *National Defense*, February 1986.

"Soviet Submarine Prospects 1985–2000." *Submarine Review*, January 1986.

"A New Defense Strategy for Britain." Proceedings of the United States Naval Institute, March 1987.

"Presence and Military Strategies of the USSR in the Arctic." Quebec Center for International Relations, Laval University, 1986.

"Real Time Targeting: Myth or Reality." Proceedings of the United States Naval Institute, August 2001.

"Missing Magics Machine Material. New Insights on December 7, 1941 and Relevance for Today's Navy." The *Submarine Review*, April 2003.

"US Naval Power and the Pursuit of Peace in an Era of International Terrorism and Weapons of Mass Destruction." The *Submarine Review*, October 2002.

"Transformation—Some Insights and Observations for the Royal Navy from Across the Atlantic." The *Naval Review*, August 2003.

"They Did Not Die in Vain. USS *Liberty* Incident—Some Additional Perspectives." Proceedings of the United States Naval Institute, March 2005.

"Royal Navy at the Crossroads: Turn the Strategic Tide. A Way to Implement a Lasting Vision." The *Naval Review*, November 2010.

"The Royal Navy Is Key to Britain's Security Strategy." Proceedings of the United States Naval Institute, December 2010.

"The Survivability of the Royal Navy and a New Enlightened British Defense Strategy." The *Submarine Review*, January 2011.

"A Strategy in East Asia That Can Endure." Proceedings of the United States Naval Institute, May 2011.

"A Strategy in East Asia That Can Endure." The *Naval Review*, August 2011. Reprinted by kind permission of the United States Naval Institute.

"The United States Navy, Jordan, and a Long Term Israeli-Palestinian Security Agreement." The *Submarine Review*, Spring 2012.

"Admiral Sir Herbert Richmond: What Would He Think, Write and Action Today?" The *Naval Review*, February 2013—lead article in the Centenary Edition of the *Naval Review*.

"Postscript to Missing Magics Machine Material—Tribute to a Great Submariner: Captain Edward Beach, US Navy." The *Submarine Review*, 2013

"Jordan, Israel, and US Need to Cooperate for Missile Defense." *USNI News*, March 26, 2103.

"A Tribute to Admiral Sir John 'Sandy' Woodward." *USNI News*, August 8, 2013.

"USS LIBERTY Document Center." Edited by Anthony Wells and Thomas Schaaf. A website produced by SiteWhirks, Inc., Warrenton, Virginia. September 2013. In April 2017, this website was transferred to the Library of Congress for permanent safekeeping for the use of future scholars and researchers.

"The Future of ISIS: A Joint US-Russian Assessment." With Dr. Andrey Chuprygin. The *Naval Review*, May 2015.

"The Zimmermann Telegram: 100th Anniversary." The *Naval Review*, February 2017 and the *Submarine Review*, 2017.

"Put the Guns in a Box." With Captain J. W. Phillips, US Navy retired. Proceedings of the US Naval Institute, June 2018.

"Quo Vadis China? A View from across the Atlantic. Part 1." The *Naval Review*. November 2019.

"Quo Vadis China?" The *Submarine Review*, December 2019.

"USS *Amberjack* and the Attack on USS *Liberty*." With Mr. Larry Taylor, ST1 USS *Amberjack*. US Naval Institute Naval History Blog, January 7, 2020.

"USS Amberjack & the Attack on USS Liberty." With Mr. Larry Taylor. The *Submarine Review*. March 2020.

"The UK's Strategic Defense & Security Review, a US Perspective." The *Submarine Review*. June 2020.

"The United Kingdom Needs a Maritime Strategy." The *Naval Review*, August 2020.

"Submarines and the Ring of Fire in the Indo Pacific Theater: A Strategic Analysis." The *Submarine Review*, December, 2020.

"UK's Defense & Security Review—Some Final Observations." The *Naval Review*. Autumn 2020.

"A Brave New World of Next Generation Technologies." *Warship World*: Volume 17, Number 2, January/February 2021.

"To Honor the Last Nuremburg Prosecutor." Proceedings of the United States Naval Institute, May 2021, Annapolis, Maryland.

"The United Nations Convention on the Law of the Sea and the United States Navy." US Naval Institute Blog, June 2021.

"Is There a Need for a New Generation of Submarine Officers Who Are Intelligence Trained and Experienced beyond Current Levels? & How Might We Learn from the Past?" The *Submarine Review*, June 2021.

"Behind the Five Eyes." *Counsel Magazine* (Justice Matters: Spotlight section), the monthly magazine of the Bar of England & Wales, London, UK, July 2021.

"Letter from the Plains." A monthly article in the Middleburg Eccentric, Virginia, since 2016 to November 2022.

Reports

"NATO and US Carrier Deployment Policies." Center for Naval Analyses, Arlington, Virginia, February 1977.

"NATO and US Carrier Deployment Policies, Formation of a New Standing Naval Strike Force in NATO." Center for Naval Analyses, Arlington, Virginia, April 1977.

"Sea War '85 Scenario." With Captain John L. Underwood, USN. Center for Naval Analyses, Arlington, Virginia, June 1977.

"Submarine Construction Program for the State of Sabah, Malaysia." RDA Contract TR-188600-OOl, December 1984. Chief Minister of Sabah, Malaysia and Government of Malaysia.

"The Application of Drag Reduction and Boundary Layer Control Technologies in an Experimental Program." January 1985. For the Chief Naval Architect, Vickers Shipbuilding and Engineering Ltd, Barrow-in-Furness, UK.

"The Strategic Importance and Advantages of Labuan, Federal Malaysian Territory, as a Naval Base with Special Reference to Its Capabilities as the Royal Malaysian Navy Submarine

Base," March 1985. Chief Minister of Sabah, Malaysia and Government of Malaysia.

"Preliminary Overview of Soviet Merchant Ships in Anti-SSBN Operations and Soviet Merchant Ships and Submarine Masking." (Department of the Navy Contract N00016-85-C-0204).

"SSBN Port Egress and the Non-Commercial Activities of the Soviet Merchant Fleet: Concepts of Operation and War Orders for Current and Future Anti-SSBN Operations." (Department of the Navy Contract 136400).

"Overview Study of the Maritime Aspects of the Nuclear Balance in the European Theater" (Department of Energy Study for the European Conflict Analysis Project). October 1986.

"Soviet Submarine Warfare Strategy Assessment and Future US Submarine and Anti-Submarine Warfare Technologies" (Defense Advanced Research Projects Agency, March 1988, RDA Contract 146601).

"Limited Objective Experiment ZERO, July 2000." The Naval Air Systems Command, US Navy, Department of Defense. 2002.

"Operational Factors Associated with the Software Nuclear Safety Analysis for the UGM-109A Tomahawk Submarine-Launched Land Attack Cruise Missile Combat Control System Mark I." United States Navy and Logicon Inc., 1989.

"Operation Bahrain," March 2003. The Assistant Director of Central Intelligence, the Central Intelligence Agency.

"Distributed Data Analysis with Bayesian Networks: A Preliminary Study for Non-Proliferation of Radioactive Devices," December 2003 (with F. Dowla and G. Larson). The

Lawrence Livermore National Laboratory, Livermore, California, December 2003.

"Fiber Reinforced Pumice Protective Barriers—to Mitigate the Effects of Suicide and Truck Bombs." Final Report and Recommendations. United States Navy, Washington DC. With Professor Vistasp Kharbari, Professor of Structural Engineering, University of California, San Diego. August 2006.

"Weapon Target Centric Model." Preliminary Modules and Applications, in Two Volumes. United States Navy, Principal Executive Officer Submarines, Washington DC, August, 2007.

"Tactical Decision Aid (TDA)," Multi intelligence capability for National, Theater, and Tactical intelligence in real time across geographic space and time. The National Intelligence Community, Washington, DC, May 2012.

"Submarine Industrial Base Model." Key industrial base model for the US VIRGINIA Class nuclear powered attack submarine, Principal Executive Officer Submarines, Washington Navy Yard, Washington DC, October 2012.

Manuals

"Astro-Navigation: A Programmed Course in 6 Volumes for Training UK and Commonwealth Naval Officers in the Use of Astronomical Navigation at Sea." Royal Navy, Ministry of Defence, UK, 1969.

"The Battle of Trafalgar: A Programmed Course in One Volume in Naval Strategy and Tactics." Royal Navy, Ministry of Defence, 1969.

"The Double Cross System: A Programmed Course In One Volume

for British, Foreign and Commonwealth Naval Officers Attending the Royal Naval Staff College, Greenwich, UK." Royal Navy, Ministry of Defence, 1973.

Unclassified Titles for Technology and Operational Areas, Covering Classified Programs—and Publications—Generic Areas

Airborne Mine Clearance

Streak Tube Imaging LIDAR

Magic Lantern Program

Tritium Microsphere Technology

Classified Applications of the Naval Simulation System

Naval Surface Fire Support and the Extended Range Guided Munition (ERGM)

Non Acoustic Antisubmarine Warfare

Battlefield Awareness and Data Dissemination (BADD Program)

Joint Stars Program Special Applications

Naval Fires Network

Littoral Surveillance System

Fleet Battle Experiment Operations (Technical Director FBE Alpha and FBE Bravo) Third Fleet, US Pacific Fleet

Ocean Surveillance (radar and optics)

Multi Spectral Applications

Space Based Sensors and Surveillance

Microwave Radiometry Applications

Detection, Locating and Tracking

Clandestine Operations and Intelligence Collection Operations

Support to Special Forces

Special Submarine Operations

Tagging Tracking and Surveillance

Battlespace Shaping and Real Time Targeting

*Covert and Clandestine Operations against Weapons of Mass Destruction
and Other Major Threats to US Security*

Special Sensor Technology

Covert & Overt Operations Planning and Execution

Reports and MOUs for Commander-in-Chief and Secretary Level Actions

Airborne Infrared Measurement System

Stealth and Counter Stealth

Counter Intelligence Operations

Tactical Exploitation System and Joint Fires Network

Asymmetric Warfare Initiative—2003

Hairy Buffalo Program

Tracking of the al Qai'da Terrorist Network and Operations

Tactical Decision Aid (TDA) for Submarine ISR Operations

Advanced Cyber Attack and Defense Technologies and Operations

Shrouded Lightning Special Program

Non Linear Junction Radar and Adaptive Regenerative Controller Special Program

Special Program in Jordan

Special Program in Malaysia

Special Program in Bahrain

Special Program in Abu Dhabi

Special Program in Saudi Arabia

Special Program with Commander United States Pacific Fleet

Special Tests at the US Naval Air Station Patuxent River, Maryland, September 2012

LISAC Special Program

Applications of the Robust Laser Interferometry (RLI) system and technology

Special Support to a Combined Cheltenham UK and Maryland US Group

Special Support for Indo-Pacific Operations

Classified Titles and Publications
1968–2018: Dr. Wells has been the author, lead author, or a key author of multiple highly classified code word documents at the top-secret SCI level in both the United Kingdom and the United States.